Whiteness and Racialized Ethnic Groups in the United States

Whiteness and Racialized Ethnic Groups in the United States

The Politics of Remembering

Sherrow O. Pinder

LEXINGTON BOOKS
Lanham • Boulder • New York • Toronto • Plymouth, UK

Published by Lexington Books
A wholly owned subsidiary of The Rowman & Littlefield Publishing Group, Inc.
4501 Forbes Boulevard, Suite 200, Lanham, Maryland 20706
www.rowman.com

10 Thornbury Road, Plymouth PL6 7PP, United Kingdom

British Library Cataloguing in Publication Information Available

Library of Congress Cataloging-in-Publication Data
The hardback edition of this book was previously cataloged by the Library of Congress as
follows:

Pinder, Sherrow O.
Whiteness and racialized ethnic groups in the United States : the politics of remembering
   / Sherrow O. Pinder.
      p. cm.
   Includes bibliographical references and index.
   1. Whites—Race identity—United States—History. 2. Whites—United States—
Attitudes—History. 3. Race awareness—United States—History. 4. Racism—United
States—History. 5. United States—Race relations—History. I. Title.
   E184.A1P56 2012
   305.800973—dc23   2011042546

   ISBN: 978-0-7391-6489-1 (cloth : alk. paper)
   ISBN: 978-0-7391-6490-7 (pbk. : alk. paper)
   ISBN: 978-0-7391-6491-4 (ebook)

Printed in the United States of America

Contents

Acknowledgments

The inspiration for this book started with the writing of a paper, "Racialized Ethnic Groups and Public Memory in the United States," for the Public Memory, Race, and Ethnicity Conference at Lewis and Clark College in October 2007. I was delighted by the questions and comments that I received from colleagues at the conference. Hence, I revised the paper and presented it under a new title, "Whiteness, Racialized Ethnic Groups, and Public Memory in America," at the Midwest Political Science Association Conference in April 2010. After a meeting with Joseph C. Parry, the acquisition editor for political science with Lexington Books, about expanding my paper into a book project, I started to think seriously about the history of whiteness in the United States and how it has shaped, and continues to shape, the unequal position of racialized ethnic groups including blacks, First Nations, Chinese, and Mexicans. In this respect, I thank Joseph C. Parry for supporting my book project. I also thank the College of Behavioral and Social Science and California State University (CSU), Chico, for its financial support. I am indeed grateful to my dear friend Nadia Louar who teaches in the French and Francophone Department at the University of Wisconsin, Oshkosh, for reading, rereading, and editing the first draft of my book.

During the time I was working on this book, I was motivated by the love and support of my family. I am somewhat deflated of words to express my gratefulness to my sisters Allison Greaves, Pauline Matthews, and Lorna Pinder-Jackson; my nieces Amber and Alyssa for listening to my endless stories about race and ethnicity in the United States; my nephews Anthony, Cory, Luxley, Jordan, and Kirk Matthews; and my uncle Bruce Wendell Richmond. In addition, I thank my friends James-Henry Holland, George Joseph, and Thelma Pinto of Hobart and William Smith colleges. My warm thanks to my friends in Canada: Michele Ball, Sheryl Thompson, and the Landau's—Ariel, Daniel, Enoch, Sophie, and Remy—for their unceasing love. I am particularly thankful for the steadfast support of my friend and colleague Cynthia Bynoe. Also, my thanks to my friends Theresa Cotner, chair of the Art Department at CSU, Chico; Jennifer Asenas and Kevin Johnson, the Communication Department at CSU, Long Beach; Jim Cotner, a MFA graduate of CSU, Los Angeles; Monica Ciobanu, the Department of Sociology at State University of New York, Plattsburgh; and Robert Stanley, the Department of Political Science, CSU, Chico. Last but not least, I thank Claire Martin, Nancy Shealy, and Elena Tzelepis for their love and support for which I am continually thankful.

Introduction: The Argument in Brief

America's commitment to "whiteness" started with the arrival of the colonists who sought to view First Nations[1] and blacks as physically different from themselves. In fact, skin color became the early form of America's racism, which differentiated immediately black and First Nations indentured servants from white indentured servants. Even though the word "racism" was not actually used then and according to George M. Fredrickson the word racism first appeared in the 1930s to describe the Nazi's prosecution of the Jews,[2] the symbolic identification of the phenomenon through naming does not prevent racism as an established system in practice from actually existing and happening. When indentured servitude ultimately legalized racism through laws and practice that determined the unequal treatment of First Nations and blacks, it established the racial paradigm that would govern the new colonies. The unequal treatment of blacks, especially, would reemerge and extend itself into legalized slavery, which provided a template for the treatment of all racialized ethnic groups.

It was not an accident that the 1790 Naturalization Act excluded all racialized ethnic groups from American citizenship. American citizenship was infested with racial particularity instead of universality. And despite the racial conglomeration on which it was founded, "whiteness," even though it was a part of the everyday practice and discourse, was institutionalized and would, in the end, fiercely orchestrate the social, economic, political, and cultural experience of those deemed as noncitizens. Chinese exclusion from citizenship, for example, was further marked by a series of acts, which culminated into the Chinese Exclusion Act of 1882. The Chinese Exclusion Act was a tyrannical policy that was modified and extended, in various ways, to Japanese, Filipinos, Koreans, and Asian-Indians in the United States. In the end, to be nonwhite in America was to be at the bottom of the racial hierarchy that was in place. The French post-colonial scholar Frantz Fanon's notion of racial hierarchy addresses the ontological complexities of nonwhites in America.[3] The victimization endemic to this racial hierarchy did not come from the mere condition of being nonwhite; it came from the condition of being nonwhite in relation to "whiteness."[4] In other words, it was not so much about *being* as much as about *not being*.

Whiteness can be defined as a system of domination that upholds a white identity "as an essential something."[5] Its meaning and status depend on racist structures that associate whiteness with normality so that whites, independent of their social status, can assert their "property rights in whiteness,"[6] as the law professor Cheryl I. Harris describes it. Whiteness as "property" operates "socio-discursively through subjectivity and knowledge production,"[7] which whites have invested in, and profited from the asymmetrical power relations between those on the margins and those in the center of power forging what the African American philosopher Charles W. Mills describes as a "racial contract." In fact, whiteness as property shields the white "self" from any ontological interruption of racial otherness. Racial otherness, while it separates the self from that which threatens the self, disqualifies the "other" as humans and precludes it from embracing the "livable live," as the feminist philosopher Judith Butler puts it.[8]

Unless the body passes for white, race is, as Fanon writes, epidermatized. It determines who qualifies as "human" and "livable." In fact, if racialized ethnic groups were seen as human, that is, equal to whites, they could transcend racial boundaries and convert to an "absolute being: a being that stands in the way of human being or a human way of being,"[9] and not regarded as inferior.[10] It is fundamental for nonwhites to be viewed as inferior for whites to be superior. This is simply how "racial naturalism" works. Blacks and other nonwhites have to be viewed as inferior for whites to be superior. Drawing on the French feminist Simone de Beauvoir's paradigm according to which "one is not born a woman but becomes one" through the process of feminization,[11] I suggest that one is not born raced, but becomes raced through the process of racialization.[12] In other words, the morphological and sociohistorical reality of race hamstrings nonwhites from moving beyond race.[13] Moving beyond race, however, does not mean that race will disappear, but merely that the signifier race will be pegged to another signified such as gender, class, or sexuality, where race remains salient.

Very often *culture* is substituted for *race*, or *class* is substituted for *race*. When the latter happens, it does so because America's class system is distinctively racialized. Therefore, it does not alter the praxeology of those who are marked by race and its signified existence.[14] The marking of race on the body allows for a return to a false biological interpretation of race. However, the cultural facts of racial assimilation in par with concepts such as colorblindness and post-racial are fundamental for understanding America's current race relations. Indeed, in the United States of America, it is a chilly climate for people marked by race. The African American historian Barbara J. Fields reminds us of the dangers of substituting *race* for *racism* or vice versa because, she writes, it "transforms the act of a subject into an attribute of the object."[15] Hence, when blacks and other people of color are labeled racists, we fail to take into account the history of America's racialization process and how it worked, and continues to work, to subjugate people of color.

The manner in which America remembers its racist past, in terms of "memory," which has inevitably shaped its futuristic ambitions associated with race relations cannot be disputed. Nathaniel Hawthorne writes that history "lies upon the present like a giant's dead body."[16] The concept of "memory" is used as a critical category across a wide range of academia disciplines, including the natural and social sciences, humanities, media studies, and the arts. The past three decades have observed a growth in the quantity of conferences that focus of "memory."[17] Books have been written, scholarly articles published, peer-reviewed journals created, and centers and programs opened.[18] "Memory," as the French historian Pierre Nora explains, "Is life, borne out of livening societies founded in its name. It remains in permanent evolution, open to the dialectic of remembering and forgetting, unconscious of its successive deformations, vulnerable to manipulation and appropriation, susceptible to being long dormant and periodically revived."[19]

Scholars working on memory traditionally have come from various disciplines and have collaborated in interdisciplinary works that have led to what is now called "memory studies." "One reason for attending to memory as a concept," as the rhetorician Kendall R Phillips observes, is "the fear of memory's failure, understood not in terms of forgetting but in terms of misremembering, or remembering differently,"[20] which is triggered by false judgment or, what Levette interprets as, "other-judging." Other-Judging, Levette writes, "differs substantively from the possibility of forgetting. While forgetting is conceived as a kind of occlusion or even erasure, the process of other-judging, or here misremembering, constitutes an active process of making knowledge claims about the past that are in error."[21] Remembrance in some cases sets itself apart from history,[22] but America's laws, epistemologies, and every day practices are meant to construct and defend a culture that was and continues to be based on whiteness in the presence of a racially and culturally diverse United States of America even though, as the African American scholar W. E. B. Du Bois tells us, that "there is no true American music but the wild sweet melodies of the Negro Slaves; the American fairy tales and folklore are Indian and African."[23] However, scholars, including Arthur M. Schlesinger and Samuel P. Huntington, argue that the origin of America's culture is "essentially European."[24]

My intention in this book is not to contribute to the fascinating field of memory studies. Some brilliant scholars have been working in this field for the past several years and even created their own journal, *Memory Studies*.[25] That said, I will rely on memory as a conceptual tool to investigate America's racist past and establish it "as a space of experience,"[26] in which memory becomes a facilitator for interpreting America's present and future race relations. I will look at the history of its antidiscrimination measures, more specifically its affirmative action programs,[27] as a form of atonement for its racist past. Drawing on the work of Pierre

Nora's *Rethinking of Memory: Rethinking the French Past*, I will retrace the history of the American nation from its birth, follow its past, observe its present, and envision its future in order to offer an account of America's race relations. According to Nora, "memory functions as a mere historical trace that can exists only as a stimulation of the past."[28] In this sense, America, remembering its racist past cannot be a calm act of "introspection and retrospection." The post-colonial theorist Homi Bhabha describes the remembering process as a painful act, "a putting together of a dismembered past to make sense of the [racial] trauma of the present."[29]

In spite of constitutional amendments, the outlawing of de jure racial segregation, the implementation of the Civil Rights Act of 1964, and the Voting Rights Act of 1965 that made blacks and other nonwhites equal to whites, at least in theory, whiteness remains the normalized, unmarked structural position that maintains white privilege and authorizes systematic power.[30] Hence, it is fundamental to highlight the relation between whiteness and white identity. In this book, whiteness as a system of domination and white identity are interrogated separately as well as together. In fact, a white identity—poor whites, antiracists, or racists—itself is not fixed and stable but flexible and, in the face of normalized whiteness, is far from simple.

Some scholars have argued that not all whites are equality whites and that whites should not be gathered into an aggregate singularity.[31] Some whites are disadvantaged because of gender, sexual orientation, and socioeconomic status. Poor whites, for example, define their status in relation to upper- and middle-class whites. In comparison, they see themselves and are viewed as "others"; but their otherness is one of "whiteness within," allowing for the liminality of whiteness. In other words, the poor whites, because of their economic inferiority, "are not quite white." Yet it is not impossible for them to indeed "become white." For blacks and other people of color, this possibility does not exist unless they pass for whites. I will return to this point later. For now, I want to suggest that race simply dislocates the liminality of whiteness. Poor whites, even though they might experience stigmatization, deprivation, and suffer in the hands of other whites, they do benefit from white skin privilege.

In this discussion, whiteness is not only about having white skin. The complex interplay of its meaning and status is intrinsically linked to the logic of white supremacy and depends on racist structures naturalizing and normalizing whiteness in the United States. Instead of freeing whiteness of its presumptive hegemony, the state, through its affirmative action programs maintains, reinforces, and articulates the dominant position of whites. I am not implying that America should revert back to its discriminatory laws and practice. Given the ways in which power works, one of the roles of a democratic state is to adhere to its legitimization function, which, in this case, is to make sure that members of marginalized groups are visibility incorporated within the power structure. Furthermore, the government has to implement antidiscriminatory laws that protect against discrimination in the workplace, for example. Because antidiscriminatory laws are widely conceived as a mask that conceals the interest of the dominant group, then, the African American activist and poet Audre Lorde's much cited remarks that "the master's tool would never dismantle the master's house"[32] remain fundamental.

For sure, whiteness has undergone some changes over the centuries. For instance, the Irish, Jews, Greeks, and Italians "became" white. However, "becoming white" has not altered the ontological specificity of whiteness as domination. It is on the basis of their whiteness that whites can assert their "property rights in whiteness."[33] In this sense, whiteness no longer needs the full and widespread support of the racist state and its laws to materialize as "an essential something."[34] In looking back at the emergence of whiteness in America, laws were in place that institutionalized and uphold whiteness as "an essential something."[35] However, whiteness continues to reinforce racial hierarchy that operates discursively through America's laws, its racial discourse, and epistemologies in order to defend and support white preeminence both as a system and as an ideology. Furthermore, whiteness is tied to a cultural practice that sanctions and protects the brutal sensibleness of white privilege and entitlement.[36]

Bearing this in mind, in an effort to free America of its racist past, it is the hope of "whiteness studies" to summon all whites to face up to their privilege. Even though there are some difficulties in generating a satisfactory definition of "whiteness studies" because of the wide range of contributions by scholars from various disciplines,[37] "whiteness studies" remains an attractive and buoyant way for many whites to think about their white skin privilege. "Whiteness studies," by questioning whiteness traditional structuring, its operating procedures, and its social, political, and economic means of distributing privilege to whites, has become a positive topic of research in order to reframe America's past and present race relations. Even though scholars of whiteness studies, like Ruth Frankenberg, Peggy McIntosh, David R. Roediger, Karen Brodkin, and Noel Ignatiev, are confronting white privilege, and propose to eliminate the conditions of whiteness existence, I am doubtful that we should be prefixing "whiteness studies" with the word *critical*. Black scholars, from W. E. B. Du Bois to Toni Morrison, have been, for a long time, *critical* of whiteness. However, for many whiteness studies scholars, "critical whiteness studies" rather than "whiteness studies" is used "to mark the explicitly analytic nature of this inquiry."[38] Given that the programs at universities and colleges, in a way, are already about whiteness, "showing the face of the white subject, then it follows that whiteness studies sustains the direction or orientation of this gaze, whilst removing the 'detour' provided by the reflections of the other."[39]

Scholars critically engage in the study of whiteness with good intentions. In fact, while colorblindness fails to see race, "whiteness studies," on the other hand, recognizes race and faces up to the privileges that whites accrue. The question that disquiets me is to what degree is "whiteness studies" a form of freeing whiteness of its normalization? In other words, how does "whiteness studies" propose to deal with the whiteness of "whiteness studies? It is true that "whiteness studies" has progressed into a form of "antiracist whiteness" that denounces racism and its multidimensional forms of discrimination.[40] However, "whiteness studies," in terms of its locationality and positionality at the center of the educational institutions and systems, runs the risk of rehegemonizing instead of dehegemonizing whiteness.

If we should conjure up a genuine assessment of the university as an institution, it is a source of knowledge and education, a place for research, and a microcosm for critical work. "Whiteness studies" is now the focal point of much critical work purporting to report on, and effect real changes in the lives of marginalized groups. Notwithstanding the presumptive presence of policies and laws that promote and privilege whiteness, one of the objectives of "whiteness studies" is that whiteness should be made visible. However, whiteness is only invisible to those for whom it benefits. And the university has not disbanded its well-known and long-standing cultural norms of whiteness. The structural power inside the university obscures the potentiality for any legitimate critique, let alone any transformation of the power structure that is soundly in place. "Whiteness studies," it has to be said, has not altered the context—meaning the university—in which these scholars identify, argue about, and evaluate white privilege. A large proportion of university professors are white. And even though "whiteness studies" allows the possibilities of antiracist projects to flourish, which is important given the direction of contemporary racism, "whiteness studies" has not really focused on trying to get outside of whiteness. This is symptomatic of the fact that there is no legitimate standpoint, to borrow from Allison Bailey and Jacquelyn Zita, "of knowing, seeing, ontologizing [and] evaluating"[41] outside of whiteness. Consequently, "whiteness studies" would have to be disrupted from within in order to imagine a denormalized form of whiteness. It is my fervent hope that we can move beyond the deadlock of "whiteness studies" and "antiracist whiteness" in order to begin the process of denormalizing whiteness and conjure up a post-white identity. Given that the self cannot exists without the presence of the "other,"[42] subjectivity, in this sense, which is produced in the act of naming and being named,[43] is engendered as a vivacious engagement with that which surpasses the self. And in fact, you can never truly understand the self unless you study the "other," which is embedded in the self.

The purpose of this book is to revisit America's history of whiteness in order to show the difference between remembering a history of human indignities and recreating one that composes its own textual memory in order to account for the never ending discrimination toward racialized ethnic groups, including blacks, First Nations, Chinese, and Mexicans. The historically reliant positionality of whiteness as a part of the everyday practice and discourse of white supremacy would, in the end, become institutionalized, and it continued to orchestrate the discriminatory practice that blacks and other racialized ethnic groups were already experiencing. Eventually, the enactment of antidiscrimination measures such as raced-conscious affirmative action programs, in an effort to address America's discriminatory practice, has only served to strengthen whiteness and encourage the uncensored display of whites' entitlement to jobs, promotions, and university admissions. "Whiteness studies" has entered the realm of academic research with the intention of exposing white privilege. Because whiteness remains normalized, "whiteness studies," presenting itself as a way of exposing white privilege, undoubtedly remains problematic. Hence, there is a need to transcend "whiteness studies" in an effort to free whiteness of its normalization. And given that "antiracist whiteness" is not enough to decenter whiteness, whiteness would have to be denormalized, that is, stripped of its presumptive hegemony. It is only when whiteness is de-normalized can we construct a post-white identity.

THE SCOPE AND STRUCTURING OF THIS BOOK

Chapter 1 examines how whiteness gained its root in America by looking at seventeenth century colonial America. I show the way the leitmotif of race and racial thinking, which were already embedded within the English psyche even before they arrived in the United States, would refashion themselves in many important ways to determine, through laws as well as cultural practice, the unequal position of First Nations and blacks under indentured servitude. While at that time, both blacks and First Nations were looked on as inferior by the Europeans' new comers, in their view, First Nations, if given the right kind of education, could in due course be culturally whitened. Blacks' inferiority was conceived as intrinsic, which became the alleged reason for blacks to be treated as lesser than whites. Accordingly, in order to comprehend the emergence of whiteness in America, it will not do to disregard the evidence that race, racial thinking, and the symbolic dimensions of racial domination were in place before chattel slavery. By extracting from Fanon's notion of racial hierarchy, one main aim of this chapter is to expose and analyze the complexity of the hyperrealism that shaped the antagonistic positions of First Nations, blacks, and nonwhites in America as inferior during the colonial period. And while nonwhites were looked on as inferior, nonwhite women's positionality was shaped and maintained by the intersectionality of race, gender, class, and ideology,[44] which became embedded in America's cognitive and intellectual traditions.[45]

Chapter 2 examines how racialized ethnic groups experienced discrimination in very specific ways. However, I want to show that the harsh treatment of blacks under slavery was a template for the harsh treatment of the other racialized groups. While it is argued by many scholars that the black–white model focuses on blacks and whites and fails to incorporate the other nonwhites into the model, I point out that in this model, black signifies nonwhites. And within the socioeconomic and political dynamics of the United States, nonwhites were positioned as unequal to whites. This positioning occurred both in language, epistemology, and cultural practice. And even though whiteness was already a cultural practice that shaped the nefarious presence of white dominance both as a configuration and ideology, I draw our attention to the first Naturalization Act of 1790 as the first step in the institutionalization of whiteness. In addition, laws such as Black Codes, the Jim Crow Laws, and the Chinese Exclusion Act show that America's history of nation building was inherently linked to white dominance. The implementations of these laws determined the positions of racialized ethnic groups.

In due course, America had to attend to its racist past. Chapter 3 looks at the implementation of antidiscrimination measures to neutralize widespread forms of prejudice that pervasively disadvantage persons based on racially constructed differences. It focuses specifically on race-conscious affirmative action programs. Is affirmative action equipped to take on the transforming and reshaping of America's racial hierarchy that is based on whiteness? Is the need by the government to address "otherness," a fully realized, and yet fragmented presence, another way to maintain "otherness" through its affirmative programs? These questions are asked in the spirit of framing the discussion in this chapter. In the end, I point out that affirmative action programs, at least not on any manifest level, have not altered or transformed the racist structures that have shaped and maintained the discriminatory practices that are in place. Affirmative action is one more tool for the state to use as an apparatus for legitimizing the power structure in place, securing white privilege.

In the 1990s in the United States, "whiteness studies" developed and flourished as a category of analysis in literary criticism and cultural studies. Since then, in many other disciplines as diverse as history, gender studies, film studies, media studies, humor studies, linguistics, art history, rhetoric and communication, material culture, and dance,[46] there has been a growing body of influential, academic literature that focuses on whiteness.[47] In chapter 4, I examine "whiteness studies" because, in part, as "whiteness studies" scholars have espoused, to leave whiteness unexamined would fail in employing a critical analysis of white privilege. There are many good reasons for scholars to critically engage in the study of whiteness. By giving serious attention to issues of whiteness, "whiteness studies" makes that which is invisible visible by drawing heavily on how whiteness, as a guarantor for impeccable privileges, is given to whites. Is "whiteness studies," then, a form of freeing whiteness from its normalization? For sure, many whiteness studies scholars are committed to the abolition of whiteness through deconstructing, naming, and resisting whiteness. Since "whiteness studies" privileges what it names, the question, then, is "whiteness studies" self-serving? Whiteness studies scholars are working within a "whiteness studies" framework and are moving toward antiracist forms of whiteness or, at least, toward antiracist approaches for a different form of whiteness. Given that antiracist projects are not equipped to relinquish the privilege that comes with whiteness, whiteness would have to be denormalized. However, the denormalizing of whiteness is an exhaustive process because the structures and systems that uphold whiteness would have to be transformed. Somewhat for this reason, chapter five focuses on how to start the process of denormalizing whiteness. Because, in the Fanonian sense, the discourse on whiteness systematically constructs the racial object as less than human so that white supremacy can assert itself, there has to be a shift in focus from white supremacy to white security. It is only when whiteness is freed of its anxiety and become secure can we construct and reconstitute a post-white identity. The post-white identity is not a finished process; it must constantly examine itself. Rather than positioning itself as external to America's racialized culture and practice, the post-white identity would have to constantly work to decenter itself from such a practice without rehegemonizing whiteness by means of becoming its own signifying influence and calling attention to itself.

This book provides for an ongoing dialogue about America's racist history, which must be attended to because to forget the past willfully is to threaten the delicate links that guide us to an understanding of America's present and future on race relations. History cannot be forgotten; it is about remembering rather than forgetting. "It is when history is [forgotten], Roland Barthes writes, "that it is most unmistakably at work"[48] to constantly resituates itself, rewrites itself and functions to challenge our understanding of the illumination of the past, which is definitive of America's present and uncertain future of race relations. Such a history must be attended to because, as the African American poet and historian Maya Angelou, in her reflective wisdom, informs us, "history, despite its wrenching pain cannot be unlived, but if faced with courage it need not be lived again."[49] This book is a good starting point for such a reflection on the past, present, and future of race relations in the United States.

NOTES

1. In this book, I am using the term First Nations to mean Native Americans. The latter, for me, is embedded with colonial implications. First Nations is one of the existing terms referring to persons registered as Indians in Canada. In Canada's Constitutional Act of 1982, Aboriginal is used to refer to indigenous people of Canada. This term is still used by some First Nations in certain geographical locations in Canada. Also, it refers to the communities of Indians in Canada. In the United States, First Nations have continued to identify themselves in terms of Mohawks, Cree, Oneida, Kiowa, Navajo, Comanche, Apache, and Wichita, for example. See Martin E. Spencer, "Multiculturalism, 'Political Correctness,' and the Politics of Identity," (1994), 557–58.

2. Fredrickson (2002), 4.

3. In 2001, during the United Nations World Conference against Racism, Racial Discrimination, Xenophobia and Related Intolerance, confronting racial hierarchy was a part of the focus.

4. For a more comprehensive reading, see Frantz Fanon's *Black Skin, White Masks*, (1967).

5. Fine et al. (1997), 9.

6. See Cheryl I. Harris, "Whiteness as Property" (1993).

7. Moreton-Robinson (2008), 85.

8. Butler (1990), 38.

9. Gordon (2002), 10.

10. I am not arguing here that race is a unifying force because some blacks, for example, vote republican or might point to the "declining significance of race" and "the end of racism."

11. For an extensive analysis on the "woman question," also, see Monique Wittig, "One is not Born a Woman," in *The Straight Mind and Other Essays* (1992). In addition, Rosi Braidotti, *Metamorphoses: Towards a Materialistic Theory of Becoming*, draws our attention to multiple becomings in term of the famine as positioned as the "other" in post-industrial Western societies.

12. I am using the term racialization to indicate the expansion of racial meanings to an earlier racially unspecified relation, social practice, or group, and as a process that has the power to deconstruct racial groups and disclose their historical meanings. Yet it is the appearance of race that was, and still is, the indicator for fluid and complicated processes of the racialization of identity markers, including gender, sexuality, and ethnicity—the illustration and definition of the "other" based on constructed differences.

13. At the beginning of America's formation, European immigrants were looked on as races. Because of their white skin, they were able to move beyond race and become white or raceless. See Karen Brodkin, *How Jews became White Folks and What That Says About Race in America* (1998), and Noel Ignatiev, *How the Irish Became White* (1995).

14. Even though the racialized body has already been interpreted by cultural meaning or social practice, for the most part, I do not mean to say that the racialized body is a passive and inert body awaiting cultural inscription.

15. Fields (2001), 48.

16. Hawthorne (1962), 162.

17. In 2008, there was a conference titled "Is an Interdisciplinary Field of Memory Studies Possible?" at the New School for Social Research in New York City; and on October 26–27 another conference, "Public Memory, Race and Ethnicity Conference," was held at Lewis and Clark College in Portland, Oregon.

18. Journals on memory include *Memory* and *Memory Studies*. In the spring of 1989, *Representations* published a special issue titled *Memory and Counter Memory*. Centers include the Center for Interdisciplinary Research in Germany and the Warwick Center for Memory Studies. Washington University in St. Louis has a program, the Luce Program in Individual and Collective Memory.

19. Nora (1989), 8.

20. Phillips (2010), 208.
21. Phillips (2010), 212.
22. Nora (1996), 9.
23. Du Bois (2003), 14.
24. For representative statements, see Arthur M. Schlesinger, *The Disuniting of America: Reflections on a Multicultural Society* (1998) and Samuel P. Huntington, *Who Are We? The Challenges to America's National Identity* (2004).
25. Yifat Gutman et al., *Memory and the Future: Transnational Politics, Ethics and Society* (2010); Kendal R. Phillips, "The Failure of Memory: Reflections on Rhetoric and Public Remembrance" (2010); *Framing Public Memory* (2004a and 2004b); Adam D. Brown et al., "Introduction: Is an Interdisciplinary Field of Memory Studies Possible?" (2009); Susannah Radstone, "Memory Studies: For and Against" (2008); Pierre Nora, *Realms of Memory: The Construction of the French Past* (1996); and Natalie Zemon Davis and Randolph Starn, ed., "Special Issue: Memory and Counter Memory" (1989).
26. White (2010), 16.
27. During most of America's history, conflicts were resolved through formal treaties, restitution, or tacit understanding. A precedential concern for addressing, at least on the surface, the rights of marginalized groups has been visible through celebrations such as Black History Month, Martin Luther King Day, and César Chávez Day. References to past injustice and suffering that marginalized groups experienced are, especially, useful because distributive policies such as affirmative action and the quota system serve to legitimize the power structure in place.
28. Nora (1996), 12.
29. Bhabha (1997), 123.
30. Hartigan (1999a), 184.
31. See Matt Wray, *Not Quite White: White Trash and the Boundaries of Whiteness*, 2006; and Neil Foley, *The White Scourge: Mexicans, Blacks, and Poor Whites in Texas Cotton Culture*, 1997.
32. Lorde (1984), 123.
33. Harris (1993), 1716.
34. Fine et al. (1997), 9.
35. Fine et al. (1997), 9.
36. Specific epistemology, ideologies, and practices are in place that systematically sanction and protect white privilege. For further reading on whiteness as privilege, see Peggy McIntosh, "White Privilege: Unpacking the Invisible Knapsack" (2007), Ruth Frankenberg, *White Women, Race Matters: The Social Construction of Whiteness* (1993); George Lipsitz, *The Possessive Investment in Whiteness: How White People Profit From Identity Politics* (1998). In addition, white homosexuals and white women, to borrow from Frankenberg, "are practitioners of white culture" (1993), 228.
37. See David R. Roediger, *Working Towards Whiteness: How America's Immigrants Became White, The Strange Journey from Ellis Island to the Suburbs* (2005); Alastair Bonnett, *White Identity and Historical Perspectives* (2000); Karen Brodkin, *How Jews became White Folks and What That Says About Race in America* (1998); Matthew Frye Jacobson, *Whiteness of a Different Color: European Immigrants and the Alchemy of Race* (1998); Ariela J. Gross, "Like Master, Like Man: Constructing Whiteness in the Commercial Law of Slavery 1800–1861" (1996); Noel Ignatiev, *How the Irish Become White* (1995); Theodore Allen, *The Invention of the White Race* (1994 and 1997); and Cheryl I. Harris, "Whiteness as Property" (1993).
38. Rasmussen et al. (2001), 17.
39. Ahmed (2004).
40. See Geraldine Harris, *Staging Femininities: Performance and Performativity* (1999).
41. Bailey and Zita (2007), 8.
42. See Toni Morrison, *Playing in the Dark: Whiteness and the Literary Imagination* (1993).
43. See Judith Butler, *Excitable Speech: A Politics of the Performative* (1997b). Not naming and being named also, for Judith Butler, constitutes subjectivity.

44. The intersectionality framework was developed by Kimberlé Crenshaw in her 1989 article titled "Demarginalizing the Intersection of Race and Sex: A Black Feminist Critique of Antidiscrimination Doctrine, feminist Theory and Antiracist Politics." For a comprehensive reading on intersectionality, see Evelyn M. Simien, "Doing Intersectionality Research: From Conceptual issues to Practical Examples" (2007); Ange-Marie Hancock, "When Multiplication Doesn't Equal Quick Addition: Examining Intersectionality as a Research Paradigm" (2007); Avtar Brah and Ann Phoenix, "Ain't I a Woman? Revisiting Intersectionality," (2004); Cheryl I. Harris, "Finding Sojourner's Truth: Race, Gender, and the Institution of Slavery" (1996); Patricia Hills Collins, *Black feminist Thought: Knowledge, Consciousness, and the Politics of Empowerment* (1990); and bell hooks, *Ain't I a Woman: Black Woman and Feminism* (1981).

45. In this context, the issue of who is a "woman" became paramount. White was what a woman was, and not white was what she had better not be. The critique of the category "woman" is at the forefront of a variety of feminist studies, including black feminism, post-colonial feminism, queer studies, and has only recently been raised within "whiteness studies."

46. Fishkin (1995), 442.

47. Matt Wray, *Not Quite White: White Trash and the Boundaries of Whiteness* (2006); Charles Gallagher, "White Reconstruction in the University" (2003); John Hartigan, *Racial Situations: Class Predicaments of Whiteness in Detroit* (1999b); Hill, Mike, ed., *Whiteness A Critical Reader* (1997); Richard Dyer, *White* (1997); Matthew F. Jacobson, *Whiteness of a Different Color: European Immigrants and the Alchemy of Race* (1998); Noel Ignatiev, *How the Irish Became White* (1995); Noel Ignatiev and John Garvey, *Race Traitor* (1996); Ruth Frankenberg, *White Women, Race Matters: The Social Construction of Whiteness* (1993); David Roediger, *The Wages of Whiteness: Race and the Making of the American Working Class* (1991).

48. Barthes (1977), 2.

49. Angelou (1993).

ONE

The Emergence of Whiteness in the United States

In colonial America in the seventeenth century, white men achieved domination over the property rights in white, First Nations, and black labor.[1] First Nations, blacks, and whites were a part of the system of indentured servitude that was practiced during that time and continued even with the institutionalization of chattel slavery in 1660. Some historians have accurately argued that slavery, as a custom and aesthetic practice, had existed before that time. T. R. Davis, for one, in "Negro Servitude in the United States: Servitude Distinguished from Slavery," produced several convincing evidence that statutory recognition of slavery started before 1660 in Connecticut and Massachusetts.[2] However, for the first time, in 1663, the word slave appeared in the title of an act, "An Act Concerning English Servants That Runaway in the Company of Negroes and Other Slaves." The historians Oscar Handlin and Mary Handlin, in "Origins of the Southern Labor System," contended that the status of the Negro was that of servants and they were identified and treated down to the 1660s."[3]

As expected, other influential historians, including James C. Ballagh, recognized that there were no laws or customs establishing the institution of slavery.[4] John H. Russell, for example, marveled at the number of "free" blacks that were in Virginia before slavery's institutionalization.[5] This, partly, prompted Ulrich B. Phillips to claim that Africans in Virginia were indentured servants rather than slaves. And while many black indentured servants, for whatever reasons, had a fixed status to serve their masters for life, that is, de facto slavery, the opposite held true for white servants.[6] Wesley F. Craven, in *The Southern Colonies in the Seventeenth Century, 1607–1689*, expressed this concern by recognizing that from the very beginning of indentured servitude, there was an emphasis placed in

1

distinguishing the conditions of black and white servitude.[7] Yet it was not until the 1660s, in Maryland and Virginia, that a legal distinction was made between white and Negro servants.[8]

Many scholars, starting with the French political thinker and historian Alexis de Tocqueville, in their epistemology of history and the hermeneutics of the emergence of racism in America, have argued persuasively that slavery is the primary contributor of America's race prejudice. Certainly, for Tocqueville, America's race prejudice is so unfathomable and enduring that it is "immovable"[9] and "cannot be willed away."[10] My concern here is not primarily about the origins of slavery. Rather, my concern is to indicate how race prejudice, which was based on the Europeans' conceptualization of First Nations and blacks as inferior to whites, defined First Nations and blacks' positions in colonial America. Also, I want to show how the practices that originate from and sustain such a conceptualization and articulation have specific racial implications. If Tocqueville, James C. Ballagh, John H. Russell, Eric Williams, Oscar Handlin and Mary Handlin, and others are correct in arguing that slavery produced racism and not the other way around, we are then faced with an understanding that race and racial thinking were not present in colonial America before institutionalized slavery[11] and, more importantly, that the inferior status of blacks did not unfold until after slavery's institutionalization.

Given that the inferior status of blacks and First Nations in America is traceable to a definable origin, if it unfolded after slavery, why then did black and First Nations indentured servants lack rights that were bestowed on white servants? Why did race distinction become an important difference in colonial America in spite of difference in language, class, and customs, for example? Did racial distinction operate prior to the degradation of black labor? Why didn't blacks and First Nations women benefit from protection in laws and customs and were treated differently from white women? Why were the free blacks treated as inferior to whites? These questions are asked in the spirit of the emergence of whiteness as a system of domination in America. Not surprisingly, with respect to whites, the "law's construction of whiteness," as Cheryl I. Harris points out, "defined and affirmed critical aspects of identity (who is white): of privilege (what benefits accrue to that of status); and of property (what legal entitlements arise from that status)."[12] While whites remained normalized and unraced, I argue that it was during the seventeenth century in America that First Nations and blacks became raced, a sociohistorical process by which racial groups are created and reinforced. In fact, if racism did not predate slavery, race, which is only assigned to nonwhites, would make no sense unless racism existed in America. W. E. B. Du Bois understood only too well the impact of race when, in school, a white girl refused to accept his greeting card.[13]

In an effort to define the hegemonic discursive practices that describe race, Michael Omi and Howard Winant, in *Racial Formation in the United States from the 1960s to the 1990s,* employ the concept of "racial formation" to explain how race, as a cultural practice, works within America's socio-political institutions and structures.[14] In this sense, by assigning race to nonwhites, the cultural production of whiteness is caught in the current of what Audre Lorde calls a "mythical norm"[15] as wholesome and pure. Hence, the continuing need to destabilize the assumption of whiteness as wholesome and pure has been underscored by those for whom whiteness is visible.[16]

More recently, there are several "whiteness studies" scholars who are working on making whiteness visible to those whites for whom it has been invisible.[17] Notwithstanding the importance of "whiteness studies" in recent scholarships, there exist practicable shortcomings of "whiteness studies" such as the recentering of whiteness. Given that whiteness has gained historical meaning in the context of white supremacy, any discussion of whiteness must, therefore, integrate its historical origins with the semantics of race and racial thinking in the United States.

Taking into consideration that race was not inimical to the historical process of normalizing whiteness as a proliferated social practice in America, if race is equated with identity and is assigned to whites, "whiteness seems to banish the troubling asymmetry that is the essence of racism."[18] It is for this very reason that "it may be useful," according to the historian Alden T. Vaughn, "to see American racism as a necessary precondition for a system of slavery based on ancestry and pigmentation."[19] Scholars, such as Winthrop D. Jordan and Carl N. Degler, have also shown in their works how racism predated slavery. Given America's racist heritage, it is no coincidence that race relations in contemporary America remain problematic. In fact, racialized ethnic groups, especially blacks, are, for the most part, responsible for America's race problem. I think this was what the sociologist Eduardo Bonilla-Silva had in mind when he acknowledges that "many whites insist that minorities (especially blacks) are the ones responsible for [America's] racial problem."[20]

The contemporary racism-slavery debate, which legitimately gives rise to the purposeful interpretation of racism's emergence, is an attempt to show that race prejudice was already inscribed in the English psyche even before they arrived in the colonies. Hence, to use the title of the postcolonial feminist scholar Gayatri Chakravorty Spivak's article, "Race Before Racism," demonstrates that the English, from the first encounter with Africans, viewed them as inferior. Later on, G. W. F. Hegel's *Lectures on the Philosophy of World History* would confer this status of inferiority on Africans. Hegel describes Africans:

> As an example of animal man in all his savagery and lawlessness, and
> if we wish to understand him at all, we must abstract from all rever-

ence and morality, and from everything we call feelings. All that is foreign to man in his immediate existence, and nothing consonant with humanity is to be found in his character. For this reason, we cannot properly feel ourselves in his nature, no more than into that of a dog."[21]

Public documents, court cases, and the works of historians have allowed for one of the most powerful ways for us to reconstruct the lives of First Nations and blacks in seventeenth century colonial America and how whiteness determined the nefarious positions of nonwhites during that time. As we will see later in this discussion, First Nations, if they survived the raiding and massacres from the Englishmen in their attempts to secure First Nations' land, were reduced to the status of servants.[22] What was it about First Nations and blacks that set them apart from whites and rendered them inferior? Because they were viewed as different in culture and phenotype, the colonists biologized the "difference," which led First Nations and blacks to be situated in opposition to whiteness, and conceived as inferior by the European newcomers.[23] Indeed, taking my definition from Orlando Patterson, in *Slavery and Social Death: A Comparative Study*, race and racial thinking is "the assumption of innate differences based on real or imagined physical or other differences."[24] Since race can easily be transformed to racial thinking or vice versa, the relationship between the two, in this sense, is symmetrical.

In due course, laws were established to promote, whiteness and white privilege, and then justify the unequal treatment of First Nations and blacks under indentured servitude. In the context of the wider revelation of America's emphasis on life, liberty, justice, equality, and freedom, its failure to live up to these professed ideals cannot be overlooked. Slavery, for example, intimately going against these ideals, would survive the American Revolution of 1775–1783; the Declaration of Independence in 1776; the Constitution of 1787; the Naturalization Act of 1790; the Bill of Rights of 1791; and the Civil War of 1861–1865. When the Civil War ended, slavery, for several reasons, which I will not discuss here, was abolished in 1865. Slavery, I maintain, was not the highpoint for race and racial thinking, but it put into practice such existing thinking.

Was heathenism a fundamental defect of First Nations and blacks, which set them apart from the Europeans as some scholars have argued? If heathenism led the colonists to perceive First Nations and blacks as "different"; if so, why were the slaves who became Christians not affranchised? One of the more reliable example discarding the heathenism argument is the acknowledgement by Virginia Assembly in 1670 that "noe negroe or Indian though baptized and enjoyed their own Freedome shall be capable of any such purchase of Christians, but yet debarred from buying any of their owne nation."[25] Within the framework of a racially structured social reality, the construction of Christianness or Englishness from which First Nations and blacks was systematically excluded was in accordance with the norms and values of whiteness.

Whiteness, as the organizing principle of social, economic, and political life in the colonies, granted privilege to whites at the expense of First Nations, blacks, and other racialized groups.[26] Interestingly enough, this distinction had racial implications and would set in motion the racial divide that Joe R. Feagin, the sociologist and social theorist, describes as the process of "white thinking into an extensive and racialized either/or framework."[27] In time, this framework would shape and indicate the "property rights of whites" in First Nations' and Mexicans land, black, Chinese and Mexican labor, and establish whiteness as a form of property that all whites possess. This aspect will be developed in chapter two, but it is sufficient to mention here that whiteness is not simply about ideology. Through symbols, images, discursive structures, foundations, and epistemologies whiteness maintains its presumptive hegemony. Overtime, laws, utilizing racial classification, were put in place to deny First Nations and black indentured servants the rights and freedom that white indentured servants secured and enjoyed. Even though, the time of indentured servitude of many blacks was over, in many cases, their services were not elapsed.[28]

My purpose in this chapter is to decipher how whiteness gained its root in America. Seventeenth century colonial America marks an important point for understanding the emergence of whiteness. However, to accomplish this task, we must first turn our attention to how, at the initial contact with Africans, the English viewed Africans as racially different. It was in this instance of differentiation that domination, in the form of white supremacy, was produced and propagated. Bearing this in mind, I want to show how race and racial thinking were already embedded within the English psyche even before they arrived in the United States and how it would refashion itself in many important ways to determine, through laws as well as cultural practice, the unequal position of First Nations and blacks in seventeenth century colonial America. The colonists' view of First Nations and blacks as inferior was also instrumental in shaping gender and class relations. While, at that time, both blacks and First Nations were looked on as inferior by the Europeans' new comers, in their view, First Nations, if given the right kind of education could, in due course, be culturally whitened. Blacks' inferiority was conceived as inherent, which became the pretext for blacks to be treated as lesser than whites. Accordingly, in order to comprehend the emergence of whiteness in America, it will not do to disregard the evidence that race, racial thinking, and the symbolic dimensions of racial domination were in place before chattel slavery. It was during pre-slavery that the construction of race became[29] to use Barbara J. Fields's phrase "the self-evident truth,"[30] and during that period it would determine the rights, liberties, and freedoms of blacks and First Nations.[31] More importantly, it was out of this construction of race and the intolerable racial difference, which evolved simultaneously that whiteness, operating without disguise, emerged and gained dominance.[32] Whiteness, as determining how First Nations and blacks were treated during that time, seems to be a profoundly inescapable fact of American history. That whiteness must be contextualized as a diachronic analysis of power, authority, and its specificity cannot be overlooked.

EUROPEANS' VIEWS OF AFRICANS

Winthrop D. Jordan, in *White Over Black: American Attitudes Toward the Negro, 1550–1812*, has provided a comprehensive and complex account of how racial thinking was transformed into simple deficiencies and was already a socially structuring principle among the English since the Negroes arrived in England in 1553.[33] The British were incapable of understanding the full complexity of the quintessential African Culture and, hence, the first contact between the British Elizabethan English and sub-Saharan Africans, for example, provided a platform for the British to describe the Africans as "blacks," particular kinds of social beings that stood in the way of human beings.[34] Physicality such as skin color, hair, and other phenotypic characteristics readily caught the English attention and they constructed and constituted an epidermal schema not only for fixing differences but also for identifying all Africans to a distinctive kind, which would eventually translate in terms of cultural and intellectual deficiencies. Later on, Thomas Jefferson, in *The Notes on the State of Virginia*, confessed that "the first difference" about blacks was "that of color," which he argued "is fixed in nature."[35] "To have color is to be visible," as Spivak remarks, is important.[36] Skin color, in the end, would function as a metaphor that was internal to the constitution of blacks' identity.

Skin color became the most noticeable characteristic of the Negro and it had certain racial implications. The words of Jefferson are important in this regard. He writes: "blacks whether originally a distinct race, or made distinct by time and circumstances, are inferior to whites in endowments both of body and mind."[37] This is exactly how racism works. As a leading idea and principle about otherness, racism establishes the "other" as essentially different. Within the parameters of difference, there is a focus on the "other" as unalterable. The "other" has become the controller rather than the inventor of race discourse. The signifying system of racism with its concept of "essential difference" remains a vital element for situating blacks and other nonwhites as inferior. In America, blacks' inferiority became institutionalized even before slavery stood as the model for the discriminatory treatment of all racialized groups in America. In chapter 2, I show how historically the black-white model of race relations extended itself to include all nonwhites. In fact, blackness became the signifier for nonwhiteness.

The Europeans were quick to forge a consensus. As is described in Frantz Fanon's *Black Skin, White Mask*, "the Negro has one function: that of symbolizing the lower emotions, the baser inclinations, the dark side of the soul . . . The Negro—or, if one prefers, the color black—symbolizes evil, sin, wretchedness, death, war, famine."[38] Racism was essentialized and perpetuated in a signifying practice. Eventually, the most commonplace definition of the Negro would make it in a Philadelphia Encyclopedia to include "idleness, treachery, revenge, debauchery, nastiness and intemperance."[39] In Fanonian terms, in the eyes of whites, the Negro had, and continues to have, "no ontological resistance."[40] I am not implying that there is an ontological specificity to blacks.[41] In fact, one has to be wary of identity categories because they are always normative and for this very reason inevitably exclusionary. Should we, therefore, rid ourselves of the category "blacks," for example? Shouldn't we ascribe a new definition to the very term "black"? Given the overloaded significance of the term black, that very term turned Africans into unintelligible beings by the Europeans and scripted how Africans, from the very moment of contact with Europeans, were already racialized. Even though the slippery meaning of "race" during that time was evident,[42] by drawing on physical differences to construct and provide meaning to racialized groups, whiteness determined how racialization, that is "the representational process whereby social significance is attached to certain biological (usually phenotypic) human features on the basis of which those people possessing those characteristics are designated as a distinct social collectivity,"[43] worked and keeps on working. Whiteness is a dialectical force, which requires the nonwhite presence in order to maintain its malignant existence.

The racial proclivity for Europeans to view Africans as the recognizable "other" would undertake considerable development and later materialized as full-blown racism. Later on, in America, for example, the Swedish sociologist Gunnar Myrdal would refer to racism as "an American dilemma."[44] Even though the word "racism" was not in used during the colonial period, this should not surpass the historical evidence that points to a specific system in life which does not appear in language. The laws and customs that were in place were symptomatic of the wider consequences of racism as a complex inter-discursive process where the language of "difference" appealed to a concealed racist description of First Nations and blacks as racially different and usually backward. American racism can only be understood in terms of race and racial thinking and not the other way around, that is, seeing racism as the precursor for race and racial thinking. The challenging concern is that if race is denaturalized and deontologized, how can we get rid of racism and its manifestation of racial injustices? Racism allowed the colonial powers to instigate and encourage the genocide of First Nations and the encroachment of their lands. Also, laws restricting the rights of First Nations and blacks under the auspices of indentured servitude were sanctioned. This is significant when one considers how racism as historically derived would determine, shape, and reinforce the harsh treatment of blacks under legalized slavery. Starting in the 1950s, specific laws and social practices were developed in an effort to confront racism.

In addition to skin color, as a representation of difference, giving way to racial distinction itself as a form of whites' disapproval, Africans were distinguished from Europeans because of Africans' religious beliefs that contrasted with Christianity. Consequently, Africans were equated with heathenism, savagery, and uncouthness. These attributes ascribed to Africans allowed for them to be viewed as inferior to Europeans, and their inferiority would thus be foremost in the justification of Africans as slaves. In fact, the establishment of an African slave trade seemed advantageous, according to English men including Emanuel Downing. In 1645, Downing, with unmitigated certainty, described, in a letter to John Winthrop his brother-in-law, the advantages of having blacks as slaves. The missive need for Winthrop to be quoted at length is to fully capture the Europeans' view of Africans during that period.

> If upon a Just warre [with the Narragansett Indians][45] the Lord should deliver them into our hands, wee might easily have men woemen and children enough to exchange for Moores, which wilbe more gayneful pilladge for us then wee conceive, for I doe not see how we can thrive until wee get into stock of slaves sufficient to doe all our business, for our children's children will hardly see this great Continent filled with people, soe that our servants will still desire freedome to plant for themselves, and not stay but for verie great wages. And I suppose you know verie well how wee shall mayneteyne 20 Moores cheaper than one Englishe servant.[46]

This letter highlights and provides valuable insights into the psyche of the English in relation to the African population.[47] Slavery, which the English modeled after their Spanish and Portuguese forerunners, was upheld. For the British, skin color (blackness) was the essential rationale for slavery and materialized into the slave rank. In fact, as Jordan acknowledged, "embedded in the concept of blackness was its direct opposite—whiteness."[48] Further, to make use of Oscar Handlin and Mary Handlin's observation, "The trace of color became the trace of slavery"[49] and color would also determine blacks' status in a society marred by the binary logics of racial antagonisms—black and white, inferior and superior, and uncivilized and civilized.

The colonists were a product of this sort of racial thinking that triumphed with the English and extended itself to other parts of Europe. The black Marxist scholar Oliver C. Cox, rightfully, has given details and complexified this very issue by demonstrating that even proceeding to the sixteenth century, Europeans "have not been content merely to accept their present social and political dominance as an established fact. Almost from the first they have attempted to rationalize the situation and to prove to themselves that their subjugation of other racial groups was natural and inevitable."[50] It is no coincidence that the English, when they arrived in the colonies, enslaved First Nations. The enslavement of First Nations achieved its momentum during the wars between First Nations and the English. The fact that an arduous service such as enslavement was established for First Nations and that a similar status was also reserved for blacks in the colonies is no surprise.[51]

In fact, in his letter to Winthrop, Downing expressed his wish to wage war against the First Nations so that the captives (First Nations) could be bartered for Moores, which as I have already pointed out, "wilbe more gayneful pilladge for [them] then [they] conceive."[52] Judging from Shakespeare's *Othello*, the English had a specific image of the Moores as pitchy black. Even though Othello himself was a Moor, and the term Moor was almost used interchangeably with Negro, the Moor, who is never named in this play, but referred to as "the thick lip"; "an old black ram"; "the devil"; "a Barbary horse"; "lascivious"; and "an extravagant and wheeling stranger"[53] was placed outside the parameters of normalcy and considered unlike the English in customs and appearance. The English, in their narrow-mindedness, constructed him as inferior so that his mistreatment may be defensible.

One of Shakespeare's most disconcerting plays is *Titus Andronicus* where the Moor character Aaron is presented as the "most relentlessly wicked [character], a black devil pure and simple."[54] Given the unwillingness of many scholars to go further than the metaphorical imagery of blackness and whiteness in Shakespearean plays, it is easy to understand why some of the scholars would dismiss the claim that race and racial thinking among the English have led them to include in plays, such as *Othello* and *Titus Andronicus*, measures of blackness against whiteness and reduce blackness to otherness so that the relations of good (whiteness) and evil (blackness) seem naturally inevitable.[55] In spite of the reformulation of race, race continues to be marked on the body as "the physical and permanent fact of color,"[56] as Alexis de Tocqueville puts it, or as Fanon names it as epidermitized.[57] In other words, for blacks and other nonwhites, race, as an assumed fixed set of natural corporeal facts, continues to be marked on the body. Yet, we have to remember that race, per se, is not a fact. In a commonly cited passage, the philosopher Kwame Anthony Appiah points out that "race, we all assume, is, like all other concepts, constructed by metaphors and metonymy; it stands in, metonymically, for Other; it bears the weight, metaphorically, of other kinds of difference . . . The truth is that there are no races."[58] Rather, the various operations of race fashion the idea of race. Without those operations, there would be no conceptualization of race at all.

More simply, in America, what Judith Butler says about gender can be said about race: it is "a construction that regularly conceals its genesis"[59] and historical specificity under pseudo biological facts. Are we then to conclude that the racialized body is a purely passive medium completely subjected to the system of racism that precedes and determines the subject itself? Is there a need to account for the various ways in which race is usually produced, reproduced, and constituted, even though race can be produced, reproduced, and constituted differently? And even though race, in some cases, is experienced differently by individuals depending on her/his situatedness, history, and cultural distinctiveness, race still becomes the arbitrary locus of other constructions such as gender and sexuality, for example, dictating the tangible consequences for non-whites' well-being and life changes. The experiences of racialized ethnic groups are not only structured by social, economic, political, and ideological arrangements; they are also implicitly racist in their orientation, and produce and structure those arrangements.

RACE AND RACIAL THINKING IN SEVENTEENTH CENTURY COLONIAL AMERICA

The epistemic tension within history and other constitutive disciplines on whether race and racial thinking or slavery came first, which Winthrop D. Jordan would describe as "the long duration and the vigor of the controversy,"[60] have generated much scholarly interest and, rightfully so, is hotly debated by many scholars.[61] In 1949, when Wesley F. Craven, in *The Southern Colonies in the Seventeenth Century, 1607–1689*, suggested that "the modern assumption that prejudice against the Negro is largely a production of slavery,"[62] he allowed for the rethinking of Eric Williams's *Capitalism and Slavery*, which for one, noted that slavery "had to do not with the color of the laborer but the cheapness of the labor."[63] When in 1987 Barbara Lewis Solow and Stanley L. Engerman produced an edited volume, *British Capitalism and Caribbean Slavery: The Legacy of Eric Williams*, its purpose was to rethink Williams's pioneering work.[64] However, Williams's argument according to which racism was a consequence of slavery was opposed by Solow and Stanley who criticized Williams for not making any attempt "to trace the subsequent path that led to racism."[65] Jordan, in the end, would try to address the racism-slavery debate by declaring, "Rather than slavery causing "prejudice," or vice versa, they seem rather to have generated each other. Both were, after all, twin aspects of a general debasement of the Negro."[66] Drawing from the insights of William Goodell, in *Slavery and Anti-Slavery: A History of the Great Struggles in Both Hemispheres, with a View of the Slavery Question in*

America, we are equipped with the knowledge that "the Negro race, from its introduction, was regarded with disgust."[67] And, given that "knowledge of whatever kind," according to Michel Foucault, "proceeded to the ordering of its material by the establishment of differences and defined those differences by the establishment of an order,"[68] by the time slavery became fixed in law, the inferiority of blacks was an already established and recognized fact.[69] In fact, how the inferiority of blacks constructed and shaped gender and class relations is important. However, Kathleen Brown's *Good Wives, Nasty Wenches, and Anxious Patriarchs: Gender, Race, and Power in Colonial Virginia* point of departure from the saliency of race and racial thinking to drawing our attention to the gender theory of racial construction, in which she argues that during the 1600s, gender defines all groups in society.[70] In this sense, for Brown, gender constructed race.

Some evidence showed that from 1640 to 1660 there was a degradation of black labor. Many historians have argued that slavery existed in the colonies even before 1660 when slavery became a legal institution.[71] According to John H. Russell, black servants "defended themselves with increasing difficulties from the encroachment of slavery."[72] In fact, while the conditions for white servants improved, the opposite held true for blacks. Yet in the "Origins of the Southern Labor System," Oscar Handlin and Mary Handlin's work has exercised a major influence on whether racism predated slavery. It has remained, for almost a decade, an important historical grounding on this issue until the surfacing, in 1959, of Carl N. Degler, "Slavery and the Genesis of American Race Prejudice," as a necessary and integral opposition to the Handlins' highly problematic formulation. In fact, the Handlins have justified blacks' exploitation by pointing out that blacks "were farthest removed from the English." Hence, they concluded that "it is not necessary to resort to racialist assumptions to account for such measures; these were simply the reactions of immigrants lost to the stability and security of home. . . . Like the millions who would follow, these immigrants longed in the strangeness for the company of familiar men and singled out to be welcomed those who were not like them."[73] The Handlins' conclusion is understandable, but it does not explain why First Nations and blacks were racialized from the beginning of Europeans arrival in the colonies.

By drawing on physical differences to construct and provide meaning to racialized groups, whiteness determined how the process of racialization worked. Given that Africans and First Nations were marked as unwhite in appearance, the Europeans' emphasis on physical difference provided us with the need to analyze the meaning of race. In so doing, we are able to gain access to the ideological core of both race theory and racism in colonial America. The racialized body served for a disturbing alterity that differentiated "us" from "them," the civilized from the uncivilized, and the superior from the inferior. In other words, the image of the racialized "other" played a primary role in seventeenth century colonial America's cultural practice, and it was, partly for this reason, as Degler points out, that First Nations and blacks were "actually never treated as an equal of the white man, servants or free"[74] during that period. The "other" has become the regulator rather than the creator of social discourse.

In spite of the Handlins' denial that race was the primary marker for discriminatory practices toward blacks, when we examine the way in which blacks were looked on and treated, we cannot help but to conclude that the colonist immediately showed a natural disgust for blacks.[75] Wesley F. Craven, in *The Southern Colonies in the Seventeenth Century, 1607–1689*, a thoughtful reexamination of the status of blacks before slavery became a legal institution, has shown that the contemptuous look Europeans had on blacks was the product of a complex historical process that took on various forms. The economic conditions of poor whites were not different from that of blacks, which, nonetheless, did not deter those in power from enacting laws that institutionalize specific forms of race and gender relations that kept whiteness unmarked, it has to be said, in a society infested with race prejudice. Observing the natural contempt that the Europeans had for blacks, Craven was led to conclude that the enslavement of blacks was earlier than 1660.[76] Even so, the disdain for blacks would set the stage for chattel slavery as a justifiable institution in the United States. Hence, the evidence that racism was in place before slavery is not fully settled until we take another look at the concept of race and racial thinking in colonial America.

ANOTHER LOOK AT RACE AND RACIAL THINKING

Race relations in the southern colonies were rather complicated in that there was a need for labor. At the beginning, First Nations, black, and white laborers toiled side by side and socialize during leisure hours. Over the long run, black servants proved to be more advantageous than First Nations because longer years of indentured servitudes could be imposed on the former; life servitude was even imposed on some blacks. In contrast, First Nations servants would end their servitude by easily slipping away from the plantation. Whites, for different reasons, proved to be as unsatisfactory a work force as First Nations since their contract as indentured servants ended after a somewhat short period in comparison to blacks.[77] Accordingly, in due course, the plantation owners developed a preference for black labor.

We cannot argue that economic needs primarily shaped race relations in seventeenth century southern colonies. We need to turn our attention to the concept of "different" in terms of phenotype that shaped the way the colonists viewed First Nations and blacks and the growing body of stature restricted the rights of First Nations and blacks. Winthrop D.

Jordan's *White Over Black: American Attitudes Towards the Negro, 1550–1812* has elaborated on these observations in what he described and labeled the "cycle of degradation" that blacks and First Nations endured in colonial society during the seventeenth century.[78] The "cycle of degradation" advanced the motifs of white men whose superiority was not even to be questioned.

Blacks and First Nations were physically different from the newly arrived European settlers, and the Europeans, especially those who settled in Virginia, were quick to point this out.[79] In fact, First Nations were looked on as the ingenuous primitives and savage beast of colonial frontiers; and blacks were seen inhuman and uncivilized. It is not surprising, then, that the colonist would resort to some form of "color prejudice," which, as I have already alluded to, was embedded in the British psyche even before they first encountered Africans in the United States. "Color prejudice" placed whites above blacks and First Nations. And even though in the colonists' minds the physical difference of First Nations and blacks was interpreted as a mark of inferiority, the crucial distinction between these two groups is that blacks' inferiority was hereditary and that of First Nations' was sociocultural.

At the beginning, the colonists interpreted First Nations' inferiority as a result of cultural and environmental factors[80] even though several evidences pointed to the fact that First Nations had a highly developed culture. In fact, First Nations "possessed elaborate religious systems, sophisticated forms of government, and trade networks that extended as far west and North of the Great Lakes . . . Most of [them] were hunters, gatherers, and primitive cultivators."[81] Yet, they were mythified by the Europeans as the "noble savages" and, hence, had to be restrained, controlled, and civilized. Partly, for this reason, the heuristic issue for the colonists was education—a process by which First Nations were to be assimilated to the white culture in order to properly function as a race. In other words, First Nations can be redeemed from savageness if they were properly schooled in the moral and cultural value of whiteness. This view is particularly promoted in the work of Joseph Boskin's *Into Slavery, Racial Decisions in the Virginia Colony*. Boskin explained that education, as the miraculous cure for First Nations' inferiority, encouraged "finances, directives, and institutions to 'civilize' and Christianize" First Nations.[82] Such beliefs lay the apocryphal foundation of white authority. It is important, then, for us to take heed to W. E. B. Du Bois' orthodox understanding of whiteness and its legal basis for the entrenchment of white supremacy in American history.[83]

Eventually, the colonists began to define First Nations as a race.[84] How race is lived in America, a point that is highlighted throughout the text, is vastly important. In fact, the colonists drew a clear racial distinction between whites and nonwhites. Out of this distinction, while being both indentured servants, First Nations and black servants were necessarily below white servants in the servitude hierarchy.[85] For instance, during this time, white women were not allowed to work in the fields. More importantly, as we will see later on, racial hierarchy placed First Nations, black, and other nonwhite women outside the category of women.[86] Racial hierarchy among indentured servants was the starting point of the normalization of whiteness. Indentured servitude, by all means, laid the groundwork for the inscription of whiteness and white privilege into the colonists' psyche and, later on, it would be actually engraved by American laws, epistemologies, and institutions.

In the following section, I want to direct our attention to indentured servitude. It is important to note here the distinction between white and black servitude. In fact, the servitude that existed in the colonies until 1619 underwent changes, which transformed servitude into slavery. T.R. Davis argues that before then servitude took on the character of informal slavery. "Slavery," he writes, "is the fact that one man is the property or possession of another."[87] In Hegelian terms, it reflected power relations as a necessary dialectic of domination and subordination between the masters and slaves. I do not mean to imply that power relations were absent within the system of indentured servitude. In fact, power relations were imposed de facto on the masters and the servants since both masters and servants accepted its term and rely on them. Hence, in some cases, servants would break away from servitude by running away. What we see here is the Foucauldian display of the interconnection of resistance and power. In other words, even though power remains indeterminate since it is this indeterminacy that is the very state of its existence, resistance, indeed, is in anticipation of power. Power and counter-power tacitly serve to generate each other.

White servitude did not measure up to the formal feature of "property" or "possession"[88] because whites worked on a contractual basis and, under no circumstance, were expected to serve their masters for the rest of their natural lives. On the contrary, most blacks were condemned to a lifetime of servitude. It is precisely for this reason that T. R. Davis contended that "white servitude and black servitude were but different aspect of the same institutions."[89] The practice of extending to blacks a lifetime of servitude "proved," according to Davis, "a significant factor in the degradation of white servitude."[90] Partly, for this reason, black servants had a higher monetary value than white servants. For instance, in 1645, "two Negro women and a boy were sold for 5,500 pounds of tobacco," which was a high price when compared to the white servants.[91] These practices would soon be materialized into laws. However, in the long run black labor was cheaper than white labor because black labor contract was, most of the time, extended, and in some cases it never ended.

INDENTURED SERVITUDE

It is clear that the system of indentured servitude in seventeenth century colonial America was a dynamic and heterogeneous one. In Oscar Handlin and Mary Handlin's essay, "Origins of the Southern Labor System," in 1950, they argued that Africans in Virginia up until 1660 were not, at the start, singled out for enslavement and black indentured servants were treated the same way as white indentured servants. Even though as early as 1640, Maryland's law "provided that 'all masters' should try to furnish arms to themselves and 'all those of their families which shall be capable of arms—which would include servants—('excepting Negroes'),"[92] many historians have already endorsed the Handlins' argument.[93] However, I think that Winthrop D. Jordan's provocative question, "If whites and Negroes could share the same status of half freedom for forty years in the seventeenth century, why could they not share full freedom in the twentieth?" is, in many ways, the most relevant question to ask because it precisely points to the different status of white and black servants.[94] In an attempt to undermine race prejudice that blatantly existed in colonial America, the Handlins' approach to America's race relations is not without its problems.[95] Judging from the evidence that Maryland in 1639, and Virginia in 1643, "enacted laws fixing limits to the terms of servants who entered without written contract, Negroes were not included in such protective provision,"[96] it is clear that black and white servants were unequally treated. In addition, for white indentured servants, the terms of service were decreased as greater reliance rested on the labor of blacks The power that was invested in the legislatures to control black labor is aptly described by Kenneth M. Stampp.[97] Eventually, Stampp acknowledges that the masters were given "absolute power and authority over his Negro[98] who were, by then, considered slaves. The master could have murdered the slaves, mutilated their bodies, refused to feed them, severely whipped, and in terms of the slave women, raped them. In fact, all these injustices, including the rape of slave women were not deemed as crimes. It was a part of a system called "stock breeding," which reduces human beings to animals.[99]

In the period from 1619 to 1629, the tendency in the colonies was a sharp distinction between blacks and the white servants.[100] Africans brought to Virginia, for example, "held from the outset a singularly debased status in the eyes of white Virginians."[101] Countless examples of white servants being treated much better than black servants have been documented by many historians. An excellent example that Carl N. Degler has drawn on, to exemplify this difference, was the treatment of three servants, two whites, "one called Victor, a Dutchman, and the other a Scotchman called James Gregory," and one black named John Punch who ran away together in 1640. After they were caught and returned to their masters, the three men were each given thirty lashes. For the white servants, an extra three years of service to their masters was administered. The black servant had to serve his said master for the rest of his natural life in Virginia or he was assigned to another master somewhere else. Also, in the same year, a Negro, named Emanuel, was singled out from a group of runaways who were brought back; six of the seven runaways who were white were assigned additional time while the Negro was not condemned to serve for the rest of his life because he was already branded with life time servitude, but received the shackle and was branded with the letter "R."[102] In other words, if one takes seriously the definition of a slave as "a man who is the property or possession of another man," these runaway Negroes became their master's property. In fact, "white servitude lacked the final and formal feature of 'property,' namely complete 'possession,' and consequently never included either perpetual service or the transformation of servile conditions to offspring."[103]

As early as 1669, the Virginia Assembly declared "WHEREAS the only law in force for the punishment of refractory servants resisting their masters, mistresses or overseers cannot be inflected upon negroes, nor the obstinacy of many of them by other then violent meanes supprest," if a Negro "by the extremity of the correction should chance to die," his masters was not deemed guilty of any felony "since it cannot be presumed that pretense malice (which alone makes murder Felony) should induce any man to destroy his owne estate."[104] The notion of blacks as property was fully incorporated into the institutional structures. Hence, if we should take literally the sociologist Donald L. Noel's summation according to which a "society is racist . . . only if the idea of group superiority-inferiority is incorporated into the institutional structure,"[105] colonial America, during the seventeenth century, was blatantly a racist society. The mere fact that the master can destroy "his owne estate," meaning his slaves, fully demonstrates what Cheryl I. Harris, in her highly significant essay, "Whiteness as Property," calls "the property rights of whites" in black labor.[106]

And even though both whites and Negro servants, when they stole, ran away, indulged in fornication,[107] or assembled unlawfully, and if they were caught, unfortunately suffered such debase punishment, including whipping[108] and branding with the letter "R," for example, which certainly reduced the servants to the status of a slave, the "Decisions of the General Court" on June 30, 1640 kept alive the proper fate of black servants as that of second class. It stated that "the court hath granted that a commission shall be drawn for John Mottrom and Edward Fleet, authorizing them to levy a party of men, or more if need require, . . . with arms and ammunition to go in pursuit of certain runaway negroes and to bring them into the governor." In acting accordingly to the state's wish, these men were reassured that they would be handsomely rewarded.[109] We can see now, far from conceiving white men's power as autonomous of state power, the noticeable feature here is that white men's power and the power of state were synonymous. White men, with the state's support, were to exercise, through violence, their authority over blacks. And when Fields remarked that "whatever truths may have appeared self-evident in those days, neither an inalienable right to life and liberty nor the founding of government on the consent of the governed were amount them,"[110] her remarks provides a clear indication of how America's democracy was fashioned and constituted on the basis of excluding nonwhites and women from democratic citizenship.

The policing of black bodies was eventually codified into law and it would, without any remorse, extend itself and find leverage during slavery, Reconstruction, the Jim Crow south, and, more recently, in the ghettoes, super ghettoes, prisons, and racial profiling. In those days, especially during Reconstruction and the Jim Crow South, the policing of black bodies was performed by those in power and ordinary white men belonging to the nefarious Ku Klux Klan. Today, it is the police officers who mistreat people on racial grounds, confident that his or her racial profiling will remain unconstrained. The very question, in its seemingly aseptic, benevolent form, "How does it feel to be the problem?" to which W. E. B. Du Bois draws our attention, in *The Souls of Black Folks*, becomes overriding because this question has materialized from whites' invention of blacks as in opposition to themselves and are always conceived as the problem. In other words, blacks are not the problem; the problem is the predisposition for the white power structure to construct them as the problem.[111] Because power, in the Foucauldian sense, and its authoritarian dimensions, conditions and limits the possibilities of blacks as is manifested through the lived reality of their daily life, in many important ways, blacks have developed resistance to such operative powers.

The same inequality was applied between white and nonwhite females. First Nations and Negro women, free or bond, were treated differently from white women even if white women were servants.[112] While First Nations and black women were used for field work because they were considered to be "wenches that are nasty, and beastly, and not fit to be so employed" as domestic servants, white women secured domestic employment.[113] Field work was recognized in the taxation policy of Virginia. As early as 1629, taxable persons were defined as "all those that work in the grounds of what qualities or condition whatsoever,"which included First Nations and black women.[114] By 1643, this policy would appear in the written record. It now stated that all adult men and women from the age of sixteen were to be taxable. Beginning in 1654, Maryland pursued a similar path.[115] And in spite of the spectrum of evidence pertaining to the condition of blacks in Virginia, the historian Winthrop D. Jordan reluctantly conceded that "there simply is not enough evidence to indicate with any certainty whether Negroes were treated like white servants or not."[116]

In colonial Virginia, for example, restrictions on sexual unions between whites and nonwhites were codified into law, and miscegenation was criminalized.[117] To take the worst possible case, in 1630, the Virginia court sentenced "Hugh Davis to be soundly wiped before an assembly of Negroes and others for abusing himself to the dishonor of God and shame of Christians because he has defiled his body in lying with a Negro."[118] By 1662, a law in Virginia punished Christian whites for fornicating with blacks. This law, with the clearest lucidity, expresses the attentiveness to separate blacks from whites by stating that "if any Christian shall commit Fornication with a negro man or woman, hee or shee offending" would be fined doubled the usual fines. Maryland was quick to follow suit and, in 1664, it banned interracial marriages between free slaves and white women.[119] The law stated "forasmuch as divers freeborne English women forgetttful of their free Condicion and the disgrace of our Nation doe intermarry with Negro Slaves by which alsoe divers suites may arise touching the Issue of such woemen and a great damage doth befall the Masters of such Negros for prevention whereof for deterring such freeborne women from the shameful Matches." Partly for this reason, any free white woman who married a slave was to serve her husband's master for the period of the slave's life, and the children would have to serve the master until he/she was thirty years old.[120] Given that a white woman can have black children and a black woman cannot have white children, this law was in no way to suppress race and racial thinking where whites were deemed as superior. More importantly, it pointed to the state's oppressive practice of fixing race on the body.

In spite of these laws, in Virginia and Maryland, for example, racial lines were neither consistently nor piercingly demarcated within social groups because there were no structural and ideological incentives for poor whites men or women to forge an alliance with the white power structure that was in place. Consequently, activities between blacks and lower-class whites were socially communal and both "seemed to be remarkably unconcerned about their visible physical differences."[121] In this regard, whites in seventeenth-century Virginia had a more flexible understanding of race and did not equate race with slavery. Nonetheless, slavery was not the exemption but the fundamental organizing principle of society, allocating social space not just to slaveholders and slaves, free blacks and poor whites, but the social white elite as well. Racial ideology continued to permeate the social, economic, and political landscapes of the slave society,[122] which was already steadfast within the edifice of indentured servitude.

In spite of the racial ideology in place, in many instances, whites and blacks would join together to oppose the rules of the plantation owners.[123] I suppose that is partly why some scholars are convinced that

"Southern racial asperities," to quote Ulrich B. Phillips, were "mainly superficial, and that the two great elements," in this case, race and racial thinking were not "fundamentally in accord."[124] In fact, it is a well-known fact that poor whites, for the most part, seemed to be at ease with blacks who occupied subservient positions so that their supremacy could be guaranteed. Nonetheless, both black and white indentured servants joined the militia formed by Nathaniel Bacon to attack First Nations who represented a threat to white settlers. A large group of freed white men, "landless, single, discontent—and well armed,"[125] who had no alliances—political, social or economic—with member of the white gentry and the Virginia legislation would later referred to as a "giddy multitude," joined the movement with the aim of getting free land and becoming farmers. Blacks, on the other hand, burdened by the presumption that revolution was the pathway to freedom from a lifelong bond-servitude joined the militia.[126] During that time there was no indication that blacks would be freed from bond-servitude.[127] Bacon's Rebellion in 1676, was instigated by black and white bond-laborers trying to put an end to bond-servitude by overthrowing William Berkeley, the colony's governor.[128]

Bacon's Rebellion was an immense threat to the social order that intended to separate poor whites from threatening blacks. Consequently, Bacon's Rebellion was instrumental in providing those in power with new intentions. Of particular concern to the elite was the possibility to reverse the familiar bonds that were previously forged between poor whites and blacks, in such a way, that whiteness, as a system of domination, would become compatible and amalgamate with a white identity. That is, poor whites had to feel superior to blacks and other nonwhites. White supremacy would later materialize as another one of the defining characteristics of, what professor Charles Mills refers to as, "the racial contract" where laws, codes, and practice work, through racial hierarchy, to maintain, reinforce, and perpetuate white supremacy. White supremacy articulated and inscribed itself by reconfiguring and restructuring the social boundaries between whites and nonwhites as absolutely indispensable. Also, women had to be viewed as subordinate to men in an effort to reaffirm racial patriarchal structures and interests. "Racial patriarchy," according to Cheryl I. Harris, "describes that social, political, economic, legal, and conceptual system that entrenched the ideology of white supremacy and white male control over women's reproduction and sexuality."[129] In fact, a Maryland Act of 1681 described marriage of white women with Negroes as, among other things, "always to the disgrace not only of the English but also other Christian nations."[130] In addition, a 1691 law in Virginia declared that a white woman, if she married a black man, would be fined or sold into servitude for five years.[131] This was simply a fierce attempt to defend and protect the idea of white woman's wholesomeness. Racial patriarchy would pose a continual challenge to black men in asserting their masculinity. In concurrence with patriarchal norms and the furtherance of whiteness and white privilege, racial patriarchy would eventually manifest itself in the property rights in First Nations' land and black and Chinese labor. Whiteness, in itself, would become a triumphal form of property that all whites possessed, and still possess, as I argue in chapter two.

In the end, Bacon's Rebellion would establish not only the subordinate position of First Nations, blacks, other racialized groups, and women but, more important, what Theodore W. Allen called "the monorail of Anglo-American historical development, white [male] supremacy"[132] was further strengthened. In other words, racism was instrumental in controlling blacks and other nonwhites; and sexism was to keep women in their places as "the second sex." And even though there is a long tradition of blacks' resistance against racism, the diabolic systems of racism and sexism, once set in motion, seem unalterable and essential for their beneficiaries. Nonetheless, instead of distinguishing and focusing on gender, race, and class as separate identities, which locate and position nonwhite women on the margin of society, I want to locate race, gender, and class as a dialectic expansion of each of these categories. It allows for a refocus on the complexity and multiplicities of the oppression of nonwhite women. The efforts of various black and other nonwhite feminists to take into account the various identity markers, including race, gender, class, sexuality, religion, and ethnicity, as working together to create the daily experiences of women of color have, more recently, brought duly attention to the intersectionality framework.

In an effort to alienate blacks from white servants and promote racial hierarchy as a logical conclusion, the white servants were entitled to land at the end of their servitude, even though some unforeseen problems in allocating the land were inevitable.[133] Differences in skincolor, which engendered the construction of racial categories, defined and shaped the unequal position between black and white servants. Yet in assessing this claim we must turn our attention to Degler's provocative essay, "Slavery and the Genesis of American Race Prejudice," as a critique of the many writings, including the Handlins's and Williams's espousing the view that race and racial thinking was not a consequence of slavery. Degler's fundamental point is that in early America, there was always contempt for Africans. For this reason, he warns that any account of the origins of slavery has to pay particular attention to, what is labeled, "the color prejudice" of America[134] because the physical description of people flows from the conception of race and not the other way around.

Slavery, the Handlins remarked, materialized "from the adjustment to American conditions of traditional European institutions."[135] Whatever the cause of the materialization of slavery, when it did emerge, "it became infused with the social attitude," encapsulated by the single predominant perception, "which had prevailed from the very beginning, namely, that Negroes were inferior," Degler writes.[136] According to countless reports, discrimination against the Negro came about before the slave standing was definite and before Negro labor turned out to be essential to the economic system.[137] As Degler points out, "The Negro has been consigned to a special discriminatory status."[138] In New England, for example, despite the relative small amount of African laborers, the lives of blacks were impaired by immense discrimination,[139] which strengthened with slavery as a legal institution. Taking seriously Winthrop D. Jordan's observation, in *White Over Black: American Attitudes Toward the Negro, 1550–1812*, that slavery was "neither borrowed from foreigners, nor extracted from books, nor invented out of whole cloth, nor extrapolated from servitude, nor generated from the English reaction to Negroes as such, nor necessitate by the exigencies of the new world. Not any one of these made the Negro a slave, but all"[140] is important to account for the working of whiteness in America's history. For the most part, whiteness is linked with rank, power, wealth, and superiority. This alliance is not symbolic; it is entrenched in America's social structure.

More importantly, the conceptualization of race and racial thinking would be clearer if we examine the status of free blacks. Race and racial thinking permeated the laws and public discourse and were embedded in the very core of American cultural consciousness. The historian Joseph Boskin offers a concise account of how blacks and slaves become homogeneous and convertible.[141] In fact, free blacks were denied the rights enjoyed by whites. When the law determined that "no Negro may carry any weapon of any kind, nor leave his master's grounds without a pass, nor shall any 'negroe or other slaves . . . presume to lift his hands in opposition against any Christian,' and if a Negro runs away and resists recapture it 'shall be lawful for such persons or person to kill said negroe or slave,'"[142] the law made clear the second class status of blacks. Degler has refined the conception of black in a particularly influential way by showing that in the colonies, a Negro, whether he or she was a servant or a free man or woman, was "treated as an inferior to white men."[143] Hence, if race and racial thinking followed slavery, laws pertaining to black servants and free blacks would have been enforced after slavery became legal in the United States.

Even though servitude continued after slavery became a legal institution in America, "servitude continued even after the institution of slavery was fully developed."[144] As servitude disappeared, legal slavery succeeded it;[145] and there was "a natural transition from Negro servitude to slavery."[146] By the end of the seventeenth century, when slavery was a fully recognized legal institution, a 1695 act in Maryland, for example, required slaves to have in their possessions passes that were signed by either their masters, or an overseer, whenever they left the plantation, even if traveling from one plantation to another.[147] A slave caught without a pass would be severely punished. Later on, Thomas Jefferson, in *Notes on the State of Virginia*, would interpret slavery as a fact of blacks' inherent inferiority. Also, the historian Ulrich B. Phillips did not see slavery as detrimental to the human condition.[148] Indeed, the laws, which were in place before slavery began, set the tone for the subjugation of blacks and First Nations. Eventually Chinese and other racialized ethnic groups in the United States would succumb to such harsh treatments.

America's unabashed public attitudes and political response to racialized ethnic groups had been prominent and continue to shape the nefarious social and cultural practices of white America. Whiteness has become the yardstick by which all nonwhites are measured against and reduced to otherness. And even though a white identity meant different things at different times—groups including the Irish, Italians, Greeks, and Jews were not considered white at one point in American history[149] —what it meant to be white drew on a definition of the constructed racialized "other" that is placed in opposition to whites. In the next Chapter, through a sustained engagement with whiteness, I want to focus specifically on whiteness itself as a form of property. Laws, including the Naturalization Act of 1790; the Indian Removal Act of 1830; the Treaty of Guadeloupe Hidalgo in 1848; the Jim Crow laws of 1876; the Chinese Exclusion Act of 1886; and the General Allotment Act (The Dawes Severalty Act) of 1887, amongst other laws, showed the working of whiteness in America. Each, in its specificity, allows for a perception into the working of whiteness within the realm of everyday existence. In the end, America would take into account, what Jordan describes and explains as "a self conscious reappraisal of its racial arrangement"[150] by implementing antidiscriminatory measures. In chapter 3, I examine antidiscriminatory measures in the United States in great detail.

NOTES

1. Blacks, in colonial America, were called "Africans, Blackamores, Moores, Negars, Negers, Negros, Negroes, and the like." See T. R. Davis, "Negro Servitude in the United States: Servitude Distinguished from Slavery" (1923), 247–48. The historian John H. Russell, *The Free Negro in Virginia, 1619–1895,* has substituted the word "Slave" for "Negro" (1923), 16. As early as the 1630s, blacks worked on plantations in Maryland. See Kenneth M. Stampp, *Peculiar Institution: Slavery in the Ante-Bellum South* (1956), 18.

2. It is noted that slavery existed in Massachusetts since 1639, when a story is told of a Negro woman held in Noddles Island in Boston harbor where her master sought to mate her with another Negro whom she kicked out of her bed and declared that such an intrusion was "beyond her slavery." (Degler 1959), 62–63. The Body of Civil Liberties of 1661, the first legal code in Massachusetts, prohibited bond slavery. Davis noted that "statutory recognition of slavery by the American colonies occurred as following: Massachusetts 1641; Connecticut 1650; Virginia 1661; Maryland 1663; New York and New Jersey 1664; South Carolina 1682; Pennsylvania and Rhode Island, 1700; North Carolina 1717; and Georgia 1755 (1923), 254. And in spite of Davis noting that slavery started in Maryland in 1663, (1923), 254. James M. Wright, *The Free Negroes in Maryland, 1634–1860,* cited two studies of Maryland that showed slavery existed there

since 1638. For instance, in 1638, in an act of the legislature, reference was also made to slaves. It stated: "Be it enacted by the lord proprietor of this province of and with advice and approbation of the freemen of the same that all persons being Christians (slaves excepted) of the age of eighteen years or above brought into this province at the charge and adventure of some other person shall serve such person... for the full term of four years." Johnson (1978), 236. Given that the act did not identify the racial identity of these slaves, it is a great possibility that First Nations and blacks could have been included under the term slave. See Jonathan L. Alpert, "The Origins of Slavery in the United States—The Maryland Precedent" (1970), 191. The record shows that an African slave was being sold in Maryland in 1644. See Helen T. Catterall, *Judicial cases Concerning American Slavery and the Negro* (1968), 8. And, according to Jonathan L. Alpert, "'an act for the liberties of people' in 1639 provided that all Christian inhabitants 'slaves excepted' should have the rights of Englishmen. In order words, it was specified that the word slave was being applied to non-Englishmen, which meant that First Nations and blacks were not excluded from Englishness."

    3. Handlin and Handlin (1950), 204.

    4. Ballagh (1902), 29.

    5. Russell, (1913).

    6. I rely here on Ulrich B. Phillips, *American Negro Slavery: A Survey of the Supply, Employment and Control of the Negro Labor as Determined by the Plantation Regime*, for an account of this postulation (1918), 74–76.

    7. See Wesley F. Craven, *The Southern Colonies in the Seventeenth Century, 1607–1689* (1949).

    8. Stampp (1956), 22. Yet some Africans were serving their masters for life in Virginia and Maryland. See Winthrop D. Jordan, *White Over Black: American Attitudes Toward the Negro, 1550–1812* (1962), 22–24. On the other hand, Alden T. Vaughan, "The Origins Debate: Slavery and Racism in Seventeenth Century Virginia," claimed that the evidence that are available before the 1640 was not enough and thus inconclusive about the origins of slavery (1972), 469.

    9. See Alexis de Tocqueville, *Democracy in America* (1945). More recently, other authors include Eric Williams, *Capitalism and Slavery* (1994); and Oscar Handlin and Mary Handlin, "Origins of the Southern Labor System" (1959)

    10. Hacker (2003), 4.

    11. Barbara J. Fields points to the fact that the concept of race emerged in American in the late seventeenth century. See "Slavery, Race and Ideology in the United States of America" (1990), 101. I want to show that the concept of race in America was transported from Europe to America with the arrival of the British arrived in America.

    12. Harris (1993), 1725.

    13. Du Bois (2003), 4.

    14. Omi and Winant (1994), 54–56.

    15. Lorde 1984. When whiteness is viewed as wholesome and pure, it endorses this phantasmatic view of itself. However, for blacks, First Nations, and other nonwhites, whiteness is nothing but terrifying. For a good overview of whiteness as terrifying, see bell hooks, *Black Looks: Race and Representation* (1992). Also, Olaudah Equiano, in his memoirs, described his first encounter with whites as he was being placed on board a slave ship. He writes, "I was now persuaded that I had got into a world of bad spirits, and they were going to kill me . . . I found some black people about me . . . I asked them if we were not to be eaten by these white men with horrible looks, red faces, and long hair. See Olaudah Equiano, *Interesting Narrative and Other Writings* (1998), 55.

    16. See W. E. B. Du Bois, *The Soul of Black Folks*, 2003; *Darkwater: Voices From Within the Veil* (1969); and *An Essay Toward a History of the Part Black Folk Played in the Attempt to Reconstruct Democracy in America, 1860–1880* (1935); Toni Morrison, *Playing in the Dark: Whiteness and the Literary Imagination* (1993); and Audre Lorde, Sister Outsider: Essays and Speeches (1984).

    17. Some of the most interesting research and proliferation of scholarships in the field of "whiteness studies" that have shown the complexity and the intensity about

whites coming to terms with their whiteness and white skin privilege in daily cultural processes include Steve Garner, *Whiteness: An Introduction* (2007); Robyn Wiegman, "Witnessing Whiteness: Articulating Race and the 'Politics of Style,' " (2004); Michael Kimmel and Abby Ferber, *Privilege: A Reader* (2003); Karen Brodkin, *How Jews Became White Folks and What That Says About Race in America* (1998); Richard Dyer, *White* (1997) and "White" (1988); Noel Ignatiev and John Garvey, *Race Traitor* (1996); Noel Ignatiev, *How the Irish Became White* (1995); Ruth Frankenberg, *White Women, Race Matters: The Social Construction of Whiteness* (1993); and David R. Roediger, *The Wages of Whiteness: Race and the Making of the American Working Class* (1991).

18. Fields (2001), 49.

19. Vaughn (1989), 353.

20. Bonilla-Silva (2007), 131.

21. Hegel (1975), 177.

22. It was not too long after the arrival of Europeans, the provincial government of Virginia encouraged the destroying of First Nations and their crops. In 1629, a peace treaty was decided by the Virginia Council but it was rejected. Later attacks in Virginia by First Nations, trying to defend themselves from European encroachment, were in 1644 and 1675. (Nash 1976, 91). In an armed conflict from 1635 to 1637, known as the Pequot War, the First Nations village, Pequot, was massacred by the Europeans. See Scott L. Malcomson, *One Drop of Blood: The American Misadventure of Race* (2000), 37. Those who survived the conflict, including women and children, were captured and sold into indentured servitude. As early as 1656, the Virginia Assembly, for example, passed the first of a series of statutes prohibiting the enslavement of First Nations. There are many reasons why First Nations' enslavement created more problems for the colonists. See Kenneth M. Stampp, *The Peculiar Institution: Slavery in the Ante-Bellum South* (1956), 23–24.

23. Few are aware that as early as 1516 about one hundred enslaved Africans were brought to the Peedee Region of Chicora (South Carolina) by Lucas Vasquez de Ayllon. Vasquez's expedition was one of the six major Spanish *conquistas* in an effort to colonize the Southern part of North America. See Eugene R. Huck and Edward H. Moseley, *Militarists, Merchants, and Missionaries* (1970).

24. Patterson (1982), 176.

25. Jordan (1976), 112. Skin color (race) was clearly mention in the Virginia Code of 1705, which stated: "And for a further Christian care and usage of all Christian servants, Be it also enacted by the authority aforesaid, at it is hereby enacted, That no negroes, mulattos, or Indians, although Christians, or Jews, Moors, Mahometans, other infidels, shall, at any time, purchase any Christian servants, nor any other, except of their own complexion, or such as are declared slaves by the act." (Jordan 1976, 112).

26. As more non–English European arrived in the colonies, the term "white" appeared and was used mainly by whites to distinguish themselves from blacks or Africans (Jordan 1976, 113).

27. Feagin (2006), 15.

28. There are some cases where blacks successfully petitioned the court to put an end to their servitude. A few well-known cases included Thomas Hagleton (1676); William Upton (1678); and Ralph Truncket (1693). Other cases were rejected such as Joyce Gidding (1693); and Tom Blanco (1694). For a more comprehensive understanding of these cases, see Whittington B. Johnson, "The origins and Nature of African Slavery in Seventeenth Century Maryland" (1978), 239–40.

29. For a comprehensive reading on the legal construction of race, see Richard Delgado and Jean Stefanic, *Critical Race Theory an Introduction* (2001); Ian F. Haney López, *White by Law: The Legal Construction of Race* (1996); Derrick Bell, *Race, Racism, and American Law* (1980); and A. Leon Higginbotham Jr., *In the Matter of Color Race and the American Legal Process: The Colonial Period* (1978).

30. Fields (1990), 201.

31. My discussion of race and racial slavery rests largely on the exhaustive works of Theodore W. Allen, *The Invention of the White Race: Racial Oppression and Social Control*

(1994); Alden T. Vaughan, "The Origins Debate: Slavery and Racism in Seventeenth Century Virginia" (1989); Lerone Bennett, *The Shaping of Black America: The Struggles and Triumphs of African-Americans, 1619–1990s* (1975); Winthrop D. Jordan, *White Over Black: American Attitudes Toward the Negro, 1550–1812* (1968); and William Goodell, *Slavery and Anti-Slavery: A History of the Great Struggles in both Hemispheres, with a View of the Slavery Question in America* (1962).

32. There are a number of ways in which race thinking unfolded and was and still is reflected in America. Thomas Jefferson, in his *Notes on the State of Virginia*, referred to blacks, whites, and First Nations as distinct races. As a matter of fact, it was fixed in Jefferson's mind that blacks and whites could never coexist in the United States of America because the difference between these two races "is fixed in nature . . . And is this difference of no importance," Jefferson reasoned in *Notes on the State of Virginia*. For Jefferson, then, "blacks whether originally a distinct race, or made distinct by time and circumstances, are inferior to whites in the endowments both of body and mind" (1999), 6. Richard J. Herrnstein and Charles Murray's *The Bell Curve: Intelligence and Class Structure in American Life* (1994), provides an illustration of the assumed inferiority of blacks and other nonwhites. Using statistical evidence, they claimed, quite unabashedly, that when compared with blacks, whites achieve higher test scores. Three years later, Lino Graglia, a law professor at the University of Texas, following in the footsteps of Herrnstein and Murray, points to the bell curve's rendition that "blacks and Mexican-Americans are not academically competitive with whites in selective institutions. See Roger Hernandez, "Racism with Good Intensions a Misguided Policy" (1997), 7.

33. Davis (1923), 248. There is not much evidence of blacks arriving in Virginia before 1619. The first Negroes, as it is documented, arrived in Jamestown, the first permanent English settlement in America, in 1619, were the "twenty negars." See Frank Craven, "Twenty Negroes to Jamestown in 1619?" (1971), 416–20; and T. R. Davis, "Negro Servitude in the United States: Servitude Distinguished from Slavery" (1923), 249.

34. In Europe, up until the eighteenth century, there were several explanations for the physical differences of people. These explanations drew from the Bible. Alden T. Vaughan draws our attention to how the English equated Africans from the Biblical "Curse of Ham." Geneses 9:20–27, states that Noah cursed Ham's son, Canaan, to a life of perpetual servitude to his brothers Shem and Japheth. The English identified Ham as the ancestor of black Africans and themselves as the descendants of Japheth (1989). The Bible is often used as support in maintaining certain groups as the "other." In terms of Christianity, the Jews are considered directly responsible for the crucifixion of Christ. According to Matthew 27:25, Jews called for the death of Christ, and after Christ's death, "His blood be upon us and our Children" was uttered in remorse by the Jews. Hence, the persecution of the Jews, as early as the First Crusader in 1096, which continued in the fourteenth century, was inevitable. Jews were seen as less than human. They were looked on as demonic and associated with the devil. The denunciation of the Jews was supported by John 8:44, "You are of your father the devil, and your will is to do your father's desire." Anti-Semitism began to show its ugly face. See George M. Fredrickson, *Racism a Short History* (2002), 17–25. Implicit in such arguments is the assumption that differences are to be explained by tracing them to particular events outlined in the Bible where God intervenes in the overtly polarized twosome of punishment and reward that is bestowed on particular individuals. Another explanation for physical differences had to do with climate and environment. Hence, people from Africa, Europe, and Asia must have had separate ancestors, which contradicts the biblical narration that we are all descendent of Adam. Given that Adam is the ancestor of the Europeans, the argument that is exposed in the Old Testament is incomplete. Hence, the debate whether human beings consisted of one or many stocks had to be considered in terms of the prevailing paradigm and, as such, was explained as a choice between monogenesis and polygenesis. See Michael Banton, "The Idiom of Race: A Critique of Presentation" (2000), 52–53.

35. Jefferson (1999), 6.
36. Spivak (1998), 45.
37. Jefferson (1999), 11.
38. Fanon (1967), 190–91.
39. Jacobson (1998), 27.
40. Fanon (1967), 110.

41. Take, for example, the category women: if one should claim that there is an ontological specificity to women as child bearers, this claim would be up for dispute because not all women can bear children. Some women might be too old or too young to bear children. In some case, women opt out of child bearing. However, Professor Gayatri C. Spivak's announcement of "strategic essentialism" draws our attention to the strategic necessity for feminists to rely on the false ontology of women as universal in order to advance a feminist political program.

42. The first major definition of race was presented in the *Oxford English Dictionary* in 1910. It defined race as "A group of persons, animals or plants, connected by common decent or origins." In England, from the sixteenth to the eighteenth century, the use of the term "race" corresponded to the preceding definition. However, already in the sixteenth century, "the notion of likeness because of decent was generalized and 'race' was used to denote instances of likeness without any claim of common descent, like Dunbar's reference in 1508 to 'backbiters of sundry races' and Sidney's of 1580, 'the races of good men.'" In the nineteenth century, the use of race, in this sense, continued with "Lamb's reference to 'the two races of men,' the men who borrowed and the men who lend, but thereafter it was less frequent." See Michael Banton, "The Idiom of Race: A Critique of Presentation" (2000), 53.

43. Miles (1989), 74.

44. See Gunnar Myrdal, *An American Dilemma: The Negro Problem and Modern Democracy* (1962).

45. According to the Body of Liberties, captivity in a just war provided legal grounds for enslavement. After the Pequot War ended in 1637, the Body of Liberties provided the conditions for First Nations to be enslaved. However, Rhode Island law of 1652 prohibited enslavement.

46. Jordan (1968), 69.

47. In spite of the fact that the distinctions in the general outline of the cultures of Africa and Europe were not huge, in that Africans became similar to the English in civilization, morality, and religion, it was fitting for Africans to be slaves. See Frank M. Snowden, *Before Color Prejudice: The Ancient View of Blacks* (1983), 101–107; and George M. Fredrickson, *Racism a Short History* (2002), 28–29.

48. Jordan (1968), 7.
49. Handlin and Handlin (1950), 208.
50. Cox (1948), 104.
51. Degler (1959), 53.
52. Jordan (1968), 69.
53. Bartels (1997), 45.
54. Sander (1992), 246.

55. See Theodore W. Allen, *The Invention of the White Race: Racial Oppression and Social Control* where Allen claims that "Othello's flaw was not his color but his male ego, made to pass for some part of 'honor' and surely calculated to evoke universal sympathy from the English audience" (1994), 6. However, Othello's blackness is another flaw that was clearly linked with animalistic lust that was out of control.

56. Tocqueville (1945), 358.

57. Race organizes and arranges concrete consequences for one's well-being and life changes. In the present of racism as a system of advantages that benefits whites, even though socioeconomic status can sometimes constructs and determines such benefits, whiteness as unmarked and unraced is a way of acknowledging the ever-present power differential that had started to exist between whites and nonwhites in seven-

teenth century colonial America. Even though a white identity changed overtime, whiteness remained beneficial to the dominant group, in this case, whites.

58. Appiah (1985), 35.

59. Butler (1990a), 273.

60. Jordan (1962), 18.

61. This discussion resonated in the works of authors in a special edition of *William and Mary Quarterly* (1997). Also, see Barbara J. Fields, "Slavery, Race and Ideology in the United States of America" (1990); Alden T. Vaughan, "The Origins Debate: Slavery and Racism in Seventeenth Century Virginia" (1989); and "Blacks in Virginia: A Note on the First Decade" (1972); George M. Fredrickson, "Towards a Social Interpretation in the Development of American Racism" (1971); Winthrop D. Jordan, *White Over Black: American Attitudes Toward the Negro, 1550–1812* (1968); "Modern Tensions and the Origins of American Slavery" (1962); Thomas F. Gossett, *Race: The History of an Idea in America* (1963); Carl N. Degler, "Slavery and the Genesis of American Race Prejudice" (1959); Stanley M. Elkins, *Slavery a Problem in American Institutional and Intellectual Life* (1959); Oscar Handlin and Mary Handlin, "Origins of the Southern Labor System" (1950); Eric William, *Capitalism and Slavery* (1944); and Ruth Benedict, *Race: Science and Politics* (1940).

62. Craven (1949), 218.

63. Williams (1994), 19.

64. The book was republished by Cambridge University Press in 2004.

65. Solow and Stanley (1987), 4.

66. Jordan (1968), 80.

67. Goodell (1968), 10. Also, see Joseph Boskin, *Into Slavery: Racial Decisions in the Virginia Colony* (1976); Alden T. Vaughan, "The Origins Debate: Slavery and Racism in Seventeenth-Century Virginia" (1989), 312; and Donald L. Noel, ed., *The Origins of American Slavery and Racism* (1972).

68. Foucault (1994), 346.

69. Vaughan (1989), 315.

70. Brown (1996). Also, see Jennifer Morgan, "'Some Could Suckle Over Their Shoulders': Male Travelers, Female Body and the Gendering of Racial Ideology, 1500–1770" (1997) where Morgan explains that Europeans, in their efforts to define race, focused on African women and First Nations. The productive and reproductive labor of First Nations and African women respectively, which, greatly contrasted with European, served to make a drastic distinction between nonwhites and whites, and it determined nonwhites' unequal position. See also Kirsten Fischer, in *Suspect Relations: Sex, Race, and Resistance in Colonial North Carolina* (2002).

71. See Wesley F. Craven, *The Southern Colonies in the Seventeenth Century, 1607–1689* (1949); T. R. Davis, "Negro Servitude in the United States: Servitude Distinguished from Slavery" (1923); James M. Wright, *The Free Negroes in Maryland, 1634–1860* (1921); Ulrich B. Phillips, *American Negro Slavery: A Survey the Supply, Employment and Control of the Negro Labor as Determined by the Plantation Regime* (1918); and John H. Russell, *The Free Negro in Virginia, 1619–1895* (1913).

72. Russell (1913), 29.

73. Handlin and Handlin (1950), 208–11.

74. Degler (1959), 51.

75. The debate over the conditions that laid the groundwork for slavery did not vanish. George M. Fredrickson, in "Towards a Social Interpretation of the Development of American racism" (1971) acknowledged that even though the colonists were antagonistic toward blacks because of the color of their skin, racism did not emerge in the colonies until the end of the seventeenth century. For Winthrop D. Jordan, in "Modern Tensions and the Origins of American Slavery," racism preceded slavery. Blacks would not have been enslaved if there had not been any need for labor in the colonies (1968), 91. It is true that Jordan would eventually retrieve his conclusions and apologetically confess in his later book, *White Over Black: American Attitudes Toward the Negro, 1550–1812*, that "Modern Tensions and the Origins of American Slavery," was

written "at a time when (as [he] now thinks) he was far from comprehending the origins of Slavery" (1968), 599. In *White Over Black*, he reformulated his argument concerning the cause of slavery by stating, "rather than slavery causing 'prejudice' or vice versa, they seemed to rather as generated each other . . . Slavery and prejudice may have been equally cause and effect." *White Over Black*, published in 1968, earned widespread approbation. In 1969, Jordan's book earned the National Book Award, the Francis Parkman prize, and the Ralph Waldo Emerson prize. In addition, it was singled out for the 1996 seminar on "Constructing Race Differentiating People in the Early Modern World, 1400–1700."

76. Craven (1949), 217–19.

77. Breen (1976), 70–71.

78. Jordan (1968).

79. Breen (1976), 72.

80. Thomas Jefferson, later on, in his *Notes to State of Virginia*, would dismiss the claim that First Nations were inferior to whites by nothing that "more facts are wanting, and great allowance are to be made for those circumstances of their situation that call for the display of particular talent only." Blacks, however, in his view, were inferior.

81. Breen (1976), 69.

82. Boskin (1976), 23–25.

83. See W. E. B. Du Bois, *The Soul of Black Folks* (2003); *Darkwater: Voices From within the Veil* (1969); and *Black Reconstruction in American* (1962).

84. See Karen Ordahl Kupperman, "Presentment of Civility: English Reading of American Self-Preservation in the Early Years of Colonization" (1997); and Joyce E. Chapin, "Natural Philosophy and an Early Racial Idiom in North America: Comparing English and Indian Body" (1997).

85. Some historians have gone so far as to argue that blacks were inherently inferior and, hence, racial domination was natural. See Roger Burlingame, *Machines that Built America* (1953), 44–46; and Jeannette Mirsky and Allan Nevins, *The World of Eli Whitney* (1952), 66.

86. The female slave, Sojourner Truth, "Ain't I a Woman?" makes clear the homogenizing and essentializing of the category "woman" to mean white women. "Ain't I a Woman," became her signifier, her mark, and the manner in which she enters American history. Eventually, "Ain't I am Woman?" would become the idiomatic manifestation of black feminists contesting the women's movement and second wave feminism. In the autumn of 1984, the *Feminist Review* dedicated an issue, "Many Voices: One Chant: Black Feminist Perspective," to the question of who is a woman in the hope of provoking future discussions and debates of black women's experience through the interconnectedness of race, gender, class, and sexuality inequalities. As I have mentioned before, black and other feminists have focused on intersectionality. In 2004, an article was published by Avtar Brah and Ann Phoenix titled "Ain't I a Woman? Revisiting Intersectionality," Cheryl I. Harris, "Finding Sojourner's Truth: Race, Gender, and the Institution of Slavery" (1996); and bell hooks, *Ain't I a Woman: Black Woman and Feminism* (1981).

87. Davis (1923), 266.

88. Davis (1923), 266.

89. Davis (1923), 253.

90. Davis (1923), 269.

91. Jordan (1962), 25. Also, see Ulrich B. Phillips, *American Negro Slavery: A Survey the Supply, Employment and Control of the Negro Labor as Determined by the Plantation Regime* (1918), 74–76.

92. Degler (1959), 57.

93. See, John H. Russell, *Free Negro in Virginia, 1619–1895* (1913); and James Curtis Ballagh, *A History of Slavery in Virginia* (1902).

94. Jordan (1962), 20.

95. Besides the case of indentured servitude, other examples of relationships that are considered racial, by those actually and directly involved, include slavery and the Jim Crow System of the racial belief of blacks as inferior given legal form in which these relationships are indeed ideologically and structurally racial.

96. Degler (1959), 57.

97. Stampp (1956), 22.

98. Stampp (1956), 18.

99. For a more detailed account on stock breeding, see Katie Geneva Cannon, "Slave Ideology and Biblical Interpretation" (2004); Patricia Williams, "Alchemical Notes: Reconstructing Ideals form Deconstructed Rights" (1987); and Angela Davis, *Women, Race and Class* (1983). By then, the importation of slaves were prohibited, partly, for three connected reasons: planters wanted to keep prices high and reduced competition, a growing slave population, and the dangers that rebellious slaves from the West Indies posed. The importations of slaves from Africa were prohibited in Delaware in 1776; Virginia in 1778; Maryland in 1783; and Georgia in 1798. South Carolina, in 1803, reopened the importation of blacks and imported 39,000 blacks laborers before a Federal action, five years later, which prohibited the importation of slaves. See Kenneth M. Stampp, *Peculiar Institution: Slavery in the Ante-bellum South* (1956), 25; and Ulrich B. Phillips, *American Negro Slavery: A Survey of the Supply, Employment and Control of the Negro Labor as Determined by the Plantation Regime* (1918), 132–49.

100. Craven (1949), 290.

101. Vaughan (1972), 469. For more on the contempt of Negroes by the colonists, see Wesley F. Craven, *The Southern Colonies in the Seventeenth Century, 1607–1689* (1949), 217–19; 402–3.

102. For a more comprehensive discussion, see the Decisions of the General Court. (1889), 236–37.

103. Davis (1923), 266.

104. Jordan (1976), 109–10.

105. Noel (1972), 159.

106. Harris (1993), 1716.

107. The servants, at first, were able to get married but marriage, for several reasons, proved inconvenient for the master. Hence, laws preventing servants from getting married were enforced. For example, in Virginia, in 1643, the right of servants to get married was restricted.

108. The master had the legal right to whip his servants. Eventually, if a Christian white servant was to be whipped naked, the master had to obtain an order from the justice of peace.

109. Decisions of the General Court (1898), 238.

110. Fields (1990), 102.

111. Yancy (2005), 237.

112. Degler (1959), 58.

113. Jordan (1976), 106; also quoted in Jordan (1962), 26.

114. Degler (1959), 57–58.

115. Jordan (1962), 26; and Craven (1949), 219.

116. Jordan (1968), 75.

117. See Edmund S. Morgan, *American Slavery, American Freedom: The Ordeal of Colonial Virginia* (1975). However, the term miscegenation was not used until 1863, when, in a pamphlet, the Democrats suggested that any support for the Republicans would bring about race mixing, which the Democrats feared. Since then, interracial marriage and cohabitation have been termed miscegenation. In the United States, miscegenation laws were in place until 1967 when the case *Loving v. Virginia* was brought to the Supreme Court.

118. Degler (1959), 56; also quoted in Jordan (1976), 107; and Jordan (1962), 28.

119. Later, laws were extended to include interracial relations between free Africans and Europeans.

120. Degler (1959), 61.

121. Stampp (1956), 21–22.

122. Fields (1990), 115–16.

123. See Morgan, *American Slavery, American Freedom: The Ordeal of Colonial Virginia* (1975).

124. Phillips (1918), 8. Also, see Kenneth M. Stampp, *The Peculiar Institution: Slavery in the Ante-bellum South* (1956); and Oscar Handlin and Mary Handlin, "Origins of the Southern Labor System" (1950).

125. Fields (1990), 105.

126. Takaki (1998), 35.

127. The best-known case of a black man being freed from bond servitude was that of Anthony Johnson. In 1621, Johnson arrived in Virginia where he was initially a servant. Later on, he married, had four children, and earned his freedom from servitude. He was a successful planter and he owned a vast amount of land, cattle, and servants. Eventually, when life for Johnson proved difficult in Virginia, he moved to Maryland where he died in 1670. After his death, Virginia courts failed to restore to Johnson's family the land he had owned on the grounds that Johnson was a Negro. In other cases, black servants/slaves sued for their freedom in the colony's court. One important case is that of Elizabeth Key, the illegitimate child of a slave woman and a white planter who, in 1656, sued the court for her freedom on the grounds of her father status as a free white Englishman, her baptism, and the expiration of her contract to serve as a servant for her present master. See Alden T. Vaughan "The Origins Debate: Slavery and Racism in Seventeenth Century Virginia" (1989), 329–30.

128. Allen (1994), 17.

129. Harris (1996), 2.

130. Jordan (1976), 107–8.

131. Many have argued that this law was to curb the growing Mulatto population that was emerging. The Mulattoes were look on as an "abominable mixture." See T.R. Davis, "Negro Servitude in the United States: Servitude Distinguished from Slavery" (1923). The Mulatto, for a while, was a distinct racial identity. Eventually, the Mulatto was considered as black.

132. Allen (1997), 178.

133. Fields (1990), 104.

134. Degler (1959), 49.

135. Handlin and Handlin (1950), 199.

136. Degler (1959), 52.

137. Sio (1965), 304.

138. Degler (1959), 62.

139. Degler (1959), 62–65.

140. Jordan (1968), 72.

141. Boskin (1976), 4.

142. Degler (1959), 61.

143. Degler (1959), 52.

144. Davis (1923), 250.

145. Davis (1923), 253.

146. Davis (1923), 261.

147. Even though the act regulated the institution of slavery, there were some advantages for the slaves. The act, for example, prohibited slaves as well as servants from working on Sundays and holidays.

148. See Ulrich B. Phillips, *American Negro Slavery: A Survey of the Supply, Employment and Control of the Negro Labor as Determined by the Plantation Regime* (1918).

149. There are several books and articles on how the Irish and Jews became white. In terms of Italians, in 1922, the case of *Rollins v. Alabama* has shown that Italians, in America, were not always considered white. When Jim Rollins, a black man, was convicted of the crime of miscegenation, the Alabama Circuit Courts of appeal noted that the state has not provided "no competence evidence to show that the woman in

question, Edith Labue, was a white woman." Because she was a Sicilian immigrant, the court held that this "can be taken as conclusive that she was therefore a white woman."

150. Jordan (1962), 20.

TWO

Whiteness as Property and its Impact on Racialized Ethnic Groups

At the beginning of America's history, the distinction between who could *have* property and who could *be* property was paramount. Whites controlled the land belonging to First Nations and Mexicans as well as the labor of First Nations, blacks, Chinese, and eventually Mexicans. As I have pointed out in chapter one, the take-over, confiscation, and extinction of First Nations' civilization were approved and sanctioned by corroborating and granting whites the rights to own First Nations' land.[1] Blacks were subjugated as slaves and treated as property. In 1793, the Fugitive Slave Acts strengthened the definition of slaves as property as opposed to person.[2] It was no coincidence that the "pursuit of property," found meaning in its relations to whiteness. Eventually whiteness would become a form of property, a "valuable asset" that all whites possess. Whiteness, "among other things, 'being white,'"[3] united all whites across class lines and defined the stricture of who should be inferior (nonwhites) and who should be superior (whites).

Even though most whites' economic position was no better than that of the free blacks or the slaves, for example, even the poor whites remained superior to blacks. After all, to be a poor white did not mean that he or she was situated outside the space of whiteness. Acknowledging this fact is useful for a critique of the liminality of whiteness.[4] In chapter 4, I address in more detail the problematics of the liminality of whiteness. For now, I draw on Wilbert E. Moore and Robin M. Williams's "Stratification in the Ante-Bellum South" to help us understand the precipitation of the sociopolitical and cultural meanings of white identity and how whiteness works. They recognized that whiteness bestowed on the poor whites a social standing superior to that of blacks and other nonwhites. The institution of slavery, for example, linked the privilege of whites to the subordination of blacks through a legal regime that converted blacks into objects of property. Furthermore, More and Williams showed how the "stratification system based on whiteness acquired priority over economic and class interests"[5] and, with intent, kept nonwhites on the margins of society—a society marred by the binary logics of racial antagonism.

This racist formulation embedded in the fact of white privilege is incorporated into the very definition of property, marking another stage in the evolution of the complicated notion of, what law professor Tracy Higgins has termed, "a property right in whiteness."[6] At its most fundamental, what made whiteness the definitive property is that "possession—the act necessary to lay the basis for rights in property—was defined to include only the cultural practices of whites. This definition laid the foundation for the idea that whiteness—that which whites alone possesses—is valuable and is privileged,"[7] and seemed, to whites at least, to have no racial foundation. Yet whiteness, most strikingly, was everything. It was the foundation of literal as well as symbolic power. Poor whites managed to reap aesthetic and psychological rewards as a result of possessing "a property right in whiteness" on which they greatly relied. In other words, whether or not, whites, as individuals, cleaved to supremacist thinking, harbored racist attitudes, or remained oblivious to the fact that they are apprehensive by the physical presence of people that are not white, whites profited and continue nowadays to profit from being white.

In due course, the institutionalization and extension of whiteness manifested itself in the first Naturalization Act of 1790. Whiteness became the active and interactive process for determining who should be citizens of the United States. Given that First Nations, blacks, Chinese, and the other racialized ethnic groups living in America at the time were not eligible for citizenship because they were not white, the nonwhite "others" lacked the rights that accompanied citizenship bestowed on whites.[8] In fact, the rights of citizenship provide us with a singular locus to reflect on the apparent disposition of whiteness, which is helpful in identifying the role of ideology and discourse in the constitution of the nonwhite "other." The "other," created in and through difference, is, nonetheless, an essential part of the self, which Homi Bhabha describes as the hybridity within the self. Yet the "other" is forever reduced to a disturbing alterity.[9] And given that the "self" cannot counteract or, at least, relentlessly brackets the values, assumptions, and ideologies of whiteness, the nonwhite "other" is constantly measured against the white "self." Whiteness, as parasitical on nonwhiteness, forges a dialogic relation between the white "self" and the nonwhite "other." The historian David R. Roediger makes two significant observations concerning the relation between the white "self" and the nonwhite "other." First, whiteness was not limited to the ways in which the racial "others" were treated; and two, it impacted "the ways that whites [thought] of themselves, of power, of pleasure, of gender." [10]

My purpose in this chapter is to examine and show whiteness as a form of property that all whites possess, and how this possession has impacted racialized ethnic groups. While, in due course, laws such as the Naturalization Act of 1790 were ratified to promote whiteness and white privilege, First Nations, blacks, Chinese, Mexicans, and other racialized ethnic groups underwent enormous subordination and were denied the liberties and rights of citizenship. In the end, whiteness had to be protected from the threat that racialized groups represented to white supremacy. No act offers a clearer illustration than the Chinese Exclusion Act of 1882. In the meanwhile, slavery allowed blacks to be defined and treated as the chattel of a master. Black Codes and the Jim Crow laws were ultimately established to reinforce white supremacy. During this period, the black-white model of race relations extended itself to include all nonwhites. Black became the signifier for nonwhite. However, room for challenging the oppressive impact of such a categorization on people of color was found and, eventually, blacks and other nonwhites had to rally against America's discriminatory practices.

In the following section, I look specifically at the Naturalization Act of 1790 to show how it defines and protects whiteness as the property of whites. The purpose of the Naturalization Act of 1790 was to fashion and organize the differences between whites and nonwhites. More significantly, the Act was to construct dominance and subordination into socioeconomic relations based on racial categories. For reasons that are apparent, in a nonchronological order, I look at the Chinese Exclusion Act and then the Black Codes.

THE NATURALIZATION ACT OF 1790 AND WHITENESS

The Naturalization Act of March 26, 1790 momentously claimed that free whites who have migrated to the United States and were able to swear under oath in the presence of a magistrate that they intended to remain in the United States for a year "shall be entitled to the rights of citizenship." [11] The lawmakers saw the 1790 Naturalization Act as inclusive rather than exclusive and it never occurred to them that legal citizenship was only limited to whites. [12] Whites were defined and envisioned as individuals and American citizens whereas First Nations, blacks, Chinese, and other nonwhites were collectively defined as members of racialized ethnic groups. Besides the authentication and consummation of whiteness in America, this act served two main purposes: to suppress slave insurrections from occurring and to reinforce and perpetuate the "property rights of whites" in First Nations' land. It was a way to discourage the resistance effort of First Nations against whites' infringement on their land.[13] For those whites entering the United States during and after 1802, a modification to the 1790 Act set a five-year residence requirement for new immigrants. However, like the racially restrictive naturalization act of 1790, the Act of 1802 restricted naturalization to an "alien, being free and white."[14] In the midst of such gross discrimination toward non-whites, which W. E. B. Du Bois named "psychological wage," a number of proliferated benefits were bestowed on all whites, strengthening, in a substantial way, whites' ongoing preeminence.

The Naturalization Act affected Chinese immigrants arriving in America in 1852, especially the Chinese who worked in the Californian mines. The California legislature passed a tax law requiring all foreign miners who were not citizens to pay three dollars a month. This law was reversed in 1870.[15] Eventually, the Naturalization Act of 1790 normalized the racist practices of America, which connected whiteness with citizenship.[16] Cheryl I. Harris, in her article titled "Whiteness as Property," analyses the changing definitions of citizenship as they are introduced in the act. The rights of citizenship were broadened such as to extend voting rights to poor white men "at the same time that black voters were specifically disenfranchised, arguably shifting the property required for voting from land to whiteness."[17] By racializing the qualification of newcomers into the United States, this act regulated free blacks[18] and First Nations, and set limits on future access to citizenship for all racialized groups in America.[19] In fact, it was the McCarran-Walter Act of 1952, which got rid of race as a basis for naturalization and some racialized ethnic groups, including East Asians and Filipinos, for example, could finally become naturalized US citizens. [20]

RIGHTS FOR WHITES EXTENDED

From 1789 to 1791, the Bill of Rights, the first ten amendments to the American Constitution, was enacted to protect and secure the liberties and rights of whites.[21] First Nations, blacks, and other racialized groups remained unprotected by these rights. First Nations were not citizens in the legalistic sense and, many blacks, at that time, were slaves. Acts, including the Fugitive Slave Acts of 1793, were implemented to strengthen and uphold the established idea that slaves were not persons but properties. These Acts were to stabilize the rights of liberty and property. For instance, a state's recognition of liberty cannot flout another state's classification of the property rights in slaves. "Any state law or state regulation, which interrupts, limits, delays or postpones the rights of the owner to the immediate possession of the slave and the immediate command of his service and labor operates, pro tanto, a discharge of the slaves there from."[22] To that end, the laws also denied lawful rights to free slaves.

Bringing to light the purposeful racist foundation of American society, in the case of *Dred Scott v. Sandford*, Justice Roger Taney acknowledged that blacks had no rights "which the white man was bound to respect." When Dr. Van Evrie announced, "for those perverse creatures among us who clamor so loudly for Negro equality, or that the Negro shall be treated as if he were a white man, only desire to force their hideous theories on others, and would rather have theirs,[23] white supremacy was confirmed. For Van Evrie, it was indeed simple; "the Caucasian is white, the Negro is black; the first is the most superior, the latter the most inferior."[24] He would then produce a coupling of scientific and religious proof to support his agonistic claim with the usual racist discourse according to which whites are supreme and, hence, white supremacy is inevitable.[25]

Race, used to exemplify difference and divergence from the social norms that have been associated with whites, was a formative factor in determining the Hegelian categories of master and slave, subject and object, the natural (normal) and the unnatural (abnormal), the self and "other," and the "us" and "them." By conceiving of white as the norm, it was the designated nonwhite "other," the "them" that became, as Toni Morrison explains, "the means of thinking about body, mind, chaos, kindness, and love; provided the occasion for exercises in the absence of restraint, the presence of restraint, the contemplation of freedom and of aggression; permitted opportunities for the exploration of ethics and morality; for meeting the obligations of the social contract, for bearing the cross of religion and following the ramifications of power."[26] The dialectically related duality at play—whiteness and nonwhiteness—throughout the process of American cultural representation and adjustment, structures and maintains power and inequality in all spheres of its institutional and social relations. It "is like a plague," to use Angela Davis's words, "it infects every joint, muscle, and tissue of social life in this country,"[27] which, to borrow from Albert Camus's *The Plague (La Peste)*, "cannot be denied . . . its poignancy."[28] And even though, in America, white identity has changed overtime, for instance, the Irish and the Jews became identified as white based on skin color,[29] non-whiteness, at the apex of embodied difference, remains the sine qua non of whites' existence. In other words, white is a relational identity, created by those in power so that whites can define and construct themselves as unlike the nonwhite "others."[30] What we see here is that nonwhiteness is awarded the prime form of otherness by which whiteness is constituted and reconstituted.

Alexis de Tocqueville, engaged as he was with "the prejudice of race," sensed that the usage of the term races was something dishonorable. He recognized that racial prejudice was stronger in those states that had abolished slavery, and even more so "where servitude has never been known." Nonetheless, he marveled at American democracy, masquerading under the pseudo-ideals of liberty, autonomy, and freedom, which incorporated white men into the body politic of America where they were allowed to exercise their political rights and civic responsibilities bestowed on them by the Bill of Rights and the Constitution. In the meantime, First Nations, blacks, other racialized groups, and women were excluded from democratic citizenship.

What really stunned Tocqueville was that blacks and First Nations "ha[d] nothing in common; neither birth, nor features, nor language, nor habits. Both of them occupy an inferior rank in the country they inhabit; both suffer from tyranny."[31] There was nothing surprising about the treatment of blacks and First Nations. It was indicative of how whiteness worked, and continues to work, to maintain the system of racial inequality.[32] Racial classification, an obvious but complex occurrence, continued its opprobrious enterprise to separate whites from nonwhites and to maintain white supremacy, which accompanied racist actions. In fact, Thomas Jefferson, the third president of the United States and the author of the Declaration of Independence, had an optimistic and clear answer of how to maintain white supremacy: shipping blacks to an all black country. The physical removal of the "other" was premised on gaining the purity of America that Jefferson and his contemporaries sought, which was tied with the untamed desire to transform America into the homogeneous society where "men" would be free to pursue their own self-interest and exercise their "inalienable rights" and liberties that was guaranteed by the Declaration of Independence to "all men." "All men" did not mean "man" as in human beings, but a particular type of manhood that drew its identity from a society that valued whiteness and maleness. When Senator Henry Clay had referred to America as "a nation of self-made men" he was speaking in a single idiom and accent that alluded to white men.[33] And since Jefferson's solution could not materialize because slave labor was deemed indispensable for the growth and survival of the cotton industry, the state "required men to kill some white people to keep them white and to kill many blacks to keep them black."[34] State violence at its core, often spontaneous and unorganized, was legitimatized through its elevation or absorption into the discourse and ideology of white supremacy.

White domination would eventually give rise to white supremacist groups such as the vicious and lecherous Ku Klux Klan (KKK).[35] The KKK pledged to protect white womanhood. In fact, it was believed that white womanhood, which was also marked and positioned as "white men's property" and associated with "the cult of femininity," would be gravely imperiled by slavery's demise.[36] Just as thriftiness had come to signify the seditious power of the Jews, sexual potency signified that of black men, and this became a potent threat to the white social body. It was partly for this reason that the images of the promiscuous, pathological "others," "the biological-sexual-sensual genital [Negro]," to borrow the stinging phase of Frantz Fanon,[37] contaminated the Klan men's minds in a particularly compelling way. The KKK's lynching of black men was justified in order to protect white womanhood as a form of property, which was considered white men's uppermost value.[38] In the face of institutionalized violence, successful challenge to white suprema-cy, for the most part, was indeed impracticable. As a commonsense ex-treme of racism, the racial divide, or what W. E. B. Du Bois labeled "the color line," was in place as a means of keeping blacks and other non-whites in their respective separate place.

Racial classification, an obvious but complex occurrence, began its opprobrious enterprise and methodically separated whites from non-whites in order to maintain racial purity. Mulattoes were viewed as an "abominable mixture."[39] There are two opposing arguments that are pre-sented to account for the mulatto classification. On the one hand, it was "to attract men who might be counted as white and who would thereby strengthen the colony's defenses against her foreign and domestic ene-mies."[40] On the other hand, "the 'mulattoes' distinction was a functional one. Being necessary and above all concerned with maintaining their ascendancy, members of the plantation bourgeoisie sometimes made ac-commodations in their thinking in the interest of having a 'mulatto' buf-fer between themselves and the plantation bond labor."[41] Eventually, the "mulattoes' policy" underwent some changes. Many scholars have exam-ined the changing in racial classifications and noted the details in the classification of mulattoes. Mulattoes' classification started officially in 1850, when the federal enumerator on the census schedule marked a person "B" (black) or "M" (mulatto).[42] According to G. Reginald Daniel, in *More Than Black? Multiracial Identity and the New Racial Order,* "the legal status of free mulattoes was ambiguous at best up to the time of the American Revolution, although European Americans had begun to chip away at their rights as early as the 1660s."[43] Eventually, with the execu-tion of the one-drop rule, Mulattoes would be considered black. The underlying principle of the one-drop rule was to illustrate boundaries between blacks and whites, but more so, it was to emphasize the domi-nance of whiteness. The absurdities of the racial classification system based on the one-drop rule are taken up by Adrian Piper's 1990 useful essay, "Passing for White: Passing for Black," where she draws on the complexities of being biracial.[44]

The Indian Removal Act in 1830 relegated First Nations to occupy Indian Reservations;[45] and with the Treaty of Guadalupe Hidalgo, which was largely dictated by the United States after the Mexican-American War (1846–1848), Mexicans became enclosed by America's expanding borders.[46] The Treaty forced Mexico to accept the Rio Grande as the Texas border and to concede the Southwest territories to the United States for fifteen million dollars. The possession of Mexico included Cali-fornia, New Mexico, Nevada, and parts of Colorado, Arizona, and Utah. The integration of the Southwest into the American economy was devastating for Mexicans who were then incorporated into a "labor-repressive system" and pushed to the bottom of the caste system of social relations.[47] In short, even though Article IX of the Treaty of Guadalupe Hidalgo granted Mexican citizens of the conquered territories full rights in the United States,[48] "the property rights of whites" in Mexican land allowed for Mexicans to be treated as "foreigners in their own land." A foreign miners' tax of twenty dollars monthly was imposed on Mexicans who worked in the mines.[49]

The inferiority of all racialized groups was articulated by the lawmakers even before the Dred Scott case in 1857, but when the Act Concerning Civil Cases was implemented in 1850. It states, "No Black, or Mulatto person, or Indian, shall be allowed to give evidence in favor of, or against a white man." In *People v. Hall* (1854), Hall, a white man charged with the murder of Ling Sing, a Chinese man, was convicted thanks to the testimony of three Chinese witnesses. But the California Supreme Court reversed the decision because, according to the Act Concerning Civil Cases, Chinese were also included in the law. Remaining within the logics of white supremacy, the Judge affirmed that the Chinese were "a race of people whom nature has marked as inferior, and who are incapable of progress or intellectual development beyond a certain point." Article XIX, Sections I–IV of the California Constitution, adopted in 1876, was very specific on how Chinese were to be treated in California.[50] A series of Acts crystallized into the Chinese Exclusion Act of 1882,[51] which was partially a solution to the "yellow peril" that made whiteness anxious. Earlier, in 1751, Benjamin Franklin made clear his desire for America to be populated with, what he calls "purely white people," which led him to raise quite provocatively, in his essay "Observations Concerning the Increase of Mankind and Peopling of Countries," the issue as to "why should [America] in the Sight of Superior Beings, darken its people."[52] First Nations, blacks, and Chinese had one thing in common, a disturbing otherness, which emerged as the essence of the nonwhite subject. It is worth noting, however, that racial otherness, or what Homi Bhabha labels "the space of the adversary,"[53] is never completely oppositional to whiteness. It is exactly what whiteness depends on for its existence.

In the following section, I want to show how the Chinese Exclusion Act was a way to deal with the "yellow invasion" and, as the critical race theorist David Theo Goldberg puts it, "keep America white."[54] Massachusetts Senator George F. Hoar was amongst the minority when he admitted that the Act discriminated against the Chinese because of "the color of their skin."[55] In addition, given the fact that the Chinese, in the eyes of whites, were seen as black, black, as the signifier for nonwhiteness, during that time, allows for the rethinking of the black-white binary of America's race relations.

THE CHINESE EXCLUSION ACT

After the Gold Rush in the 1860s, the question of what to do with the large number of Chinese coming into America mostly to work was debated by those in power. It became a burning issue in the 1870s, in the wake of the economic slump. Before 1869, the issue had been of interest only to the frontier states and territories located along the pacific coast and the Rocky Mountains because these areas were mostly where a large number of the Chinese who were working on the transcontinental railroad in America resided. With the completion of the transcontinental railroad in May 1869, the Chinese began moving east. As a result, what to do with the Chinese population became a National issue. Chinese were compared to blacks. The *San Francisco Alta*, for example, was upfront and denounced the Chinese by claiming that "every reason that exists against the toleration of free blacks in Illinois may be argued against that of the Chinese here."[56] In a letter to the *New York Times*, Horatio Seymour, then governor of New York, acknowledged that America "do[es] not let the Indians stand in the way of civilization, so why let the Chinese?"[57] "Ought we to exclude them?" Senator James G. Blaine of Maine asked on February 14, 1879. A week later, in a widely reprinted letter to the *New York Tribune*, Blaine would refer to Chinese as "vicious, odious, abominable, dangerous, and revolting."[58]

Blaine's debasement of the Chinese was not unusual. In 1824, Ralph Waldo Emerson, for one, would describe China as a "disgustful . . . booby nation" whose civilization is a "besotted perversity."[59] As if these descriptive markers were not demeaning enough, Blaine contended that "if as a nation we have the right to keep out infectious diseases, if we have the right to exclude the criminal classes from coming to us, we surely have the right to exclude that immigration which reeks with impurity and which cannot come to us without plenteously sowing the seeds of moral and physical disease, destitution and death." In the end, he confessed, "I am opposed to the Chinese coming here; I am opposed to making them citizens: I am opposed to making them voters."[60] The Chinese Exclusion Act of 1882 was partly the answer to "the yellow peril" of which Blaine and others were so utterly afraid. The act suspended all Chinese immigration for at least the next ten years,[61] and denied citizenship to Chinese who were already in America. In addition to these legal clauses, lynching, boycotts, and mass expulsions added to the anti-Chinese sentiments.[62] In fact, during the debate of the Chinese Exclusion Act of 1882, Governor Horatio Seymour of New York wanted to know why, if First Nations could be located on reservations, the Chinese could not.[63] Like blacks and First Nations, Chinese were characterized as "sensual and lustful." This presumptive characterization of Chinese presented them also as sexual threats to the purity of white womanhood. Sarah E.

Henshaw wrote in *Scribner's Monthly*, "No matter how good a Chinaman may be, ladies never leave your children with them, especially little girls." Also, white parents were warned not to send their daughters on errands to the Chinese laundry because horrifying "things happened to white girls in the back rooms."[64]

In 1889, the Supreme Court deemed the Chinese Exclusion Act constitutional because, according to Justice Stephen J. Field who was deeply influenced by the openly racist climate of his time, Chinese are of a different race.[65] Accordingly, it was impracticable to Americanize Chinese. The Justice proceeded to claim that if the Chinese were not restricted, this "Oriental invasion [would be] a menace to [America's] civilization." The Chinese Exclusion Act was part of a tyrannical policy that was modified to include Japanese, Filipino, Korean, and Asian-Indian persons residing in the United States. Renewed in 1892, the Chinese Exclusion Act was extended indefinitely in 1902. It was not revoked until 1943 when Congress repealed the Chinese exclusion laws and allowed quotas for Chinese immigration. The implementation of the Immigration and Nationality Act Amendments of 1965 ended the quota system for Chinese.[66]

The supposed racial inferiority of Chinese was on a par with the supposed racial inferiority of blacks and First Nations. The racial binarism based on the "black vs. white" model led to consider black as an apt metaphor for uncivilized. Black meant nonwhites, and nonwhites were distinctively centered in white racist imagination as archetypal "others."[67] It was the foundation for America's political, economic, and social life, the very sovereignty of America's cultural tradition fixed in a hefty dosage of whiteness, which in the end would imprison and determine the position of all racialized ethnic groups in American society. This form of imprisonment is clearly existential and, thus, whoever is included in a racialized group is relentlessly confronted with the question: who am I? For Frantz Fanon, in *Black Skin, White Masks*, this question is a question of being and knowing, a question of the Freudian narrative of desire: "what do [nonwhites] want?"[68] Bearing witness to the fact of the crippling effects of normalized whiteness on nonwhites' self identification, Fanon ascertains that what a person of color desires is a liberation from one's self because the self is not a self of his or her own making. "What is often called the black soul is a white man artifact" he concludes.[69] Would the denormalization of whiteness liberate the nonwhite subject from itself? This question is taken up in chapter 5.

With the end of slavery, the white power structure in place had to find ways to maintain and support the hegemony of whiteness. No law offers more compelling evidence than the Black Codes, which were implemented during Reconstruction to deprive emancipated slaves to work, vote, and move around as "free" people. The Civil Rights Act of 1866, which was passed over the veto of President Andrew Johnson, stated that "All persons born . . . in the United States and not subject to any foreign power, excluding Indians, are declared to be citizens of the United States."[70] However, the Black Codes restricted ex-slaves from pursuing freedom, the rights of citizenship, and economic, social, and political autonomy.

In the following section, I will examine, in brief, the Black Codes only to show that it was a way of reinforcing white supremacy.

BLACK CODES

Slavery contradicted the self-evident truths that all human beings "are created equal." Even after the Thirteenth Amendment outlawed slavery and the Fourteenth Amendment bestowed on blacks, at least in theory, the rights of citizenship, there remained a desperate effort to maintain white supremacy. Besides the effective strategy to keep blacks subservient, which was to recruit them into either "debt servitude" as sharecroppers, tenancy, or peonage, blatant discriminatory laws such as the Black Codes supplemented an intrinsic and definitive white authority. Ignoring the Civil Rights Act of 1866, which stated that blacks and other racialized groups would benefit from the same rights "enjoyed by white citizens," the Black Codes were implemented in the former Confederate States in order to define blacks' new rights and responsibilities[71] and, more importantly, to create, what Michel Foucault refers to as "docile bodies."[72] For example, the Codes required that "ex-slaves employed by a white person" could not change jobs without permission from their employers.[73] Mississippi, identified by the historian Neil R. McMillen as "the heartland of American Apartheid,"[74] and South Carolina, toward the end of 1865, enacted the first and most cruel Black Codes. The other Confederate States hurriedly followed suit and the Black Codes were also enacted in those states.[75] The Black Codes, an effortless portrayal of how whiteness worked, in their fraught attempt to give a boost to the post-slave system of uncontestable white supremacy, constrained blacks from enjoying their newfound freedom and restricted their life opportunities by maintaining them in structural subordination and dependency.

The Freedmen's Bureau, derived from the American Freedmen's Inquiry Commission, oddly enough, was to emancipate "blacks from the old condition of forced labor to their new state of voluntary industry."[76] The political scientist Rogers M. Smith's point, and one of the most critical investigations of the Freedmen's Bureau reveals in great detail that the Freedmen's Bureau was a reaction to the Black Codes, which was beginning "to transform the subjugating racial stratification in the nation's economic and cultural arrangements[77] by endorsing civil and political rights to black men through suffrage. Because of the racism of the South, the work of the Freedmen's Bureau, ultimately, was viewed as compromising the underlying facets of white supremacy and it had to end. "So the Freedmen's Bureau died," as W. E. B. Du Bois explained it, "and its child was the Fifteenth Amendment."[78] Irrespective of its intention, this amendment was mere window dressing in relations to the Declaration of Independence according to which: "all men are created equal, that they are endowed by their Creator with certain unalienable rights, that among these are life, liberty, and the pursuit of happiness."

When we think of equality of rights, it reminds us that America was founded and consolidated at the height of Lockean liberal individualism, which proved disadvantageous for analyzing and understating structures such as racism, sexism, classism, ableism, and homophobia as systems of oppression. And, sadly so, individuals' attitudes are frequently examined to determine the level of racism in American society, for example.[79] In the end, such an examination only bolsters classic comments as "the end of racism," or racism has nothing to do with me, "I am not racist." "I don't see color, just people." "I applaud Dr. Martin Luther King's "I have a Dream" speech in that "people are judged by the content of their character, not by the color of their skin." "I strongly support diversity of all kind, including racial diversity in higher education."[80] And it is not far stretched to suspect that similar measurements are employed to determine the extent to which individuals in society are homophobic or sexist. The fundamental question remains: how does one test racial attitudes that are based, for example, on conjectures stemming from racist stereotypes that shape the ways in which American social, political, and economic institutions operate to oppress, humiliate, dehumanize, and exploit nonwhites? In fact, in terms of racist ideology, one does not have to be racist in order for such an ideology to work. These days labeling everyone, including blacks, Mexicans, and other people of color as racists has become a paroxysmal epidemic in America. Explicit in this acknowledgement is the peculiar logic that since everyone is racist then no one is racist. What we have here, as is aptly termed by the sociologist Eduardo Bonilla-Silva, is "racism without racists"[81] or, to borrow from Judith Butler, no "doer behind the deed."[82]

Even though, having black men electorate would have encouraged agency and self-determination for blacks and other nonwhites, the Fifteenth Amendment proved to be nothing more than rhetoric. The right to vote was limited for black men by barriers such as the poll taxes, literacy tests, the grandfather clause, and gross intimidation from the Ku Klux Klan (KKK). Black men were, in effect, for the most part, wittingly debarred from electoral politics.[83] Nonetheless, much like others before them, writers influenced by William Dunning and John W. Burgess's school of thought on Reconstruction translated the intimidation and limitations imposed on Black votes into "Negro incapacity" and their inability to affirm their political rights of citizenship and exercise their suffrage.[84]

Whiteness, as having the power to speak for the constructed social "other," is revealed when Thomas Andrew Bailey, a professor of history at Stanford University, and self-appointed defender of the Black Codes, in his defensive haste, eagerly put forward the argument that the Black Codes were to guard the Negro from his own capriciousness.[85] While Bailey found no reason for inquiry into the ethic, perception, or wants of the ex-slaves, his justifiable formulation that the average ex-slaves were virtually helpless and not prepared to live as free people allowed for a ring of truth. However, his analysis bore no references to the fact that blacks, under the slave regime, were reduced to chattel, property, and eventually to three-fifths of a person for determining a state's share of the national taxes and its number of seats in the House of Representatives "according to the sacred script of the Constitution."[86] In spite of the plethora of evidence demonstrating blacks' capabilities, Bailey, casting ex-slaves as socially, politically, and emotionally immature,[87] which disqualified ex-slaves from some form of agency as "free" people, can permits one to conclude an implacable intransigence on Bailey's part. Bailey merely failed to recognize the remarkable capabilities of blacks and slaves.[88] Thus, in an effort to comprehend how and why Bailey was seduced by these misconceptions about blacks, we will have to turn our attention to the obvious fact that the Black Codes were in place to reinforce oppressive ideologies that circumscribed blacks' freedom and hamstrung them from upward socioeconomic mobility and keep white supremacy intact. During slavery, nothing was more threatening to many whites than a slave who did ascend his or her social position. Slaves who learned to read and write, for example, were severely punished. White supremacy allowed for the legitimization of knowledge and, for the most part, denied such legitimacy to those who were not white.

In many ways, "the enforcement of these Black Codes had encouraged free slaves to move to the North, bringing them into direct competition for jobs with Irish immigrants who were also facing tremendous discrimination because they were not culturally whitened and, thus, were viewed as nonwhites."[89] The historian David R. Roediger traces the process by which Irish workers defined themselves as white in order to obtain the privileges enjoyed by white people, which they could not have obtained as Irish. In attacking blacks and Chinese, who had no political representation, the Irish workers secured their position by identifying with the dominant white culture. The descendants of the first generation of Irish immigrants were better educated and enjoyed better occupational mobility than their parents. President Abbot Lawrence of Harvard University draws our attention to the fact that the Irish, on the basis of their whiteness, have rapidly assimilated into America's dominant culture. "Universal political equality," President Lawrence said, "should not be applied to 'tribal Indians,' 'Chinese,' or 'Negroes,' but only to whites who can assimilate rapidly."[90] First Nations, blacks, Chinese, and other racialized groups were inherently incapable of being assimilated. They were bestowed with a difference in the corporeal sense, that is, race was marked on the body as the material location for nonwhites' social and subjective existence. And it is precisely for this reason that "the contour of difference," according to Homi Bhabha, "is agonistic, shifting, splitting, rather like Freud's description of the system of consciousness which occupies a position in space lying on the borderline between outside and inside, a surface of protection, reception and projection."[91]

The North, in terms of racial hierarchy, "for blacks was not the promised land"[92] and, on the contrary, it was no different from the South.[93] While blacks in the South were reduced to ex-slaves, in the North they were pariahs.[94] Whites intentionally attempted to uphold an unbridgeable social and symbolic gulf with people who were black.[95] Blacks were increasingly separated from whites by a congealed color line in "employment, education, especially housing,"[96] and public transportation. For example, in New York City, there were separate buses for whites and blacks; in Philadelphia, blacks were allowed to ride only on the front platforms of streetcars.[97]

As early as the 1840s, the term "Jim Crow" was used by Abolitionist Newspaper to illustrate the separate railroad cars for blacks and whites.[98] However, as a way of characterizing blacks, the term "Jim Crow" originated in minstrelsy in the early nineteenth century. A white minstrel, Thomas "Daddy" Rice, popularized the term.[99] In the historian Leon F. Litwack's account of Jim Crow, Litwack is concerned with how a dance created by a black stableman from Louisville, Kentucky was reproduced by a white man in the minstrel show for the amusement of whites would become associated with a system designed by whites to segregate themselves from blacks.[100] This is an important consideration on Litwack's part. To get to the heart of Litwack's concern, we have to focus our attention on how whites responded to blacks. Given that minstrel shows were attempts at ridiculing blacks, whites who attended these minstrel shows would walk away with a distorted perception of blacks, which provided whites with a vision of blacks as the "other."[101] In due course, Jim Crow laws would embark on social customs and practice that ensured white domination and the subordination of nonwhites. It would span for more than half of a century. And, in spite of blacks and other nonwhites' opposition to whiteness, the "separate but equal" Jim Crow laws, which started in the 1890s continued until 1954 when the court's decision in *Brown v. Topeka Board of Education* ended segregation in public schools and rendered the "separate but equal doctrine" unconstitutional.

In the following section, I examine specific characteristics of Jim Crow laws only to show another aspect of the institutionalization of whiteness.

JIM CROW LAWS

Leon L. Litwack, in *Trouble in the Mind: Black Southerners in the Age of Jim Crow*, has demonstrated the assertiveness of blacks in the struggles against Jim Crow laws.[102] Also, during this period, many black organizations, including the National Medical Association (NMA), 1895; the National Association of Colored Women (NACW), 1896;[103] the National Negro Business League (NNBL), 1900;[104] the National Bar Association (NBA), the National Hospital Association (NHA), 1923; the National Association of Colored Graduate Nurses (NAGGN), 1908; the National Association for the Advancement of Colored People (NACCP), 1909; Committee of Racial Equality (CORE), 1942; and the Student Nonviolent Coordinating Committee (SNCC), 1960—were created, partly as responses to whiteness and its restlessness. In some cases, these organizations appeal to progressive whites for support.

A few years later after the implementation of Jim Crow laws, the Fourteenth Amendment claimed that it was unconstitutional for any of the states to deprive anyone of the rights of citizenship. As previously mentioned, the Fifteenth Amendment allowed for the recasting of the conception of citizenship in a participatory manner by bestowing on black men the right to vote. The idea was that they could not be denied that right based of their race or former condition of servitude. Yet, in 1883, Justice Joseph Bradley struck down Congress's 1875 ban on racial discrimination in all places of public accommodations. For example, the Louisiana legislature, in 1890, passed a law that provided that "all railway companies carrying passengers . . . in this State shall provide separate but equal accommodations for white and colored races." One of the greatest victories that pertained to the institutionalization of white privilege was the decision to separate the so-called superior race from the inferior race in the 1896 landmark case *Plessy v. Ferguson*.[105] Blacks had to ride in separate carriages on the train.[106]

In fact, the defense of Plessy and the review of the Louisiana statute were in the hands of four influential white men, Albion W. Tourgée, M. J. Cunningham, attorney general of Louisiana, and two other lawyers who assisted Cunningham in defending the statute. Justice Henry B. Brown delivered the majority opinion of the court. Understandably, Justice John Marshall Harlan, relatively isolated in his position, sensed that "the majority decisions violated rather than affirmed the Constitution."[107] Through an in depth engagement with Harlan's opinion of the court case, what is revealed is not only blacks' ontological status as second class citizens, but, more importantly, how whiteness shaped the nefarious positions of blacks, which for good reasons, unsettled and frightened Harlan. Precisely for this reason, Harlan must be quoted at length.

> There is a race so different from our own that we do not permit those belonging to it to become citizens of the United States. Persons belonging to it are, with few exceptions, absolutely excluded from our country. I allude to the Chinese race. But, by the statute in question, a Chinaman can ride in the same passenger coach with white citizens of the United States, while citizens of the black race in Louisiana, many of whom, perhaps, risked their lives for the preservation of the Union, who are entitled, by law, to participate in the political control of the state and nation, who are not excluded, by law or by reason of their race, from public stations of any kind, and who have all the legal rights that belong to white citizens, are yet declared to be criminals, liable to imprisonment, if they ride in a public coach occupied by citizens of the white race. [108]

Engaged as Harlan was with the plight of blacks, his concern suggests that the black–white model of race relations in America excluding—in this case—Chinese. However, it is clear from Harlan's speech that the Chinese were "absolutely excluded" from citizenship. With minor exceptions, the model extended itself to include all nonwhites. For example, when Chan Yong, a Chinese man residing in San Francisco challenged the Naturalization Act of 1790 because it denied him American citizenship, the court conferred in its ruling that the 1790 Act limited citizenship to whites. Years later, in *State v. Wong Kim Ark*, the Chinese were considered to be part of the "colored race" and was frequently identified with First Nations and blacks. Furthermore, as Ronald K. Takaki noted, "The Chinese migrants found that racial qualities previously assigned to blacks quickly became 'Chinese' characteristics . . . White workers referred to the Chinese as 'nagurs,' and a magazine cartoon depicted the Chinese as a bloodsucking vampire with slanted eyes, a pigtail, dark skin, and thick lips. Like blacks, the Chinese were described as heathen, morally inferior, savage, childlike, and lustful." [109] Dr. Arthur B. Stout, as cited by Ronald Takaki, claimed that allowing blacks and Chinese to be a part of American society was like "a cancer" in the "biological, social, religious and political systems." [110]

After the Civil War was over and slavery had been eliminated in 1865, a *New York Times* editorial advanced the notion that both Chinese and blacks posed a threat to America's cultural homogeneity. [111] It wrote:

> We have four million of degraded negroes in the South . . . and if there were to be a flood-tide of Chinese population—a population befouled with all social vices, with no knowledge or appreciation of free institutions or constitutional liberty, with heathenish souls and heathenish propensities, whose character, and habits, and modes of thought are firmly fixed by the consolidating influences of ages upon ages—we should be prepared to bid farewell to [America's cultural homogeneity]. [112]

Nonetheless, we cannot say for sure how the Chinese would have been treated on the segregated train because, to my knowledge, there is not much evidence to that effect.[113] As early as 1852, the *Daily Alta California* wrote that the Chinese are "debased and servile coolies, inferior to the Negroes morally—more clannish, deceitful, and vicious, and immeasurably lower than the Indian." In addition, Horace Greeley of the *New York Tribune* depicted Chinese immigrants as "uncivilized, unclean and filthy beyond all conception, without any of the higher domestic or social relations . . . Pagan in religion, they know not the virtues of honesty, integrity or good faith"; and Bayard Taylor, in 1855, wrote in a frequently cited passage that "The Chinese are, morally, the most debased people on the face of the earth . . . [with a] depravity so shocking and horrible that their character cannot even be hinted."[114] What we do know for sure, and W. E. B. Du Bois summed it up exceedingly well, is that in the "Jim Crow Car . . . the races were mixed together." The "white coach was all white."[115] Du Bois goes on to explain, "The color line—the relation of the darker to the lighter races of men in Asia and Africa, in America and the sea" is the separation of colored people from the whites.[116] The Canadian theorist Will Kymlicka suggests as much when he acknowledges that "whenever African or Asian delegates to the United Nations in New York drove down to Washington to talk to American government officials, they passed into the land of Jim Crow, and were forced to use racially segregated restaurants and washrooms."[117] The color line, a daily actuality supported by institutional patterns of racial pre-eminence, was so rigidly drawn that all nonwhites had to accept the status of blacks unless they could pass for white as some blacks did. Even though in 1915 *The Birth of a Nation* depicted black as the problem, I take my cue from Du Bois: "How does it feel to be the problem?" where, in *The Souls of Black Folk*, he explains and describes the experience of being viewed as nonwhite, especially black, as the problem of American race relations.[118] Given that "how does it feel to be the problem?" was not a question asked only of African Americans, but of all nonwhite people, the overall answer to this question would be clearly revealed in *People v. Hall* in 1854, when the California Supreme Court determined that a California statute preventing Indians and Negroes from testifying in court cases concerning whites also applied to Chinese Americans. To properly grasp this process and further contemplate this issue, we must return to George Yancy's suggestion that when nonwhites:

> Are asked the same question by white American, "how does it feel to be the problem?" the relations of being . . . [nonwhite] and being a problem is non-contingent. It is a necessary relation. Outgrowing this ontological state of being a problem is believed impossible. Hence, when regarding one's existence as problematic, temporality is frozen. One is a problem forever. However, it is important to note that it is

from the white imaginary that the question "How does it feels to be a problem?" is given birth.[119]

Hence, when Richard Wright, shortly after World War II, was asked by a French reporter about his opinion on the "Negro Problem" in America, without much searching, Wright incisively responded, "There's isn't any Negro problem; there is only a white problem."[120] In other words, the problem is not of blacks and other nonwhites, but one of whites—for it is they who replicate and uphold whiteness as the regulating system of domination that makes such a question feasible.[121] Blacks, First Nations, and other nonwhites cannot break away from the objective frame of power and its authoritarian dimensions, which is exercised on the lived reality of their daily life. This is the tragic fact of nonwhiteness, of racial discrimination, and of anguish in America. Given that blacks and other nonwhites are subjugated to whites through a practice of racial "othering," blacks and other nonwhites must always posit themselves or be posited in relations to whiteness. In this sense, people of color have no ontological resistance in the presence of whiteness. Suddenly, they have been given two frames of references within which they have had to place themselves.[122] This is what W. E. B. Du Bois called the "double consciousness." Blacks, First Nations, Chinese, Mexicans, and other racialized ethnic groups are, sadly so, always confounded by this "peculiar sensation"[123] of having to simultaneously confront and modify their behaviors in the face of whiteness.

In the variety and multifaceted nature of America's racial and cultural heterogeneity im the black–white model of race relations, black unmistakably meant nonwhite. More recently, the sociologist Joe Feagin has examined anti-black racism, and saw that the black-white racial model is fundamental for an analysis of the impact of racial discrimination on other racialized ethnic groups.[124] Given that racialized ethnic groups are not immune to racial oppression,[125] it was quite telling, as Frank H. Wu, a law professor, reported that during World War II, on the night of the Harlem riot, a Chinese laundryman "hurriedly posted a sign on his store window which read: 'Me Colored Too.'"[126] The laundryman display of his sign provides a revealing example of how when various nonwhites, Chinese, blacks, First Nations, and Mexicans called themselves and each other colored, they invoked a shared political identity. This is not to say that solidarity is assumed on the basis of race; it is forged in the historical, social, and legal practice of America's racism. Instead, if anything, the connotations of the term colored was constructed from the dominant codes of racial discourse and reformulated as signs of grouping and unity among isolated groups of people sharing common experiences historically framed within the psychic representation and the social, economical, and political reality of America's racism.[127] Therefore, discourses about race and racism are not simply about the black-white model of race relations, as it understood and argued by many scholars, to exclude other racialized ethnicities from the model.

As I have mentioned before, blacks, as a discursive constructed group, both legally and conceptually, signifies nonwhites in term of their object status in a structure that is racist. Hence, in the advancement of any form of an antiracist project, the racial gaze, which unequivocally articulated, for example, in the child's idiom, "Mummy, see the Negro! I am frightened,"[128] has to be directed from the racial object (nonwhites) to the racial subject (whites). Gunnar Myrdal's *An American Dilemma: The Negro Problem and Modern Democracy* captured the necessity to examine the prejudice of white Americans, in his words, "what goes on in the minds of white Americans."[129] The methodology for such a move is imagined in the prolific wave of "whiteness studies." As a framework, the field of "whiteness studies" normally alleges an antiracist viewpoint to the point that it is as much a political project as a critical framework. I return to "whiteness studies" in chapter 4. For now, I will suggest that "whiteness studies," instead of decentering whiteness, seems to be recentering whiteness as an essential something."[130]

BLACKS AND OTHER NONWHITES' RESPONSE TO WHITENESS

In many instances, race consciousness among African Americans was used to challenge Jim Crow laws. A. Philip Randolph's Negro March on Washington, DC, in 1941 and the Southern Christian Leadership Conference created by Dr. Martin Luther King, Jr. in 1957, aimed at achieving the full rights of citizenship and equality for blacks and other nonwhites, and the integration of blacks and other nonwhites in all aspects of American life were illustrative. Nonetheless, those who challenged whiteness and white privilege were, as a rule, severely penalized. For instance, Marcus Garvey and Claudia Jones were exiled; W. E. B. Du Bois and Paul Robeson were relentlessly hassled and denied passports; Henry Winston, Angela Davis, and Angelo Herndon spent years in jail; Fannie Lou Hamer and John Lewis were viciously beaten; and Malcolm X, Martin Luther King, and Fred Hampton were assassinated.[131] Under the Jim Crow laws, everything was separate, but nothing was equal. The de jure segregation in the South was matched by a de facto segregation in the North. In the North the "official" rules of segregation were pronounced in housing, schooling, entertainment, and employment. In this sense, racism does not require the full support of the state and its laws. Racial discrimination by individuals and institutions persisted and even flourished in the North.

The subordinate position of blacks and other nonwhites was the "natural" outcome of white supremacy as a structure formed over time through an ensemble of legal and social mechanics and processes that were, and still are, solidly in place. In fact, blacks and other racialized ethnic groups were not on the opposite side of the racial binary. All that mattered was white skin. Even the lowest of the lowest whites on the social white ladder had something that a nonwhite person could never possess, that is, white skin. Skin privilege was tied to a certain status that all whites enjoyed simply, according to W. E. B. Du Bois, "because they were white." Poor and degraded whites "were admitted freely, with all classes of white people, to public functions [and] public parks . . . The police were drawn from their ranks and, the courts, dependent on their votes treated them with leniency."[132] The institutionalized violence of the KKK toward blacks and other marginalized groups, giving way to the presumptive hegemony of whiteness, cannot be ignored. By the 1920s, the KKK achieved a terrifying public presence, operating not only in the South but also in the heartlands of the Midwest. In fact, lynching, then, was not criminalized.[133]

Given that white supremacy has been planted within American institutions and systems from the very beginning of America's formation, white supremacy has also encountered resistance from individuals and groups, mobilizing around racial particularities, in the form of what Gayatri C. Spivak labels as "strategic essentialism."[134] This mobilization, for the most part, has been located outside of the racist state. Far from being the opposite of power, power generates it own resistance, which is how Judith Butler describes power as the "double valence of producing and subordinating."[135] Appropriately, that is to say, power, morphing itself into a whole host of lexis, is what gives resistance its strength. In due course, with the formation of groups such as the National Association for the Advancement of Colored People (NAACP), resistance, although opposed by those in power, became more organized and articulated. Later on, other organizations, including CORE, SNCC, the Civil Rights Movement, the Asian American Movement of the 1960s and 1970s, the American Indian Movement founded in 1968, the Chicano Movement of the 1960s, a growth of the Mexican American civil rights movement, which began in the 1940s, the National Council of La Raza created in 1968 in Washington, DC, and the Organization of Chinese American founded in 1973 were formed to address the rights of racialized ethnic groups. Black Nationalists, including Martin R. Delany[136] and Marcus Garvey, and later on other militant blacks such as Stokely Carmichael and Charles V. Hamilton, for example, focused their usual attention on promoting "Black Power." The Black Power movement arose out of its discontentment with integrationism.

The Black Panther Party, taking its inspiration from "Black Power," as championed and defended by black nationalists, was a good example of an antiracist impulse, which challenged the intertwining of whiteness and American racism. Racial oppression in America, for the members of the Black Panther, was viewed as "internal colonialism." Internal colonialism, in this respect, is best explained and described as a structure of social relations based on a complicated and comprehensive control and mistreatment of First Nations, blacks, Chinese, Mexicans, and other racialized ethnic groups in the face of a irrefutable hegemonic whiteness. It is a direct result of pervasive dehumanization, a product that supports and maintains whiteness at the expense of nonwhiteness. It provides an effective entry point for analyzing racial oppression in the United States through the invocation of a colonial model.[137] In fact, more recently, many scholars have unmasked and exposed the simple, extraordinarily disturbing fact of black ghettoes, super ghettoes, and other congested and rat-infested "ethnic enclaves," for what they really are, America's internal colonies. Many individuals and groups, located within America's internal colonies, were, and continue to be placed, outside of, as well as inside, the racialized working class and have been advanced to an underprivileged class, which lately is referred to as the "underclass," a racially charged term.

When, in 1963, Gunnar Myrdal, in his book *Challenge to Affluence*, used the term the underclass, it was, in its entirety, to explain and describe the position of the chronically unemployed, underemployed, and the underemployables that were created by the post-industrial society. While the underclass in this sense was used as an economic concept, it does not mean that it escaped its racial characteristic since economic relations are not freed from the process of racialization. In fact, the process of racialization is interconnected with black ghettoes, super ghettoes and so on. Mickey Kaus, senior editor of the *New Republic*, has been specific and foremost in defining the "underclass" as a racialized concept.[138] Without reservation, the political scientist Adolph Reed Jr. indeed criticizes Kaus for joining in the declaration that "the underclass is the black lower class for which the work ethic has evaporated and the entrepreneurial drive is channeled into gangs and drug-pushing."[139] Kaus's image of the underclass, as the major organizing cryptogram of poverty, is within a culture that for Reed is "ghetto-specific."[140] Reed, once again, decries this notion of the underclass as resting "on fuzzy and disturbing assumptions about poor people, poverty, and the world in which both are reproduced."[141] Furthermore, poverty, as a systematic problem, has been an unpopular view within mainstream discourse. In this discourse, the poor are blamed for being poor.[142]

The internal colonial perspective, in opposition to the triumphalist approbation from the New Right that colorblindness should prevail in America and the ideological challenges that it presents, upholds the saliency of race. Also, it provides a fundamental challenge to the issue of race, rooted in America's race history in which racialized ethnic groups were discriminated and continue to experience gross discrimination. With the aftermath of the Civil Rights Movement, urban violence and social unrest, the development of Black Power and the Black Panthers

Party, race relations were beginning to take center stage. It was for good reason that Michael Banton, borrowing from Robert Miles, labeled the 1960s as "the race relations problematic."[143] A decade of social unrest prompted the government in the 1960s to pass landmark legislations that dealt with race relations in America.

The Civil Rights Act of 1964 and the Fair Employment Opportunity Commission attempting, in process, to affirmatively put an end to discrimination in employment are important. In spite of many antidiscrimination measures that have been effectively executed to encourage, in principle, racial equality, nonwhites in America continue to be overwhelmed by America's perpetual and unbearable race problems. One precise reason for this is the manner in which these antidiscrimination measures continue to uphold the white power structure that is in place. Whiteness and white privilege determine who should have power and who should subscribe to such a power. However, power allows for members of marginalized group to challenge its hegemonic rule. Hence, concessions, in the form of antidiscrimination measures, as a marker of a civilized society, are necessary to appease the marginalized and, at same time, to support and uphold the power structure that is in place. In this sense, power's paradoxical milieu is revealed.

In a society premises on the able-bodied, white, masculine symbolic, concessions are symptomatic of what Professor Louis F. Mirón calls "the moral exercise of power."[144] In fact, antidiscriminatory measures allows for visible representation of nonwhites, women, homosexuals, the disabled, and immigrants, for example, to occupy positions of power. And even though in America, a black man, Barack Obama, holds the highest position of power as the president, whites continue to disproportionately occupy positions of power. Power produces certain forms of knowledge that are substantial; and it legitimizes and extends the interests of those serve by the possession of the operative power. In other words, power is tyrannical. And it is only through embodying the very contingent norms of the power that marginalize and stigmatize a nonwhite person that individual can gain some access to power and find his or her partial expression in "honorary whiteness."

Honorary whiteness allows for blacks and other nonwhites to acquire a certificate of whiteness and become an honorary white, an identity that is somewhat established or instituted. It is different from "passing for white" because "becoming white" is not absolute; it is a continuous process; it is never settled. An honorary white remains white in so far as his or her presence does not intrude on the white social body. In other words, even as an honorary white, you should not intrude on white social space. To become an honorary white, as Simone de Beauvoir usage of the verb "becoming" for the construction of women's identity, is a tough enterprise because it is never commensurable to whiteness as is marked on the body. Although, whites are willing to accept honorary whites, there is a detail about the "those" (nonwhites) that bothers the "us" (whites). The way race is epidermatized, the way it is marked on the body means that race "stands out as a visible social sign." Whiteness, which is no less social, is, nonetheless, "part of the taken-for-granted visual field, a sign of its presumptive hegemony."[145] At its most elementary level, honorary whiteness requires one to transcend nonwhiteness and free oneself from the labels and stereotypes that are linked with nonwhites; taking on a lifestyle that permits the association of white images; presenting oneself, or being presented to whites in a way that make them feel secure and unsusceptible. It is not astounding, then, that if honorary whiteness can be granted, it can also be withdrawn. In the end, the sad part is that honorary whiteness is the result of the way whiteness "interpellates" the "us" as nonwhites—First Nations, blacks, Asians, and Mexicans. The epidermatization of race accentuates and renders the "them" as aliens no matter how much "them" are culturally whitened and try to assimilate "us."

In a society marred by normalized whiteness, power fastens nonwhites to an image that signifies otherness, an image that imprisons and determines social status. This is precisely how Frantz Fanon describes otherness, as "the lived experience of [nonwhites], "the fact of [nonwhiteness],"[146] as marked on the body. I do not mean to imply that an individual from a racialized ethnic group shares a set of physical characteristics that joins that individual to the other members of his or her group; on the contrary, there is no true essence to First Nationness, Chineseness, Mexicanness, or blackness. However, racial authenticity matters not so much conceptually but practically. The aura of an authentic blackness, for example, feeds a special kind of comfort in America; it guarantees the status of whiteness. "And since race in itself—in so far as it is anything in itself—refers to some intrinsically insignificant geographical/physical difference between people, it is the imagery of race that is played out."[147] What makes blacks, for example, black, is the communal understanding of being visually or cognitively acknowledged as black by a society that is racist, and the disciplinary and destructive effects of that classification, giving strength to the signifying practice of normalized whiteness, which raises the inevitable questions below.[148]

Are antidiscrimination measures accountable to normalized whiteness? Can they address unlawful behavior based on patterns of hiring in the workplace? For example, if a company decides to limit blacks and Mexicans from working with that company or working in areas of the company that is predominantly staffed with white workers by requiring high test scores or a high school diploma, is this an unlawful practice? How can we determine unlawful behavior in the workplace? Is the function of antidiscriminatory measures to enable us to accept the consequences of whiteness presumptive hegemony? Any discussion of such measure must first take into account whiteness as property and how it has intricately bound up with issues of power and powerlessness. Even though in the next chapter, the preceding questions will form the basis for my discussion, my focal point, however, is to examine the trajectory of race-conscious affirmative action programs as a way of foregrounding America's remembering of its racist past, which provides a full grasp into its future on race relations.

NOTES

1. Harris (1993), 1716.
2. African women were equated with other household property that white men owned. Laws, establishing slavery in colonial Virginia, imposed taxes on African but not on European women. See Kathleen M. Brown, *Good Wives, Nasty Wenches, and Anxious Patriarchs: Gender, Race, and Power in Colonial Virginia* (1996). Also, laws imposed taxes on children of First Nations and European parentage and First Nations and black couples. See Kirsten Fischer, *Suspect Relations: Sex, Race, and Resistance in Colonial North Carolina* (2002). Fischer's analysis is in dialogue with Brown's even though she does not come to the same conclusion as Brown that gender was the decisive marker for defining groups in colonial Virginia. Like Brown, however, Fischer examined gender construction in colonial America. Both Brown and Fisher's contribution to race and racial thinking in colonial America is their feminist analysis that is, most of the time, lacking.
3. Arnesen (2001), 7.
4. Another form of white identity is antiracists, which I discussed in chapter 5.
5. Moore and Williams (1942), 351.
6. Bell, Higgins, and Suh (1997),107.
7. Harris (1993), 1721.
8. If rights, as liberal theorists argue, define the realm of privacy within which the individual resides, this realm must be safeguarded if one's autonomy is to be preserved. To curtail one's rights is to diminish one's existence. As is shown in *Dred Scott v. Sandford* in 1857, the Supreme Court held that blacks could not be citizens and, therefore, could not enjoy the rights of citizens.
9. Bhabha (1994).
10. Roediger (1994), 75. In the defining and shaping of gender roles and expectations, whiteness attempts to control gender by infusing the positive association of whiteness with gender norms and expectations. As in the case of nonwhite women, as a socially constituted homogeneous group, their subjectivity was often associated with immorality and promiscuity. Such constructions would later on be appropriated, for example, in black communities. Instead of moving away from such an essentially crippling notion of black women, the National Association of Colored Women (founded in 1896) comprised mostly of middleclass black women, was very much focused on black womanhood. Black women who were members of this organization were profoundly concerned that black women were immoral and promiscuous. In the meanwhile, white women's characterization was the antithesis to these characteristics assigned to nonwhite women.

White women were associated with purity and innocence, as elements of the repressive confinement of domesticity and the cult of true womanhood rooted in the socially institutionalized heteronormativity that strove to restrict women of libidinous pleasure, especially, if it was not centered on procreation. In other words, white women were placed on a podium of sexual inaccessibility if sexuality was not centered on procreation. And inasmuch as white women were epitomized as sexually unknowing and unavailable, it was Ida B. Well-Barnett who actively decried the conceptual purity of white women in her editorial, in *Memphis Free Speech*, where she declared that some white women freely engaged in sexual contact with black men (2005, 8). Nonetheless, in *Black Skin White Mask*, as Fanon reminds us, whiteness is looked on as desire. Whiteness, as desire, makes allowance for white women's apparent desire for black men to operationalize the terrifying assumption that black men are on the whole not to be trusted around white women. To sum it up, black men are trapped by their assumed desire for white women and were seen as sexually aggressive and hypermasculine, which presented an assumed threat to white manhood. The stereotype of the exotic, the promiscuous, and the accessible black male "other" promotes simultaneously anger against, and fear of, black men. The dualism of fear and desire is a dangerous combination that black men encounter, putting them at continuous risk of social castration.

11. See Annals of Congress, *Abridgements of Debates of Congress, 1789–1856* (1857), 184.

12. See Annals of Congress, *Abridgements of Debates of Congress, 1789–1856* (1857), 553–58.

13. Jacobson (1998), 25.

14. This clearly contradicted George Washington's idea of America being open to all immigrants. He wrote in 1783, "The bosom of America is open to receive not only the Opulent and respectable Stranger, but the oppressed and persecuted of all Nations and Religions." In 1870, the law of naturalization was extended to "aliens of African nativity, and to persons of African descent." Quoted in Arthur Mann, "From Immigration to Acculturation" (1992, 75).

15. "A foreign miners' tax of twenty dollars monthly was in practice a 'Mexican Miners' Tax.'" Miners who came from Mexico as well as Mexicans living in America (American citizens) had to pay the taxes. See Ronald Takaki, *A Different Mirror: A History of Multicultural America* (1993), 178.

16. Jacobson (1998), 31.

17. Harris (1993), 1776. The Naturalization Act of 1795, which continued to deny American citizenship to white women and all nonwhite people, superseded the Naturalization Act of 1790. Certainly, the expansion of the eligibility of nonwhites into the incorporation of American citizenship has been sluggish. Naturalization was not extended to blacks until 1870. It was not until the implementation of the Magnuson Act, or the Chinese Exclusion Repeal Act of 1943 that Chinese could have become naturalized citizens of the United States. East Asians and Filipinos could not naturalize until 1952, with the passage of the McCarran-Walter Act, which restricted immigration into the United States.

18. Yet, free blacks were only free in the sense that they were not slaves. Many free blacks were not allowed to live in certain states. Slaves who were emancipated had to move to other states and could never return. Many restrictions were placed on free blacks exercising their rights. See Leon F. Litwack, *North of Slavery: The Negro in the Free States, 1790–1860* (1965).

19. Blacks could not obtain citizenship until 1870; First Nations until 1924; Chinese after 1943, and Japanese after 1952. However, whites were never barred from claiming citizenship. Until 1931, a woman could not naturalize if she was married to an alien that was barred from citizenship because he was nonwhite. And, if she were to marry such an alien, she was automatically stripped of her legal citizenship. See Ian F. Haney López, *White by Law: The Legal Construction of Race* (1996, 15–16). In 1855, Congress declared that an alien woman "automatically acquired citizenship upon marriage to a US citizen, or upon the naturalization of her husband." The automatic citizenship of women through marriage ended in 1922. See Haney López (1996), 46–47.

20. In 1922, a Japanese American, Takao Ozawa, failed in his attempt to persuade the Hawaii's district court as well as the Supreme Court that he was eligible for naturalization based on the premise that he was culturally whitened. Both argued that Ozawa was yellow by law, which points to the fact that in America, the law constructs race as a reality. For a more comprehensive overview of this case, see *Ozawa v. the United States*.

21. Later on, Alexis de Tocqueville, when he arrived in the United States to research the American prison system, would marvel at American democracy. In the end, Tocqueville ended up writing two books on democracy in America.

22. Harris (1993), 119.

23. Van Evrie (1863), 91.

24. Van Evrie (1863), 90.

25. Dr. J. H. Van Evrie popularized the scientific basis of white supremacy. In his book, *Negroes and Negro Slavery*, he drew on such human attributes as skin color, hair, physique (figure), features, and brain as "facts that separate the races" (1863, 132) which would, in the bitter end, determine power relations. In the end, he asked "what are [blacks'] natural relations to whites? He wrote, "if the natural relations that men bear to each other are thus misunderstood in Europe, it may well be supposed that they are wholly ignorant of the natural relations of races, and without even the remotest conception of the relations that naturally exist between white men and negroes [in America]" (187). And if scientific evidence was not enough, he turned his attention to Christianity and blazingly claimed, "God has made the negro different from, and inferior to the white man" (189).

26. Morrison (1993), 47.

27. Davis (1974), 34.

28. Camus (1948), 153.

29. For a more comprehensive discussion of how the Irish became white, see Noel Ignatiev, *How the Irish Became* (1995); and how the Jews became white, see Karen Brodkin, *How Jews Became White Folks and What That Says About Race in America* (1998).

30. See Karen Brodkin, *How Jews Became White Folks and What That Says about Race in America* (1998); Richard Dyer, *White* (1997); Noel Ignatiev, *How the Irish Became White* (1995); Theodore W. Allen, *The Invention of the White Race: Racial Oppression and Social Control* (1994); Toni Morrison, *Playing in the Dark: Whiteness and the Literary Imagination*, (1993); and David R. Roediger, *The Wages of Whiteness: Race and the Making of the American Working Class* (1991).

31. See Alexis de Tocqueville, "Democracy in America" (1999).

32. It is from this very basis that American democracy was later looked on by scholars, including Gunnar Myrdal, as compromising America's creed: liberty, equality, and property for all because of the way nonwhites, especially blacks, were treated in America. See Myrdal's masterpiece, *An American Dilemma: The Negro Problem and Modern Democracy* (1962). In 1968, the Kerner Commission Report would point to the fact of institutionalized racism. This was old news. Frederick Douglass, already, had observed the inconsistency that existed between America's democratic values and its racial practices. One of the main tasks of a democratic government is to make sure that all members of a society are protected from harsh treatment from individuals, groups, or even the state.

33. In addition, "I think God made all people good," declared the 1992 Republican presidential nominee Pat Buchanan, "but we had to take a million immigrants in, say, Zulus, next year, or Englishmen and put them in Virginia, what group would be easier to assimilate and would cause less problems for the people of Virginia?" Buchanan obtrusively asked. And he would offer a conclusion that "there is nothing wrong with sitting down and arguing that issue, that [America] is a European country" (Hing 1993, 863–64) as a rationale for his own deep-seated bigotry. While America continues to be viewed as a "white country," more recently, the political scientist, Samuel P. Huntington and his contemporaries have persuaded many scholars that nonwhites are threats to America's cultural homogeneity. See Samuel P. Huntington, *Who Are We? The Challenges to America's National Identity* (2004); *The Disuniting of America: Reflections on a Multicultural Society* (1998); Nathan Glazer, *We are all Multiculturalists Now,* (1997); and Dinesh D'Souza, *Illiberal Education: The Politics of Race and Sex on Campus* (1991).

34. Benette (1975), 73.

35. The assumption of whites' racial purity gave rise to Nazi Germany.

36. Some feminists view women's position in society as similar to the history and practices of slavery. However, bell hooks, rightfully, points out that "theoretically, the white woman's legal status under patriarchy may have been that of 'property,' but she was in no way subjected to the dehumanization and brutal oppression that was the lot of the slaves" (1981), 126.

37. Fanon (1967), 202.

38. See George M. Fredrickson, *Racism a Short History* (2002); Lisa Cardyn, "Sexualized Racism/Gendered violence: Outraging the Body Politics in the Reconstruction South" (2002); and William L. Katz, *The Invisible Empire: The Ku Klux Klan's Impact on History* (1986).

39. Gossett (1963), 30. See Richard Mayo-Smith, "Assimilation of Nationalities in the United States" (1894), 429–32.

40. Jordan (1968), 169.

41. Allen (1994), 14.

42. Daniel (2002), 40.

43. Daniel (2002), 41.

44. Also, see Gerald Early's edited volume, *Lure and Loathing: Essays on Race, Identity, and the Ambivalence of Assimilation* (1994).

45. Later on, during World War II, Japanese American would also be relegated to "location centers," which disadvantaged them from securing economic and political resources.

46. Takaki (1993), 11.

47. Takaki (1979), 162.

48. Article IX stated:

> The Mexicans who, in the territories aforesaid, shall not preserve the character of citizens of the Mexican Republic, conformably with what is stipulated in the preceding article, shall be incorporated in the union of the United States, and be admitted at the proper time (to be judged by the Congress of the United States) to the enjoyment of all the rights of citizens of the United States, according to the principles of the Constitution; and in the mean time shall be maintained and protected in the free enjoyment of their liberty and property, and secured in the free exercise of their religion without restriction. (Hill 2008, 121)

49. Takaki (1993), 178.

50. For a detailed reading of Sections I-IV of Article XIX, see Section 95 in the Congressional Quarterly's Guide to the U.S. Supreme Court (1979), 631.

51. For a thorough reading of the Chinese Exclusion Act of 1882, see Sucheng Chan, *Entry Denied: Exclusion and the Chinese American Community in America, 1882–1943* (1991a); Sucheng Chan, *Asian Americans: An Interpretive History* (1991b). With the implementation of the Page Law in 1875, Chinese women were barred from entering the United States.

52. Franklin (1961), 234.

53. Bhabha (1994), 109.

54. Goldberg (1994), 5.

55. Takaki (1979), 222.

56. Quoted in Takaki (1979), 217.

57. Takaki (1979), 220.

58. Takaki (1979), 3.

59. Takaki (1979), 17.

60. Takaki (1979), 3.

61. The Scott Act of 1888 allowed Chinese officials, teachers, students, merchants, or travelers for pleasure or curiosity to enter the United States. See Wu Tingfang, *America Through the Spectacles of an Oriental Diplomat* (1914), 48.

62. Higham (1994), 25.

63. See Dan Caldwell, "The Negroization of the Chinese Stereotype in California" (1971).

64. Takaki (1979), 217.

65. By the eighteenth and nineteenth century many thinkers, that is, the founding fathers of racial classification and racial theory, including Francois Bernier (1625–1688), Carl Linnaeus (1707–1778), Comte de Buffon (1707–1788), Johann Friedrich Blumenbach (1752–1840), Georges Cuvier (1769–1832), and Arthur de Gobineau (1816–1882), attempted to classify humans by biological races based on physical attributes. And when, in 1896, Frederick L. Hoffman, *Race Traits and Tendency of the American Negro*, continued his analysis within the racist pseudoscience framework as a synthesis of these earlier works and suggested that blacks were biologically inferior, he was totally discredited by some scholars and progressive reformers. In 1899, starting with W. E. B. Du Bois' path breaking book, *The Philadelphia Negro: A Social Studies*, where Du Bois positioned himself against the biological notion of race and argued that blackness, for example, was constructed so as to promote racial classification and stratification. He continued to explain that black communities are the outcome of severe environmental constraints and not black assumed inherent inferiority. Also, see S. T. Joshi's *Documents of American Prejudice: An Anthology of Writings on Race from Thomas Jefferson to David Duke* (1999), 51–52. More recently, many scholars have rejected the concept of race all together. In 1942, Ashley Montagu, *Man's Most Dangerous Myth: The Fallacy of Race*, argued that physical characteristics do not provide the basis for placing human beings into rigid racial categories. In a frequently cited passage, Anthony K. Appiah, in "The Uncompleted Argument: Du Bois and the Illusion of Race," takes on a different approach to the understanding of race. He argues, quite persuasively, that race has no real meaning and reference. "The truth is that there are no races: there is nothing in the world that can do all we ask 'race' to do for us." (1985, 35). Walter Benn Michaels points to the fact that some scholars refuse to recognize race altogether, claiming that race has no meaning if it is not a scientific fact. See Michaels, "Autobiography of an Ex-White Man" (1998); "Posthistoricism: The End of History" (1996); and "Race into Culture: A Critical Genealogy of Cultural Identity" (1992). What this points to is the throwing out "the baby of race with the bathwater of racism." See Winthrop D. Jordan, "Modern Tensions and the Origins of American Slavery" (1962). However, more recently, *Scientific America* captioned its 2003 report on the results of the recent completed Human Genome Project with the title "Science Has the Answer: Does Race Exist? Genetic Results May Surprise You" and claimed that races do exist. See Jane H. Hill, *The Everyday Language of White Racism* (2008), 10.

66. It also ended the Asiatic barred zone that was created by Congress in 1917 to exclude all persons from Asia to enter the United States. During the same period, a bill was passed by the Senate to exclude "all members of the African or black race." Because of the lobbying efforts of the National Association for the Advancement of Colored People (NAACP), the bill was defeated in the House.

67. In Nazi Germany, Eastern European Jews were perceived as black. Also, in the post-war period, Southern Italians who migrated to Australia were considered black before they finally became white.

68. Fanon (1967), 8.

69. Fanon (1967), 14.

70. This Act was firmly tested in *Elk v. Wilkins* in 1884 when the Supreme Court denied citizenship to First Nations on the grounds that First Nations did not acquire citizenship upon birth. Even though the Nationality Act of 1940 bestowed citizenship "to a member of an Indian, Eskimo, Aleutian, or other aboriginal tribe," born in the United States, it was not until 1924 did Congress pass an Act granting citizenship to First Nations. Also, it was tested in 1898, in the case *United States v. Wong Kim* where the Supreme Court declared that Chinese who were born in the United States and resided here were citizens of the United States.

71. The Codes authorized blacks to acquire and own properties, marry, make contracts, sue and be sued, and testify in courts in cases involving only blacks. Howev-

er, some of the more severe features of the Codes included written evidence of employment and being subjected to arrest by any white person. For a detailed reading of the implementation of the Black Codes during Reconstruction, see Eric Foner, *Reconstruction: America's Unfinished Revolution, 1863–1877* (1988), 199–201.

72. Foucault (1977), 138.

73. Katz (1986), 19.

74. McMillen (1990), 11.

75. The former confederate states are Alabama, Arizona, Arkansas, Florida, Georgia, Kentucky, Louisiana, Maryland, Mississippi, Missouri, North Carolina, South Carolina, Tennessee, Texas, Virginia, and West Virginia.

76. Du Bois (2003), 21.

77. Smith (1999), 329.

78. Du Bois (2003), 41.

79. See David O. Sears, "Symbolic Racism" (1988); Howard Schuman et al., *Racial Attitudes in America: Trends and Interpretation* (1985).

80. See James Traub, "Forget Diversity" (2003).

81. For a careful consider of the term "racism without racists," see Eduardo Bonilla-Silva, *Racism Without Racists: Color-Blind Racism and the Persistence of Racial Inequality in the United States* (2006).

82. Butler (1990b), 142.

83. Black women experienced similar fate with the enactment of the nineteenth Amendment.

84. Foner (1988), 20.

85. Bailey (1982).

86. Wacquant (2002), 45.

87. Bailey (1982).

88. Countless examples that have provided the most profound insights of blacks' responsiveness have served to mediate Bailey's critique. Surely, Bailey must have been aware that in the War of 1812 with Britain, freed slaves joined with mercenaries and burnt down the White House. In addition, slaves made some attempts at insurrection, including under Gabriel in Virginia in 1800; under Vesey in Carolina in 1822; and on August 22, 1831, it was the slave Nat Turner who, for two days in Virginia, led seventy other slaves in a ferocious insurrection where sixty whites were found dead. Also, about 189,000 black men were recruited from the slave states to fight in the Civil War. Abolitionists, including Frederick Douglass (himself a slave), David Walker, and Henry Highland, were black men and some of the most forceful opposing voices against the conditions of the slaves. In addition, black women who were ex-slaves fought to improve the conditions of black women in America. Anna Julia Cooper published A Voice from the South by a Black Woman of the South, and Sojourner Truth, an ex-slave, famous for her speech, "Ain't I a Woman." I suppose, then, that Bailey's claim about blacks, masquerading as "truth," is astonishingly numb to the otherwise countless evidence. In sum, Bailey's valorization of the Black Codes as tools to curb the capriciousness of ex-slaves is precisely what Nancy Fraser refers to as a "false antithesis."

89. Casey (2003), 51. There were two conditions by which slaves were to be freed. The first was that a slave had to prove that he or she had a maternal ancestor who was First Nations, because, in the United States, slavery "descended matrilineally," freeing white men from their responsibilities for children borne by black women. Second, the slave had to provide proof that the maternal ancestor was not enslaved between 1679 and 1705 because during this period First Nations were slaves. See Adrienne D. Davis, "Identity Notes, Part One: Playing in the Light" (1997), 232.

90. Takaki (1993), 163. Also, quoted in Stephen Spencer, "The Discourse of Whiteness: Chinese-American History, Pearl S. Buck, and the Good Earth," 2002.

91. Bhabha (1994), 110.

92. Takaki (1993), 110.

93. See Stetson Kennedy, *Jim Crow Guide to the U.S.A.: The Laws, Customs, and Etiquette Governing the Conduct of Nonwhites and Other Minorities as Second-Class Citizens* (1959).

94. Litwack (1965), 234.

95. Wacquant (2002), 49.

96. Massey and Denton (1993), 30.

97. Litwack (1965), 120.

98. Litwack (2004), 7.

99. For a more comprehensive reading of the emergence of the term Jim Crow, see Leon F. Litwack, "Jim Crow Blues" (2004), 7. Also, the rise, manifestations, and implications of Jim Crow have been documented by scholars, including C. Vann Woodward, *Origins of the New South, 1877–1913* (1951); and *The Strange Career of Jim Crow* (1951). This is not to say that blacks and other nonwhites did not experience discrimination before the institutionalization of Jim Crow. The implementation of the Black Codes is a case in point.

100. Litwack (2004), 7.

101. David R Roediger, in *The Wages of Whiteness: Race and the Making of the American Working Class* (1991), explains how the role that minstrelsy, blackface performance in the supposedly Negro Style, in the nineteenth century, helped in the assimilation of Irish because some of the well-known performers in blackface were Irish.

102. Litwack (1998).

103. The forming of the National Association of Colored Women (NACW) was a response to the discrimination against black and other nonwhite women that existed in General Federation of Women Club. The National Federal and the National League of Colored Women came together to form, in Washington, DC, the NACW.

104. The organization was founded by Booker T. Washington after he realized that blacks were barred from white controlled league.

105. Homer Plessy was a mulatto. On June 7, 1892, he bought a first class ticket on the East Louisiana Railway for a trip from New Orleans to Covington, Louisiana. The first class ticket provided seats in the "white section" of the train. Plessy was convicted of violating the 1890 statute. His appeal was useless. The Supreme Court of Louisiana upheld the conviction.

106. George Washington Cable draws our attention to the state of the public accommodations for Negroes. He said that "the negroes compartment on a train was in every instance and without recourse, the most uncomfortable, uncleanest, and unsafest place . . . [and these conditions] are a shame to any community pretending to practice public justice" (quoted in Gossett 1963), 275.

107. Harlan (1997), 34.

108. Harlan (1997), 58.

109. Takaki (1979), 219.

110. Takaki (1979), 219.

111. America's cultural identity as white came about early in its history. Even though there was a social practice in place that defined America as white, none offers a more powerful description than the Naturalization Act of 1790, which granted citizenship only to whites.

112. Quoted in Takaki (1979), 216.

113. Wu Tingfang, *America Through the Spectacles of an Oriental Diplomat*, recounted in his 1914 memoir how he was treated at the train station in Washington, DC. Although a porter led him to the "white area" of the station, he was not sure whether he belonged in the "white area."

114. Gyory (1998), 17.

115. Du bois (2003), 113.

116. Du bois (2003), 115.

117. Kymlicka (2007), 116.

118. In Du Bois' deep analysis, he writes:

Between me and the other world there is ever an unmasked question: unmasked by some through feelings of delicacy; by others through the difficulty of rightly framing it. All, nevertheless, flutter round it. They approach me in a half-hesitant sort of way, eye me curiously or compassionately, and then, instead of saying directly, How does it feel to be the problem? They say, I know an excellent colored man in my town; or, I fought at Mechanicsville; or, Do not these Southern outrages make your blood boil? At these I smile, or am interested, or reduce the boiling to a simmer, as the occasion may require. To the real question, How does it feel to be a problem? I answer seldom a world. (2003, 3–4)

119. Yancy (2005), 237.
120. Tardon (1946).
121. Owen (2007), 110.
122. See Frantz Fanon, "The Fact of Blackness," in *Black Skin White Masks*, where he notes that "not only must the black man be black; he must be black in relations to the white man" (1967, 110).
123. Du Bois (2003), 5.
124. On the importance of the Black-White model of race relations as impacting other racialized ethnic groups, see Joe R. Feagin, *Racist America: Roots, Current Realities, and Future Reparations* (2000).
125. See Andrew Hacker, *Two Nations: Black and White, Separate, Hostile, Unequal* (2003).
126. Wu (2002), 19. African American filmmaker Spike Lee, in his 1989 movie *Do the Right Thing*, used the same scenario. See Frank H. Wu, *Yellow: Race in America Beyond Black and White* (2002), 19.
127. See Kobena Mercer, "'1968': Periodizing Postmodern Politics and Identity" (1991), 426–27.
128. Fanon (1967), 112.
129. Myrdal (1962), 51–52.
130. Fine et al. (1997), 11.
131. Marable and Mullings (2009), 29.
132. Du Bois (1962), 700–01.
133. On January 26, 1922, the Dyer Bill was passed by the House of Representatives. Nonetheless, the very idea of protecting blacks from lynching mobs prompted a large number of white supremacist senators to use filibuster, which succeeded in preventing the bill from ever reaching a vote in the Senate. It was not until the 1930s with the proposal of Costigan-Wager Bill that efforts were made to pass similar bills. The aim of this Bill was to make sure that sheriffs who failed to protect their prisoners from mob violence were punished. President Franklin D. Roosevelt, because he was afraid of losing the support of the white voters in the South, which meant losing the 1936 presidential election, refused to support the Bill. In 1937 and again in 1940, another anti-lynching bill, the Gavagan Bill, was passed in the House. In both cases, it died in the Senate because of Southern filibusters. See Sherrow O. Pinder, "Anti-Lynching Movement" (2007), 162.
134. See Gayatri C. Spivak, "Diasporas Old and New: Woman in Transnational World" (1996).
135. Butler (1997a), 4.
136. In 1852, in *The Condition, Elevation, Immigration and Destiny of the Colored People of the United States and Official Report of the Niger Valley Exploring Party*, Delany beseeched African Americans to emigrate because "We love our country; dearly love her; but she doesn't love us—she despises us, and bids us begone, driving us from her embraces; but we shall not go where she desires us; but when we do go, whatever love we have for her, we shall love the country none the less that receives us as her adopted children" (2004, 216).

137. For a concise understanding of the colonial model, see Frantz Fanon, *The Wretched of the Earth* (1963) and *Towards the African Revolution: Political Essays* (1964); and Paulo Freire, *The Pedagogy of the Oppressed* (2000).

138. The main argument of William Julius Wilson's book, *The Declining Significance of Race: Blacks and the Changing American Institutions*, is that the dynamic of class, more than that of race, created the apparent underclass. I think that it is dangerous not to recognize the interlocking of race and class, which blacks have been forced to share. Wilson fails to recognize the significance of racism in the deepening of poverty and its monstrous outcomes. See Sherrow O. Pinder, "Notes on Hurricane Katrina: Rethinking Race, Class, and Power in the United States" (2009).

139. Reed (1992), 23.

140. Reed (1992), 24.

141. Reed (1992), 24.

142. For proof of the widespread efforts by the government, especially, for blaming the poor for being poor, see, for instance, Sherrow O. Pinder, *From Welfare to Workfare: How Capitalist States Create a Pool of Unskilled Cheap Labor (A Marxist-Feminist Social Analysis)* (2007); and Herbert Gans, "Deconstructing the Underclass" (2007).

143. Banton (1991), 117.

144. Mirón (1999), 85.

145. Butler (2001), 79.

146. See Frantz Fanon's chapter 5 in *Black Skin, White Masks* (1967).

147. Dyer (1997), 1.

148. Piper (1992), 30–31.

THREE

Antidiscrimination Measures and Whiteness: The Case of Affirmative Action

In America, First Nations, blacks, Chinese, and Mexicans have long fought for equality. The Black Power Movement, for example, was created because of the overwhelming frustration with the many barriers, whether social, economical, or psychological, that prevented blacks from being equal to whites. Eventually, to concede to America's discriminatory past, various antidiscriminatory measures were undertaken by the government to redeem itself and palliate to the problems of inequalities faced by culturally, sexually, and socially marginalized groups. Title VII Section 703a of the 1964 Civil Rights Act, for example, prohibits employment discrimination on the basis of "race, color, religion, sex, or national origins."[1] An employee is required to base his or her judgment about the suitable applicant for a job outside of these identities. Historically, identity markers such as race and gender were employed by the law and social customs to oppress nonwhites and women. Title VII, for instance, is intended to protect individuals from such forms of discriminatory practices.

As a rule, antidiscriminatory measures present themselves according to the very distinctive logic of promoting equality, at least in theory, in American institutions, systems, and workplace. This explicit logic emanates from an unyielding commonsense of the social reality of America's deep seated prejudice.[2] Under Title VII, for example, an employer may discriminate on the basis of race or gender in instances where race or gender "is a bona fide occupational qualification reasonably necessary to the normal operation of that particular business or enterprise."[3] The question, which remains paramount, is whether these antidiscriminatory measures, when left to their own device, are maintaining the interests of those that benefits from the power structure that is in place. In fact, antidiscrimination measures are supposed to counterbalance prevalent forms of prejudice that pervasively disadvantage individual members of marginalized groups such as First Nations, blacks, Chinese, Mexicans, other racialized minorities, women, the disabled, and homosexuals.[4]

More recently, without taking into accounts the systems and practices of discrimination that have brought about Title VII in the first place, blindness to race, sexuality or gender, for example, is a mainstream discourse that is uncritically employed to mean race, gender or sexuality nonrecognition. It is politically operational in the way it signifies the basic and fundamental unanimity of people, linking them all beyond all differences including race, gender, sexually, ethnicity, religion, physical and mental abilities, and age. Blindness, in terms of race, for example, or what is referred to as colorblindness, is the idea that if we look beyond mere appearances of race, equal opportunities for all members of a society would avail themselves regardless of their race. It is only then can we foster a merit-based society. In the end, blindness, taken to its fullest logics, as Ruth Frankenberg puts it, is a "power-evasive discursive repertoire in play."[5] Blindness, while maintaining the status quo, is "what sets men at odds and allows them to be guided by their prejudices."[6] While blindness is fully justified, what it basically dismisses is that discriminatory structures such as racism, sexism, classism, homophobia, ageism, and ableism have not disappeared and are not even hidden from our view.

From the preceding analysis, antidiscriminatory measures such as affirmative action programs are intended and designed to support and give, in part, opportunities to individuals who have been unequally treated precisely because of these discriminatory structures. However, affirmative action has become the hotbed for debates about race relations in American politics, and it propels individuals and state government to be for or against affirmative action.[7] My intention is not to enter the current debate. Rather, I want to focus on how the presumptive hegemony of whiteness has informed and continues to inform these debates. Given the manner in which whiteness functions in American society, it is not coincidental that the University of California Board of Regents ruled, in 1995, that race could not be a factor in University admission. In 1996, in the case *Hopwood v. Texas*, the court claimed that affirmative action discriminated against whites. In 2003, in the case *Gutter v. Bollinger*, Kirk O. Kolbo, the attorney for the plaintiff argued that to use race as the primary reason to enroll students into law school was unconstitutional.

Race, even though it matters in the United States,[8] cannot be used as one of the factors in "a highly individualized, holistic review of each applicant's file, giving serious consideration to all the ways an applicant might contribute to a diverse educational environment."[9] It is amazing that a number of uncritically established arguments establish that affirmative action programs put whiteness at risk because of the obligation an employer or a university now has to hire or admit a nonwhite person rather than a white person. Historically, when whites felt threatened by social changes, group mobilization have occurred, for instance through white supremacist groups such as the Ku Klux Klan, immigration restriction movement, or the White Citizens' Councils. In the 1960s, as blacks increased their political presence, whites' resistance to comprehensive desegregation intensified and blacks' support for protest action mushroomed. As we will see later, power itself engenders the overindulgence of resistance from the dominant group to incorporate any changes that, in their minds, seem in opposition to their interests. As Slavoj Žižek explains, "the power edifice itself it split from within, that is, to reproduce itself and contain its Other, it has to rely on an inherent excess which grounds it."[10] In daily social practice, which repeats, acts upon, and makes unrestricted its personal cathexis in whiteness, race is a central point in which power relations continue to be configured and reconfigured.

In this chapter, I have no intention to engage in a defense for or against affirmative action. I will rather extract from these opposing viewpoints in order to show how affirmative action programs are derivative of America's antidiscriminatory measures and present a dogmatic turn from exclusion to inclusion of racialized ethnic groups within America's social, educational, political, and economic institutions for the benefit of the masses. And even though affirmative action programs are ostentatiously necessary to partially combat America's past and present discriminatory practices, these programs are fundamental for keeping the power structure in place. Whiteness, as property, works in a setting where whites are free to enjoy rights to their property (whiteness) and rights against coercion or interference with their property. For this reason, it is easy for the opponents of affirmative action to argue that affirmative action programs put whiteness at risk, or signify "the abolition of whiteness."[11] Given that affirmative action programs are necessary in order to maintain the legitimacy of the dominant class and the continuation of its domination and exploitation, it is inevitable that these programs have no recourse but to leave white privilege marked and uncontested. The hullabaloo over affirmative action is just another way of maintaining the dominant class position and reinforcing whites' entitlement to their "property rights in whiteness."

As I have already showed in chapter 2, America's first Naturalization Act of 1790 conferred American citizenship as the property of whites.[12] In other words, whites are *disciplined*, in the Foucauldian sense, to view America as a white possession that instills them with a sense of entitlement and ownership. When the Civil Rights Act of 1866 granted citizenship to blacks and permitted them to own property, enter into contracts, testify in courts, and enjoy equality before the law, President Andrew Johnson vetoed the act. His claim that blacks, having the same rights as whites, would "'break down the barrier that preserves the rights of the states,' that it would empower federal officials 'whose interests it would be to foment discard between the races,' and, most pertinent to present concerns that it would 'operate in favor of the colored and against the white race,'"[13] points to the possessiveness of whiteness.

As aforementioned, at the very beginning of America's formation, blacks and First Nations, under the system of indentured servitude, were viewed as inferior to whites. Eventually the enslavement of blacks became legalized and blacks were treated as the master's property. Indeed, the subordination of blacks carried with it a mark that would justify the discriminatory treatment of them after slavery ended. During the emancipation period in both the North and South, employers were reluctant to hire blacks. In the South especially, if blacks were hired and were discontented with their position they could not change jobs without authorization from their employers.[14] Even newly arrived immigrants from Europe were given hiring preferences over blacks and other nonwhites.

Many blacks, in various ways, have retaliated against their subordinate position during and after slavery as well as in the Jim Crow South. Eventually, for a brief period, Dr. Martin Luther King's nonviolence civil disobedience proved highly effective, particularly, in pressing the federal government to eliminate segregation laws. It led to the Supreme Court decision in *Brown v. Board of Education*[15] to desegregate schools and to the passing of the Civil Rights Act of 1964 and the Voting Act of 1965.[16] However, blacks, other people of color, women, and homosexuals, for example, continued to be denied job opportunities. The need for affirmative action programs, it is argued by proponents was, and is necessary, to protect, at least in theory, job discrimination toward individuals belonging to marginalized groups. We can see that one of the major sources of discontent about affirmative action stems from the notion of *laissez faire liberalism*. In other words, for the laissez faire liberals, the fact that the state gets involved in such matters as to whom an employer could hire interferes with the market mechanism. The idea is that a lack of government interference with the market mechanics enables the market to provide the most efficient use and allocation of resources. In fact, it is a grave mistake to rely on market forces to address social inequalities because, as Wood explains, "the market has a force of its own, which it imposes on everyone, capitalists as well as workers, certain impersonal systemic requirements of competition, accumulation, and profit-maximization."[17] Hence, the notion of *equality of opportunities* takes the place of *equality of results*.

In fact, affirmative action is supposed to deal with racial barriers. For example, historically, secured employment, job promotions, and admissions to institutions of higher education had generally been allocated to whites. These benefits are still predominantly accorded to whites today because the goal of affirmative action rather than dismantling white privilege or entitlements that whites have become accustomed, affirmative action seemingly appears as a form of "reverse discrimination," which, in the end, only serves to reinstate whiteness. And since "reverse discrimination" expresses the idea that whites are victimized whites, white privilege is concealed and not critically analyzed. In the following section, I examine specific characteristics of affirmative action in order to point to the many misconceptions of the goals of affirmative action programs.

DEFINING AFFIRMATIVE ACTION

The United States Commission on Civil Rights defines affirmative action as any "measure, beyond simple termination of a discriminatory practice, adopted to correct or compensate for past or present discrimination or to prevent discrimination from occurring in the future." Affirmative action programs take numerous forms, ranging from making recruiting efforts in racialized ethnic communities to permitting that a definite number of positions be put aside for individuals from racialized minorities, the disabled, homosexuals, and white women. It aims at promoting visible representation in the work place. It is common knowledge that affirmative action programs have been advantageous in advancing the careers of white women in higher education.

Why is gender left out of the debate?[18] It has often been argued that affirmative action is "reverse racism." Affirmative action programs are indeed about equal access to employment, education, and opportunities for promotion in the labor market, but that same market precisely strives on occupational segregation based on race and gender, for example. For decades, blacks, other nonwhites, as well as women, the disabled, and homosexuals were denied such equal job opportunities. As I have already mentioned in the previous chapters, blacks were their masters' property and women were white men's property. However these two forms of ownership are not reducible to the same phenomenon. It is true that white women were, and still are, oppressed under patriarchy,[19] but they were never equated as chattels or represented three-fifths of a person according to the Constitution.[20] Yet, white women, like blacks and other nonwhites, were denied the opportunity to compete on an equal footing with white men on the job market. While patriarchal dispositions subjugated women to the status of "the second sex," black and other women of color had to, and continue to, endure the intersectionality of race, gender, and class.[21] For instance, when the Equal Pay Act of 1963 was enacted, it was intended to benefit only white women.[22] Most black and nonwhite women who worked outside of the home were mostly domestics in white households. In fact, gendered bodies have been, and continue to be, regimented in racialized ways that reinforce whiteness.[23]

For whatever reasons, affirmative action programs are viewed as correlated with race, especially blacks. The prevailing argument is that these programs violate a fundamental tenet of the American creed of "liberty, equality, justice, and fair opportunity for everyone."[24] In other words, affirmative action amounts to devoid the individual "the freedom to fulfill his own purposes."[25] Hence, the Supreme Court, over the last several decades, in a series of cases, has been grappling with the question whether the American Constitution encourages such measures as are spelt out in the American creed.[26] Affirmative action programs are viewed as preferential programs benefitting the racial and social minorities, truly illiberal and, thus, are antithetical to meritocracy. This raises a fundamental question: what kind of a meritocracy would deprive blacks and other racialized groups, women, the disabled, homosexuals, and immigrants from acquiring resources so that they can compete with heterosexual, white males? Furthermore, the nature of merits is determined by the needs of society and undergoes a constant process of reformation as a result of economic and social changes. So in the end, a society presumably operating on meritocratic principles shamelessly justifies the inherent inequalities that are determined by social outcomes.

Even though opponents of affirmative action are convinced that with "hard work, effort, and persistence" the American dream always avails itself to these individuals, it is known that students receive points for admission to the university if one or both of their parents are alumni of that university. But this factual privilege is not taken into consideration when admission is claimed to be based on merits. In fact, the alumni status, while seemingly race neutral, it privileges whiteness and disadvantaged many First Nations, blacks, Chinese, Mexicans, and other nonwhite applicants who are statistically more likely to be first generation college students. In the presence of normalized whiteness America's doctrine of racial exclusion is once again brought to the forefront. In this sense, affirmative action is not equipped to work against white privilege. This is a severe charge, and it rests on the very fact that affirmative action programs spring from an original positioning of multiple and complex set of historically situated, inflected, unmediated, and constituted social relations of white dominance. Hence, there remains the intractable problem of dealing with the historically generated and maintenance of normalized whiteness.

Given that whiteness is endemic to America's sociocultural foundation and inheritance—to its laws and political, social, and economic structures, to its epistemologies and daily customs[27] —whiteness has certain implications for the nonwhite "other." It would be a mistake to suppose that antidiscriminatory measures, including affirmative action programs, work in opposition to modes of normalized whiteness. As an indicator of a civilized society, antidiscriminatory measures are necessary to keep the power structure in place. Affirmative action programs form the basis for a defense against the disproportionate use of power to secure white privilege. In the end, the most impoverished in the nations—First Nations, blacks, Mexicans, and other racialized groups—are unaffected by affirmative action programs. After all, to be nonwhite is one thing, but to be nonwhite and poor is quite another thing.[28] As Hurricane Katrina showed, when made aware of the threat of flooding, many blacks were unable to afford public transportation to a safe spot.[29]

AFFIRMATIVE ACTION: ORIGINS AND FOCUS

The term "affirmative action" has its roots in a complex genealogy of America's discriminatory practice. It first appeared as a part of the 1935 National Labor Relation Act (NLRA) in which an employer who was found to be discriminating against union members or union organizers would have to abandon such a practice. In addition, the employer was ordered to place those workers in jobs that would prevent any form of discrimination. The 1937 case, *NLRB v. Jones & Laughlin Stell Corp*, where the Supreme Court supported a federal law barring discrimination against employees or job applicants on the basis of anti- or pro-union activities, appeared to have opened up the door to employment discrimination. With the outbreak of World War II, the distinguishable racism that had infested America's social, political, and economic relations from the very beginning of its formation as a nation was once again brought to the forefront.

Black and white soldiers served during the Second World War in racially segregated units commanded by white officers as they had done during the Civil War. Many blacks were obviously angered and, as a result, black communities, speaking through black media and groups such as the National Association for the Advancement of Colored People (NAACP), began to pressure the government to lift the restrictions placed on blacks in the defense industry. In addition, A. Phillip Randolph, head of the Brotherhood of Sleeping Car Workers, campaigned against racial discrimination in the defense industry and government. His campaign led to the March on Washington Movement. Embarking on a new course, members of the movement, seeking support from black organizations, threatened to march on Washington in the summer of 1941. The NAACP did support the march and organized its members for the march.

Given that the federal government feared the disruption that the march would have created, it reluctantly became attentive to *racism* in the defense industry. Hence, in June 1941, President Theodore Roosevelt requested the Office of Production Management to end the exclusion of blacks from the defense industry. For A. Phillip Randolph and the other members of the Movement, this order was not enough. Consequently, they continued to organize the March. The day before the march, President Roosevelt issued the long overdue Executive Order 8802, which publicly admitted, as President Lyndon Baines Johnson, almost twenty-five years later, in his speech at Howard University, would announce that "discrimination based on race was repugnant to the Constitution, and therefore void."[30] Executive Order 8802 ordered an end to employment discrimination by race in the defense industry, and the march was cancelled. As a result of this Order, the Fair Employment Practices Committee (FEPC) was formed to hear and address complains that the Executive Order 8802 had not been disregarded, remedy discriminatory employment complaints, and propose enforcement measures of fair employment practices to federal agencies.

It was the fervent hope of blacks, as Hayward "Woody" Farrar observed, that "the Executive Order 8802 and FEPC would force defense contractors to hire black workers."[31] When in 1944, three years after Executive Order 8802, the National Opinion Research Center asked whites, "Do you think Negroes should have a chance as white people to get any kind of job, or do you think white people should have the first chance at any kind of job?" Less than half—forty-four percent—contended that blacks should have an equal chance. A year later, in 1945, a Gallup poll asked, "Do you favor or oppose a law in this state which would require employers to hire a person if he is qualified for the job, regardless of his race or color?" According to the poll, forty-three percent were in favor, forty-four percent were opposed, and thirteen percent had no opinion.[32] And even though with the Executive Order 8802 blacks did make some gains in securing employment, blacks continued to be treated as second class citizens; to experience widespread legal and economic discrimination, high unemployment and underemployment, inadequate health care and housing, and negative cultural representation. Against this background, many whites continue to oppose programs that are supposed to bring about some form of racial equity.

Lurking underneath the veneer of a civilized American society, the harsh reality of being black in America was once more brought to the forefront in 1946. That year, a black man, Herman Marion Sweatt applied to the University of Texas Law School and was refused admission because the state law mandated that only whites could attend the University of Texas Law School. The Supreme Court declared that under the Fourteenth Amendment of the American Constitution, the state law violated Sweatt's rights. Given that it was not easy for blacks and other nonwhites, at that time, to acquire resources that would aid in the suing of universities for promoting racial discrimination, Sweatt, five years later, with the help of the National Association for the Advancement of Colored People's lawyer Turgood Marshall, was able to sue the University of Texas. The landmark decision in the case *Sweatt v. Painter* is foundational in the history of America's race relations. It paved the way for the landmark decision in *Brown v. Board of Education*, which finally desegregated the public school system. Later on, in the case *Swann v. Charlotte-Mecklenburg*, the guidelines for desegregation were upheld.

In the case of *Sweatt v. Painter*, the Court based its decision on *Plessy v. Ferguson* in which the notion of "separate but equal" was constitutional. The cases, *Plessy v. Ferguson* and *Sweatt v. Painter*, were good examples of how institutionalized whiteness worked in separating the superior (whites) from the inferior (blacks). And in an effort to continue its vile practice of keeping blacks and other nonwhites separate from whites, as the Supreme Court decided in the case of *Gaines v. Canada* in 1938,[33] the Court mandated that Texas hurriedly built an accredited law school for blacks only. One should ask here a vital question: why did the university publicly resist admitting black students? There is only one possible answer to this question. It was not that black students posed a sincere threat to white students but, on the contrary, it was because of an irrational fear of blacks and other people of color as the constructed social "others," as a deviation from the regulatory norms of whiteness, harboring itself in the beings of many whites and lending credence to the very question: what was truly feared?

Richard Dyer has made some helpful observations in voicing and highlighting this fear, that is, whiteness would be exposed for its "emptiness, absence, denial, or even kind of death."[34] Far from being superior and secure, whiteness displays an incessantly reformulated anxiety over the social and theoretical construction of "us" and "them," and the suspected defining presence of the "them" within the "us." Whiteness, then, by asserting its privilege with the help of state sponsored racist practices such as slavery, Chinese Exclusion Act, First Nations' allocation to Indian reservation, Jim Crow South, National Housing Act of 1934,[35] and Japanese internment camps, responds to this feared emptiness by legally separating whites from nonwhites. The principle of racial hierarchy, as Frantz Fanon puts it, "is thus but one aspect of a systematized hierarchization implacably pursued" to reinforce and maintain whiteness presumptive hegemony.[36] Thus, in order to maintain whiteness presumptive hegemony, affirmative action, at the beginning, had to openly adhere to the interests of whites, and continues, in a less obvious manner, to maintain whiteness.

As I will show in the following section, affirmative action has not always been race-conscious. I am using the term race-conscious, because, as many scholars have shown, in America, at the very beginning of its formation, affirmative action programs were in place to benefit whites.

WHEN AFFIRMATIVE ACTION WAS FOR WHITES

Affirmative action for whites began with the conquest of America and the promotion of "the property rights of whiteness" in First Nations' land. In other words, First Nations' land was transferred to European settlers. This is how W. Avon Drake puts it in "Affirmative Action at the Cross-roads: Race and the future of Black Progress": "[t]he long, brutal acquisition of Native American resources and the subsequence transfer to the settler community were no less an expression of racial preference than the seat at the UC Davis School of Medicine once held in reserve for minority students." [37] Nonetheless, affirmative action in medical school admission was, in part, to guarantee blacks, for example, trained as doctors, who would later work in poor black communities. [38]

In addition, affirmative action programs were visible in the GI Bill of Rights, which was referred to as the 1944 Serviceman's Readjustment Act. The rights for veterans included preferential hiring, low interest home loans, loans for starting businesses, and educational benefits such as tuitions and living expenses paid for while attending college or university. And even though, all veterans were supposed to benefit from such a bill, in fact, white male veterans were the sole benefiters. In this sense, white affirmative action or affirmative action for white, to draw on Ira Katznelson's book, "when affirmative action was white," one of the main goals of affirmative action was to maintain whiteness presumptive hegemony. Even though whiteness is tied to privileges that are associated with membership into the privileged group, more recently the race component of affirmative action programs is being translated to mean nonwhites, especially blacks. [39]

How race-conscious affirmative action programs came about is fundamental. In the following section, I look at the emergence of raced-conscious affirmative action to help us locate how affirmative action has seemingly transformed itself from being *white* to meaning *black*.

RACE-CONSCIOUS AFFIRMATIVE ACTION

Affirmative action appeared again in March 1961, in President John F. Kennedy's Executive Order 10925, which mandated "affirmative action to ensure that applicants are employed, and that employee are treated during employment, without regard to their race, creed, color, or national origins." [40] This order established the President's Committee on Equal Employment Opportunity. Shortly after, following the ratification of the Civil Rights Act of 1964, the President's Committee on Equal Employment Opportunity became the Equal Employment Opportunity Commission, which President Ronald Reagan would later on consider as "a bad piece of legislation." [41] One of the goals of the civil rights leaders, including Dr. Martin Luther King, Jr. and Malcolm X, was to pressure the government to make every effort to eliminate barriers, such as segregation laws, discrimination in America's judicial system, employment procedures, and policies, which prevented blacks and other racialized ethnic groups from attending colleges and universities and prevented the advancement of people of color.

In its attempt to adhere to the pursuit of the aforementioned goals, in Title VII of the Civil Rights Act of 1964, affirmative action appears in the paragraph: "If the court finds that the respondent has intentionally engaged in or is intentionally engaging in an unlawful employment practice . . . the court may . . . offer such affirmative action as may be appropriate, which may include, but not limited to, reinstatement or hiring of employees, with or without back pay . . . or any equitable relief as the court deems appropriate."[42] At the historic black institution, Howard University, on June 4, 1965, in his speech to the graduating class titled, "To Fulfill These Rights," President Lyndon Baines Johnson contended that:

> Nothing is more frightened with the meaning than the revolution of the Negro American . . . In far too many ways American Negroes have been another nation: deprived of freedom, crippled by hatred, the door of opportunity closed to hope . . . But freedom is not enough. You do not wipe out the scares of century by saying: Now you are free to go where you want, and to do as you desire, and choose the leaders you please. You do not take a person who, for years, has been hobbled by chains and liberate him, bring him up to the starting line of race and then say 'you are free to compete with all others', and still justly believe that you have been completely fair . . . This is the next and the more profound stage of the battle for civil rights. We seek not just freedom but opportunity. We seek not just legal equity but human ability, not just equality as a right and a theory but equality as a fact and equality as a result . . . To this end equal opportunity is essential but not enough, not enough . . . And I hope, and I pray, and I believe, it will be a part of the program of all Americans.[43]

After his speech on September 24, 1965, President Johnson issued Executive Order 11246, which required equal employment opportunity for blacks, other nonwhites, and women.[44] It "prohibits federal contractors and federally assisted construction contractor and subcontractor, who do over ten thousand dollars in government business in one year from discriminating in employment decisions on the basis of race, color, religion, sex or national origins."[45] Morris B. Abram, quoting professor William Van Alstyne, observed that Executive Order 11246 "is affirmative action (i.e., action of a positive character, discriminating against none, dispreferring no one, involving neither quotas or queues nor targets or presumptions of what the 'right' mix or proper share of each according to their race . . . It is an action undertaken consciously . . . to vindicate more effectively a commitment opposed to racial discrimination in all its form."[46] Executive Order 11246 complemented President Kennedy's Order 10925. In reality, the main aim of affirmative action was to make sure that every avenue of power remained in the hands of white men. Its aim was to incorporate blacks, other racialized minorities, and women into white male mainstream America.

Blacks and other people of color, for a long time, have acted with "impressive restraint" from whites' encroachment and have "peacefully protested and marched, entered the courtrooms and the seats of government, demanding justice that has long been denied."[47] Indeed, for President Johnson, if African Americans were to achieve true freedom, affirmative action, as "designed to make equal opportunity a reality," is needed. This view, in 1978, would later manifest itself in the Supreme Court case of *Regents of the University of California v. Bakke.*[48] The idea, as was espoused by Justice Harry Blackmun, is that "in order to get past racism we must first take account of race. There is no other present way. And in order to treat some persons equally, we must treat them differently."[49] This is what Iris Marion Young considers as "special rights"[50] for people belonging to "specially disadvantaged group."[51] For example, the poor and unemployed are entitled to governmental assistance through welfare programs,[52] and senior citizens, in some cases, can use the transit system at a lower cost. As Young argues, "Special rights for oppressed or disadvantage groups are appropriate."[53] Are "special rights" a way of de-normalizing rights in an attempt to preserve the ethical fundamentals of "equality in difference"? And even though, "equality in difference" reminds me of "the equal but separate" doctrine of the Jim Crow laws that targeted blacks and other nonwhites, resulting in most extreme form of discrimination, denormalizing rights, I think, are important because, in the United States, rights were and are always, tied to whiteness and maleness. Yet when blacks, First Nations, other nonwhites, women, homosexuals, and other individuals belonging to the non-dominant groups are given rights, these rights are nothing but what Frederick Douglas once referred to as America's "boasted [right]," "an unholy license" that can be retrieved at a whim.[54] "Special rights" would take into consideration race, for example, as an identity that maintain racial differences between whites and nonwhites. However, for opponents of affirmative action, taking race into consideration for jobs, university admission, or promotions means that blacks and other people of color are placed into positions for which they are less qualified. For us to think and behave as if racial differences are a proxy for access to the social good is to reestablish the notion of whiteness as entitlement.

In the face of normalized whiteness, affirmative action programs are needed as legitimization tools for America's racist, sexist, homophobic, ageist, and ableit structures. Nonetheless, the implementations of antidiscrimination measures in the United States, as "another triumph for freedom" of the oppressed and marginalized, were important for President Johnson. Affirmative action programs are "not the end. It is not even the beginning of the end. But it is perhaps, the end of the beginning. That beginning is freedom."[55] In effect, whiteness, socially and systematically, holds freedom for blacks and other nonwhites captive because of it power "to reinforce and re-inscribe white supremacy,"[56] as is traced by bell hooks in *Black Looks: Race and Representation*. As a way of rehegemonizing whiteness, affirmative action programs have been discredited by many prominent scholars, politicians, the media, commentators of various political persuasions, and many ordinary citizens.

The most prejudicial and prevailing misunderstanding is that race plays a salient part in hiring practices, university admissions, and promotions. In 1989, in the case, *City of Richmond v. J. A. Croson Company*, the Supreme Court argued that under the Equal Protection Clause in the Fourteenth Amendment,[57] the city of Richmond granting preference to minority business enterprises in awarding city contracts was unconstitutional. In the same vein, in 1995, the University of California Board of Regents ruled that race could not be a factor in university admission. Again, in 1996, in the case *Hopwood v. Texas*, the court simply maintained that affirmative action discriminated against whites. In 2003 in the case *Gutter v. Bollinger*, Kirk O. Kolbo, the attorney for the plaintiff, concluded that to use race in order to enroll students into law school is unconstitutional under the Equal Protection Clause of the Fourteenth Amendment. These examples point to the process I identify as the rehegemonizing of whiteness, a process to which I will return to later. For now, the Supreme Court's negative response of affirmative action programs as unconstitutional is a cause for concern because it was the very constitutional measure designed to guarantee equality for blacks and other nonwhites that is based on the Court's continual rejection to dismantle the institutional protection of benefits for whites at the expense of blacks and other nonwhites. As a result, the strictures of suitable cures are not ordered by the scope of the damage to people of color, but by the extent of the infringement on normalized whiteness.[58]

Race in America, as Cornel West reminds us, matters so much that it "has become almost impracticable to think outside of racial category"[59] and decontextualize or ahistoricize the concept of race. To declare that America is post-racial, then, is to deny the palpable force of race in the lives of blacks, First Nations, Mexicans, Chinese, and other nonwhites who try, according to Henry Louis Gates, "to function everyday in a still very racist America."[60] It is important to think and rethink how blacks and other racialized groups are enmeshed in the realm of a corporeality that unmistakably inscribes race on their bodies, "and are judged irrespective of their social or educational attainment."[61] The current president of the United States, Barack Obama, even though he is a black man, sadly does not disrupt the power structure that is in place. The predominant positions of power remain occupied by whites at all levels of government, in corporations, at the universities, in the court house, the police force, and the media.

In the following section, I look at some arguments against affirmative action programs. I want to show how these oppositions are recentering rather than decentering whiteness and, therefore, pose an enormous problem for race relations in America.

AGAINST AFFIRMATIVE ACTION: THE REHEGEMONIZING OF WHITENESS

Affirmative action programs, since its manifestation, have captured the attention of a growing number of academics, politicians, the media, and the American public as a whole. While there are many misconceptions about what affirmative action programs actually are, the conservatives as well as the liberals have campaigned to end affirmative action programs on the pretext that they are discriminatory against whites. Ever since the 1970s, in the case, *Regents of the University of California v. Bakke*, race-conscious affirmative action programs have been subject to an increasing disavowal from all segments of the society, including black conservatives.[62] Antagonistic reactions to affirmative action appeared regularly in the newspapers, journals, and books. Nathan Glazer's 1987 book, *Affirmative Discrimination: Ethnic Inequality and Public Policy*, is a notable contribution to this debate. In this book, the author flogs affirmative action as morally incorrect and socially coercive because admission guidelines take race into account in hiring practices and college admissions. Other scholars and public figures disagree and point instead to the advantages of affirmative action programs not only for blacks and other racial minority, and women but, in fact, for the American society as a whole. In their minds, affirmative action programs are a way for America to deal with its racist and sexist past. For opponent of affirmative action, is it only through a colorblind society that white America can maintain its commitment of promoting a nonracist environment where individuals "are judged not by the color of their skin but the content of their character."[63] Patrick J. Buchanan, in his book, *The Death of the West: How Dying Populations and Immigrant Invasions Imperil Our Country and Civilization*, suggests that "the time for apologies is past" and it is "time to say" no to affirmative action[64] because affirmative action works in opposition to equality of opportunity and meritocracy.

Rather than thinking of these measures as a way to promote blindness to race, it is essential to think of them as color/race-conscious because the implications of race is not fictional it is real because race is marked on the body; it is "epidermatized" as Frantz Fanon writes. Colorblind projects aim toward a willful blindness to America's racial truths and seek to hide the fact that America has, since its birth, operated on a colorblind basis. Its first Naturalization Law, in 1790, granted citizenship only to white men. In America, the uniqueness of race, its historical flexibility and propinquity in the daily experience of nonwhites, and social conflicts are ubiquitous.[65] Colorblindness, that is being racially invisible, puts emphasis on the very reality of the construction of race that it purports to eliminate. Nonetheless, for the opponents of colorblindness, racism can be eliminated if one moves beyond race, which does not mean that race has disappeared. Race has taken on new meanings such as a racial false consciousness, which turns racial discrimination into a defense for whites' advantages and denies stratified racial differences.

The language of colorblindness is but one more manner of talking about race, in that, it appeals to the social and economic facts of racial stratification in the course of rejecting its normative implications. Further, in terms of permissible discourse, that of "reverse discrimination" or "preferential treatment" for nonwhites at the workplace or in college admissions, race is openly discussed. Colorblindness pretends not to see race and promote the liberal notion that "we are all the same," which makes it difficult to challenge white supremacy. Even though white supremacy does not manifest itself in the same way it did during indentured servitude, slavery, Reconstruction, and Jim Crow South, it still pervades society in the philosophy of customs and habits. It has transformed itself from de jure to de facto. All the affluent schools and neighborhoods are reserved for whites, and whites' access to jobs and university admissions are just a fact of life as a white person.

While colorblindness is loaded with rhetoric, its main aim is to maintain and protect whiteness presumptive hegemony. Nathan Glazer has been upfront in pointing out that a detour away from colorblindness to embrace affirmative action is what he sees as "affirmative discrimination" which "will enable citizens as well as scholars to better understand and evaluate policies for achieving social justice in a multiethnic society."[66] Without taking into consideration the nature of white power and how it works, Glazer assumes that the only way to combat exclusion and degradation of blacks and other racial minorities is to promote, to borrow from Marion Iris Young, "equal rights that are blind to group differences."[67] As Stuart Hall observes a few years ago, "the capacity to live with difference is, in [his] view, the coming question of the twenty-first century."[68] Racial discrimination makes indeed the material existence, at best, uncertain and, at worst, unendurable for nonwhite people in the United States.[69]

If colorblindness is the ultimate goal of American society, why is there a need for antidiscriminatory measures to combat and prohibit discrimination stemming from race identity? To make any sense of colorblindness one would have to believe that there is "a declining significance of race"[70]; that racism has ended and that opportunities and resources are allocated and distributed in a race-blind fashion. We would have to buy into the rhetoric of equality of opportunity and free choice for all and arrive at very problematic conclusions: the reason why First Nations, blacks, Mexicans, and other racialized group remain poor in this society is because they lack the entrepreneurial drive and Weber work ethic and its moral principle of discipline, sustainability, imagination, and hard work. Thus, concepts such as the "welfare queen" would not be critically assessed as a concept embedded within a racist idiom.

It has become easy to equate black single mothers as "welfare queens"; and to talk about poor people with an invidious racist subtext. In the end, colorblindness only perpetuates, reinforces, and maintains oppression on the basis of race. Racial oppression extends itself to oppress and disadvantage other groups including women, homosexuals, immigrants, the poor, the aged, the disabled, and linguistic and cultural nondominant groups. Instead of being blind to these differences, it is essential to acknowledge these differences (which some scholars have argued, are the basis for affirmative action programs in the first place).[71] In other words, blindness would be viable if, and only if, we were living in a society that is freed from prejudices stemming from differences. This is not the case. Consequently, affirmative action programs do not dismantle the power structure that is in place, benefiting whites and it does not give more opportunities to the majority of nonwhite people.[72] Many First Nations, blacks, Mexicans, and other nonwhites are unaffected by affirmative action programs. Because of their positioning, as poor and underprivileged, many of them are high school dropouts, and/or are working in minimum wage jobs.

In order to appease the marginalized groups and maintain stability within the system, antidiscrimination measures such as affirmative action programs through visible representations are important. Highly qualified professors from marginalized groups are hired to teach in programs such as Black Studies, Ethnic Studies, Women's Studies, and Sexual Minority Studies, at Ivy League universities. Some of them even hold very high positions at these universities, but these institutions still retain their white male elitism. In this sense, there is a moral obligation for a civilized society to include individuals from marginalized groups into positions of power. Yet, as we understand from Michel Foucault's theory of power, power must remain unsettled since it is this unsettledness that is the state of its existence.

The countermovement on affirmative action has, in part, manifested itself in the so-called crisis of whiteness, a crisis that Charles Gallagher identifies as a "transformation of whiteness."[73] What makes this a crisis, in the first place, is, of course, the impression that we are living in a period of interference and challenge to white supremacy. Starting with the Reagan administration's decision to support the idea of raceblindness, this crisis first expressed and inscribed itself within the colorblind discourse. President Reagan declared, as Kennedy observed, "We want what I think Martin Luther King asked for. We want a color-blind society."[74] Reagan clearly failed to understand Dr. King's speech within the context of America's history of racialization and racism. Keeping in par with President Reagan's interpretation of Dr. King's speech, California's Governor Pete Wilson, in his campaign for the republic nomination for president, attacked affirmative action as failing to live up to King's dream of a colorblind America. Both President Reagan and Governor Wilson willfully missed Dr. King's basic point by omitting from their analysis that Dr. King was aware of the discriminatory treatment of blacks and other nonwhites because of their skin color. Dr. King, during that same period, would announce, quite provocatively,

> Among the many vital jobs to be done, the nation must radically readjust its attitude toward the Negro [and other people of color] in the compelling present, but must incorporate in its planning some compensatory consideration for the handicaps [they have] inherited from the past. It is impossible to create a formula for the future which does not take into account that our society has been doing something special against the Negro [and other people of color] for hundreds of years. How then can [they] be absorbed into the mainstream of American life if we do not do something special for [them] now, in order to balance the equation and equip [them] to compete on a just and equal basis?[75]

Not taking heed to Dr. King's concern, on June 1, 1995, Governor Wilson issued Executive Order W-124-95 "to end preferential treatment and to promote individual opportunity based on merits . . . and to take all necessary action to comply with the intent and the requirement of the order."[76] What comes to mind is the famous case in 1978, the *Regents of the University of California v. Bakke*, in which the popular argument was made, and still is frequently made, that Allan "Bakke has a right to be judged by his own merits. That Allan "Bakke has a right to be judged as an individual rather than as a member of a social group"[77] in no way constitutes a sufficient explanation of Bakke's denied admission to University of California, Davis medical school. Apparently, Bakke was competitive enough to compete with those applicants who were "educationally or economically disadvantaged minorities."[78] Significantly, merits are not correlated with race as long as Bakke was competing with other whites; whiteness, indeed, did not rule him out of the competition. Yet, when he was competing with nonwhiteness, race then became a "suspect classification" and was subjected to "strict scrutiny" under the Equal Protection Clause.

What we see here is that whiteness cannot sustain itself unless there is a nonwhite presence. Whiteness, according to Toni Morrison, "is mute, meaningless, unfathomable, pointless, frozen, veiled, curtailed, dreaded, senseless, and implacable."[79] In a word, there is a symbiotic relationship between nonwhiteness and whiteness. In the end, in the case *Regents of the University of California v. Bakke*, the Supreme Court's decision to cancel out race, as in university admission, perfectly captures the performative power of the ruling ideology, which illustrates, without any irony, how white ascendancy continues to function systemically. Canceling out race, useful as it is for creating a more equitable society, does not eliminate race. Race remains explicitly embedded in the bogus notion of "reverse discrimination."[80] The decisions of the Supreme Court, in the case of *Regents of the University of California v. Bakke* and other affirmative action cases,[81] point to the protection of whiteness; an ideal born out of systematic white supremacy and nurtured through the years by various laws and systems that continue to be a central part of the judicial system.

Whiteness continues to be unmarked; and as the dominant position it remains invisible. I do not mean to say that whiteness is hidden. Whiteness is only hidden to those who "own" it. However, in the active process of re-hegemonizing whiteness, it becomes performative and de facto entitles white males. It is so natural for white men to forgo the ignominy of speaking about one self with an authoritative "I" that asserts its authority though its mere enunciation: "I" am a white male therefore "I" am. The first person position for the white man subsumes the dominant viewpoint. It is inconceivable that this specific "I" can no longer totally rely on its automatic privilege of whiteness and maleness as a guarantee in competing for a job. In the minds of white men, the unconscious shift from entitlement to adjustment is creating a backlash against their entitlement, which embodies a tremendously among of anxiety for whiteness. A good illustration is a white sergeant Ed Kirste with the Los Angeles County Sherriff's officer unwarily made known the creation of the Association of White Male Peace Officers (AWMPO). The goal of the AWMPO is to defend the rights of white officers who are "distinctively averse to the proposal that, as a class, we be punished or penalized for any real or purported transgressions of our forbears.[82] And while the present here is a recycled updated past of white supremacy, Kirste is not alone in his explicit injunction of white supremacy.

The former Republican Louisiana State Representative David Duke's proposal to create white student unions on college campus and an organization called the National Association for the Advancement of White People is another example of white entitlement. What we see, in this effort to protect whiteness, is its fear and anxiety that it might disappear. The Society for the Prevention of Niggers Getting Everything (SPONGE), comprising of disaffected whites in the Canarise section of Brooklyn, New York, shows white entitlement. Even though SPONGE is a white supremacist group, it is ignored by the media and provokes no public outcry.[83] In the end, angry white men's supposedly denied access to the common good such as education and employment is nothing but a farce. It repeatedly misrepresents the actual opportunities of blacks and other nonwhites to succeed in these areas. However, we need to understand the root of such hostility. It simply stems from the ideology of white supremacy.

Whenever whites shamelessly defend their group interests, they are described as psychologically adequate—with, of course, the voiced exceptions of openly white supremacist groups such as the Ku Klux Klan (KKK), the White American Resistance (WAR), the Aryan Nations, the Silent Brotherhood, the Church of the Creator, and the National Association for the Advancement of White People. Whites, in this case, instead of thinking of themselves as actors within a racist system see blacks and other nonwhites striving to secure rights that they are denied, to be an infringement on their "property rights in whiteness." Alongside this backdrop, white privilege has its foundations in a racial hierarchy that is established such as to socially, culturally, economically, and politically protects, reproduce, and advance whiteness. The implication of "reverse discrimination," merely works to conceal the existing racial inequalities. When whites are conceived as the group that is discriminating against, their *majority* status is conceivably shifted to *minority* status and racial hierarchy becomes neutralize in order to maintain and secure the benefits accruing to whites.[84] Whites' self-racialization or, what the social theorist Ghassan Hage labels "identity fetishism," that is, this obsession with their "possessive investment in whiteness," is nothing but appalling.[85] It must be seen, for what it is, an organizing imperative that regiments the social discourses of race and racial thinking by privileging whiteness and ignoring multiethnic America.

Ironically, since whites are now claiming to be the victims of "reverse racism," it means that if blacks and other nonwhites are allowed to form groups and mobilized in the name of racism, so are whites. Most white Americans cannot grasp, "what the fuss is about,"[86] when whites seemingly feel disempowered. And with race-conscious affirmative action programs, nonwhites are taken seriously as applications for admission to higher learning, jobs, and promotions. However, we cannot discard what George Lipsitz defines as whites "possessiveness investment in [their] whiteness,"[87] which affirmative action programs do not alter but maintain. Especially, when the favored applicant for a job is nonwhite, this possessiveness operates within the realm of intra-subjectivity, where whites have control over nonwhites' being, ideas, and feelings.[88] This, without a doubt, is what Frantz Fanon had in mind when he drew on the fact that in the presence of whiteness, "the [person] of color encounter difficulties in the development of his [her] bodily schema." Fanon goes on to describe and explain the various moments of the nonwhite body in the presence of white social bodies, which "are made not out of habit but out of an implicit knowledge." Hence, it seems to Fanon that "consciousness of the body is solely a negating activity. It is a third-person consciousness. The body is surrounded by an atmosphere of certain uncertainty."[89] The nonwhite body becomes a decidable racial text, fixed, and unambiguous, which is opened to the hermeneutics of aberration and terror. Whiteness becomes the disciplinary force, in the Foucauldian sense, where the nonwhite body is constantly interpellated by the white gaze.

A good example of nonwhites being interpellated by the white gaze is when nonwhite students attend predominantly white institutions. Many nonwhite students experience this discursive silence in the many ways in which whites invade their "psychic space" with indifference, an automatic manner of classifying, primitivizing, and humiliating them with comments suggesting, "What are you doing here."[90] This intrusion, it seems, is having a negative effect on their actual social status. While blacks and other nonwhite students continue to be silenced and marginalized, the policing of social norms that are based on whiteness stigmatizes and discredits student of color. Hence, the question remains, how has affirmative action dealt, or is dealing with, the phallocentric logic of the ideology of white supremacy? This question cannot be fully answered unless we try to understand how whiteness as property works. In other words, are whiteness studies scholars providing us with an adequate picture? I argue, in chapter 4, that whiteness studies scholars might be recentering rather than decentering whiteness because they are not immune to the inevitability of white privilege, which they are trying to decipher. It was W. E. B. Du Bois, in *Black Reconstruction: An Essay Toward a History of the Part Black Folk Played in the Attempt to Reconstruct Democracy in America, 1860–1880*, who provided us with the greatest insights and most necessary background for an understanding of white privilege, the unwarranted benefits that flow to whites at the expense of First Nations, blacks, and other racialized minorities, when he draws our attention to the "public and psychological wage" that is enjoyed by all whites, even poor whites.[91] In other words, having white skin is a colossal benefit, which many whites hold on to by expressing their superiority over blacks and other people of color.

Adhering to the governor's request, the University of California Board of Regents met on July 20, 1995 and wrote a resolution with the title "Policy Ensuring Equal Treatment—Admissions." It stated: "Believing California's diversity to be an asset, we adopt this statement: Because individual members of all of California's diverse races have the intelligence and capacity to succeed at the University of California, this policy achieve a UC population that reflects this state's diversity through the preparation and empowerment of all students in this state to succeed rather than through a system of artificial preference."[92] Judging from the resolution, the motivation of its authors was to bring about a new kind of preferential treatment that was not based on *race* and it now to be based on a different set of criteria that would take into account the "suffered disadvantage economically or in terms of [individual's] social environment (such as an abusive or otherwise dysfunctional home or a neighborhood of unwholesome or antisocial influence),"[93] and are staggering on the edge of society. These new criteria applied to a vast numbers of people, including whites, serve however its primary purpose, which is to eliminate *race* as the decisive factor in hiring, admittance to universities, contracting, and promoting. The elimination of *race*, within a racialized social system, is one of the most helpful ways to heighten our awareness of the workings of whiteness.

Governor Wilson defended the University of California regent's decision by concluding that "it was the right thing to do" and added that "racial preferences are by definition racial discrimination."[94] This explicit twist is characteristic of white privilege, and it participates in the effort to uphold whiteness. Governor Wilson's conclusion is per se discriminatory. In fact, discrimination does not take place only when it is deliberately intended. That discrimination is assisted and supported when admissions measures fall short to take into consideration the significance of "cultural, sexual, and racial diversity in the building of an academic community"[95] is fundamental. However, echoing Governor Wilson's defense, Dinesh D'Souza, for one, complains, "One can hardly maintain that preferential policies strictly serve the goals of social justice."[96] Given that merits, in themselves, are multifaceted forms of subjective preferences created and overdetermined by operative white privilege, racial preference is unmistakably "a form of social justice" and should be absolutely indispensable.[97]

In his famous speech, "Why We Can't Wait," Dr. Martin Luther King warned us that "whenever the issue of compensatory or preferential treatment for the Negro is raised, some of our friends recoil in horror. The Negro should be granted equality, they agree: but he should ask nothing more. On the surface, this appears reasonable, but it is not realistic."[98] Arguments that are presented against "racial preference" in university admission, for example, merely ignore what the Hispanic Coalition on Higher Education, in "An Open Letter to the Regents of the University of California," describes as "a robust, healthy educational environment."[99] And even though diversity helps to intellectually and socially enrich students' learning processes and the universities as a whole, the Regent's timid proclamation on diversity is redolent of the worrisome notion of blindness. A 2003 *Los Angeles Times* poll examined thoughts about admissions in higher education and found Democrats uniformly divided; "Forty-six percent thought colleges and universities should only consider a student academic records; forty-six percent thought that 'geographic location, ethnicity, and Gender' to 'balance the student body'"[100] are important. In spite of America's history of racial discrimination, *race*, here, is not given any serious thought.

When antidiscriminatory measures such as affirmative action programs are challenged by the mainstream and the state adheres to these challenges, it is to protect the interests of the dominant class. In the meanwhile, blacks, First Nations, Mexicans, other racialized minorities, women, the disabled, homosexuals, and other individuals from disadvantaged groups are impacted. With the implementation of Proposition 209, applications from black and other nonwhite students to University of California's Berkeley Law School, for example, were drastically curtailed. Instead of taking into account the great need for increasing the number of First Nations, blacks, Hispanics, and other racialized minority at the traditionally white institutions, there is this outcry that minority students, especially blacks and Hispanics, are lowering the standards of the universities. The continuing whitening of the university is what I call whiteness unbounded and unmarked. I do not mean that affirmative action can help to denormalize whiteness. On the contrary, one of the fundamental goals of affirmative action is to keep whiteness intact. An excellent illustration was offered by Audrey Lorde when she reminded us that "the master's tool would never dismantle the master's house."[101] In fact, these antidiscrimination measures are not put in place to remedy past or present discrimination. Resistance to the power structure creates instability within the system and, as such, given that those in power benefit from adhering to minority interests, the implementation of antidiscrimination measures are put in place to stabilize the extent power structure. The government's responses to the civil rights movements of the 1950s and 1960s with laws such as Civil Rights Act of 1964, the Voting Rights Act of 1965, the Immigration Act of 1965,[102] and presidential executive orders are illustrative. These antidiscriminatory measures enfolded within the problematic concept of justice, unavoidably renouncing the ideals of the rule of law, "a law that would treat people equally but do not seek to make them equal."[103] Antidiscriminatory measures, in the face of an unmarked and boundless whiteness, are necessary, at least on the surface, to address discriminatory practices that are endemic within the white power structure. Whiteness protects and secures its ascendancy by remaining unraced and unmarked, "seeming not to be anything in particular," as Richard Dwyer puts it,[104] and never having to admit to its role as a systematizing principle in America's social, economic, legal, and political relations. More recently, whiteness advances and maintains its power with an emphasis on race neutrality and colorblindness.

WHITENESS UNBOUNDED AND UNMARKED

When judicial challenges in the 1980s and the middle of the 1990s failed to end affirmative action programs, opponents turned to voters by putting the elimination of affirmative action programs on state ballots. California's Proposition 209, the first to end affirmative action program, stated that "the state shall not discriminate against, or grant preferential treatment to, any individual or group on the basis of race, sex, color, ethnicity, or national origin in operation of public employment, public education, or public contracting." California has an increasing racially heterogeneous and multiethnic population, and it is a cause for white anxiety.[105] In 1996, Proposition 209 was approved by voters by fifty-six to forty-six votes.[106] The implementation of Proposition 209 brought about immediate and dramatic results. University of California Board of Regents met on July 20, 1996 and as of January 1997, "race, religion, sex, color, ethnicity, or national origin" would no longer be employed "as a criterion for admission to the University or to any program of study."[107] Washington followed suit in 1998. In November 2006, Michigan voters approved an amendment to the state constitution "to ban affirmative action programs that give preferential treatment to groups or individual based on their race, gender, color, ethnicity, or national origins for public employment, employment or contracting purposes."[108] In these three states, California, Washington, and Michigan, the ballots were called "civil rights initiatives," reversing the struggles of marginalized groups for civil rights in America.

The first public university on July 20, 1995, to end affirmative action program and replace it with other admission policy was the University of California.[109] Soon after, other states including Florida,[110] Michigan, Georgia, and Texas followed suit. In Texas, Justice Lewis F. Powell's decision, in the case of the *University of California v. Bakke*, that "preferring members of any one group for no reason other than race or ethnic origins is discrimination for its own sake . . . would hinder rather than further attainment of genuine diversity,"[111] was further elaborated in the case of *Hopwood v. Texas*. The Fifth Circuit held that the University of Texas "may not use race as a factor in law school admissions." This was not surprising; until 1980, an investigation by the Department of Health, Education, and Welfare's Office for Civil Rights concluded that Texas still had "failed to eliminate vestiges of its former de jure racially dual system of public higher education, a system which segregated blacks and whites." *Hopwood v. Texas* has attracted national attention. This was, of course, mainly because the court's logic calls into question the constitutionality of applying race-conscious affirmative action policy into the guidelines for admission to public university.

Whether affirmative action remains necessary, whether it has accomplished such goals as promoting a diverse community of students, scholars, practitioners, educators, supervisors, directors, and administrations, is a moot point because white supremacy is still flourishing. Of course, racialized ethnic groups, women, homosexuals, and the disabled, for instance, have added tremendously to the resources of businesses, educational institutions, and social, political, and economic systems. And given that indigenous knowledge emanating from the marginalized individuals and groups is important for enriching the lives of members of the dominant group, what counts as institutional knowledge remains fundamental. However, these days, especially at the university level, syllabi, curricula, and scholarships mark a shift from the focus on the works of dead white men to now include a more diverse array of authors and texts.

Even the student bodies have become more diverse in terms of racial and cultural differences, which pose an enormous problem for white entitlement. And, if any kind of social changes are to occur in the university and society as a whole, what is being taught, by whom, and for whom, for the most part, is fundamental. In the case, *Regents of the University of California v. Bakke*, even though race or ethnic origins should not be the primary basis for university admission, according to Justice Powell, who, however, recognized the important of having a diverse student body, which, I think, is very tied to broader issues of the production and dissemination of knowledge.[112] At the same time, Justice Powell was convinced that if *race* was the only factor for admission, it was discriminatory and would "hinder rather than further the attainment of genuine diversity." Diversity, at its most radical, seems to centrally concern itself with issues of *race* and other identity markers such as ethnicity, sexuality, age, and physical disabilities. It involves the amalgamation of people and cultures. The Powellian model of diversity, presenting itself as if race was not constituted and contested through multifaceted hierarchies of power, remains limited and becomes meaningless in the adherence of race-conscious affirmative action programs. What is even more disconcerting is that, in a further development of the Powellian model of diversity, it, indeed, introduces the idea, as Sandra Foster observes that:

> An institution could assign a "plus" to economically advantaged white male students over minorities once it has a sufficient "mix" of minorities or women in that institution. . . . Ironically, then, diversity could be used both to justify the inclusion of an otherwise disadvantaged minority group at one time and to justify its exclusion at another once it is sufficiently represented in the student body.

113

What is obvious, yet unable to grasp, is that even though no other Justice joined Justice Powell's opinion, it is telling that Powell's opinion on diversity has been treated as the opinion of the Court and, as such, would influence other Court decisions on such cases. The aspiration of diversity at the university level offers, at one point, some hope for the democratization of the dominant culture but, at another, serves as an assimilation process for the "other" to adhere to perfomative whiteness. Whiteness, once again, takes center stage.

Although Justice Sandra Day O'Connor came later, in the case *Grutter v. Bollinger*, in her majority decision, she followed Justice Powell's interpretation of diversity. In her optimism, she held that diversity is central to the American dream and the legitimacy of the dominant class. And the goal now, on college and university campuses, is to "diversify"; to embrace other changes such as multiculturalism and interculturalism. Generally, interculturalism is supposed to promote positive interaction among people from different cultures so that they can learn from each other and gain a better intercultural knowledge.[114] The chance to meet people from diverse backgrounds and cultures cannot be disavowed. It allows students to discover the construction of those differences and to learn to communicate across cultural barriers. In most universities, undergraduate students are now required to complete a nonwestern class as a requirement for graduation. Since in the 1990s, the Task Force on Minorities for New York, for example, called attention to the importance of a culturally diverse education.

Looking back at Justice Powell's understanding of diversity where he concluded that race and ethnic minorities are needless to accomplish a diverse student body, diversity, in this sense, has narrowed its scope to exclude race and racialized ethnicities and broaden its scope to include gender, sexuality, physical and mental abilities, religion, and, as Justice Powell puts it, "the robust exchange of ideas."[115] However, the question remains, how is the goal of diversity satisfied if the focus is not on racialized ethnic groups who are systematically disadvantaged? Are race-conscious affirmative action programs equipped to address this new emphasis on diversity, or the hybrid diversity model falling prey to economic and social marginality, which should be subject to critical scrutiny? Is the focus on hybrid diversity another way of retreating toward whiteness, which is the problem in the first place? Does it, to borrow from Sandra Foster, "affirmatively promote and treat all differences the same?"[116] Can it take into account how racial differences and its historical association of the superior (white) and inferior (nonwhite), for example, determined the position and unequal treatment of those who are viewed as inferior? Given that racial difference stems from the dialogic relation between whiteness and nonwhiteness, which, when nonwhiteness is measured against whiteness is reduced to otherness, as Foster points out, "by treating all differences the same," hybrid diversity model is blind to the saliency of racial differences in this society "by extracting differences from the sociopolitical contexts"[117] where *race* is replaced with *class* even though we very well know that America's class system is distinctively racialized. The fact of the matter is that race-conscious affirmation programs rarely apply to poor blacks and other poor nonwhites because, for the most part, these individuals do not attend university. In thinking about affirmative action and whiteness, these are some of the concerns that need to be explored.

Even though many of the nontraditional programs and departments, such as Black studies, women's studies, and Asian studies, had to materialize to deal, in part, with the whiteness of academic disciplines, they continue to exist under substantial tensions and real challenges. As a way of creating a more inclusive and integrated America, the emphasis on diversity, is not an end in itself, but means for enriching students' university experience because the university is, as professor Henry Louis Gates reminds us, "an institution of legitimization—establishing what counts as knowledge, what counts as culture." [118] As a matter of fact, I think that a class on Western History can be just as "productive" as a class on race and ethnicity if, in the Western history class, students are able to read about Western civilization with and against works that conform to the traditional codes and models of white dominance. What would follow, then, is for students to unlearn and relearn what they have been taught about the supremacy of Western civilization in comparison to nonwestern cultures—African, Asian, Middle Eastern, Latin American, and the Caribbean—for instance. Arthur M Schlesinger, for one, by denying the influences of nonwestern cultures in their polymorphic historical variation on civilization sees Western culture as the pinnacle of civilization, unlike nonwestern cultures, which, for him, are "based on despotism, superstition, tribalism, and fanaticism." [119] This is a good example of what Professor Charles W. Mills refers to as "a 'bleaching' of the multicultural roots of human civilization." [120] In the end, it would be a mistake not to recognize that the educational system is still rooted in the prerogative of whiteness, and is the only legitimate site for knowledge production.

At the universities, in the face of normalized whiteness, First Nations, blacks, and other minorities continue to be totalized by their minority status, their nonwhiteness, which works to maintain and strengthen a set of social dynamics and historical formations that fasten nonwhites to the status of the "other." Otherness becomes a framework, an epistemic provision for determining and measuring accomplishment and merits. Because America has failed to live up to "the America creed," and have placed legal, cultural, economic, and political barriers that prevent nonwhites, women, and other marginalized groups from embracing such a creed, it has created, what Gunnar Myrdal, in 1944, had called "an American dilemma." [121] Notwithstanding the fact that the most disadvantaged members of marginalized groups do not benefit from affirmative action programs, I do think that affirmative action, once it is finally admitted that it constitutes a realistic response to the reality of white skin privilege and its implications for nonwhites, are important for employers, especially, taking seriously job applicants that are members of marginalized groups.

Affirmative action programs have produced and reproduced a new form of whiteness that is consistent with the logics of colorblindness. Given the racialist ontology from which race-conscious affirmative action has evolved, it cannot detach itself from the legacy of normalized whiteness. Placing a time limit on affirmative action, as professor Orlando Patterson has suggested, [122] or to get rid of it all together as Proposition

209, for example, did, is not the answer for addressing whiteness presumptive hegemony. A policy, such as Proposition 209, only serves to rehegemonize whiteness instead of dehegemonize whiteness. In spite of the many disturbing arguments that affirmative action puts whiteness in crisis, whiteness, in terms of privilege, stealth narcissism, egotism, self-centeredness, entitlement, and power, far from being in crisis, continues to advance into something monumental. Hence, in order for America to fulfill its creed of equality, liberty, and justice for all, whiteness and white privilege would have to be exposed. Is "whiteness studies" a form of exposing whiteness and white privilege? This question is examined in the next chapter.

NOTES

1. This effort has been fraught by a lack of clarity and controversy as to what are the specific goals that are intended to guide the proper utilization of Title VII. The Equal Employment Opportunity Commission (EEOC) and the courts have been faced with a huge problem of interpreting employers' violation and lack of compliance with the law. In two cases, *Washington v. Davis* and *U.S. v. South Carolina*, the court rejected the EEOC's guidelines for compliance by claiming that these guidelines, even though they might be helpful, the guidelines are not binding on either employers or the court. *Griggs v. Duke Power Company* seemed to have set precedence on how companies can enforce Title VII. The Duke Power Company placed all of its black employees in one department called the "labor department," which had the lowest paying jobs in the company. In complying with Title VII, the company requires that all new applicants to formerly "white departments" would have to have a high school diploma or certain test scores. Has the company violated Title VII? According to the district court, the company did not discriminate in terms of race. In writing for the majority, Chief Justice Burger stated that "What is required by Congress is the removal of artificial, arbitrary, and unnecessary barriers to employment when the barriers operate individually to discriminate on the basis of racial or other impermissible classification."
2. Post (2001), 10.
3. The statute states: "Notwithstanding any other provision of this subchapter, (1) it shall not be an unlawful employment practice for an employer to hire and employ employees . . . on the basis of his religion, sex, or national origin."
4. Post (2001), 10.
5. Frankenberg (1994), 64.
6. Rawls (1971), 57. John Rawls's "original position" behind "the veil of ignorance" is very much in harmony with the notion of blindness to race, gender, or sexuality identity markers.
7. Scholars who oppose affirmative action, for whatever reasons, include Dinesh D'Souza, *Illiberal Education: The Politics of Race and Sex on Campus* (1991); Glazer, Nathan, *Affirmative Discrimination: Ethnic Inequality and Public Policy* (1987); and Charles Murray, "Affirmative Racism" (1984).
8. See Cornel West, *Race Matters*, (2001).
9. Barkan (2008), 50.
10. Žižek (1997), 34.
11. See David R. Roediger, *Towards the Abolition of Whiteness: Essays on Race, Politics, and Working Class History* (1994).
12. Also, see the case of *Scott v. Stanford* (1856).
13. Kennedy (1986), 1342 n. 51.

14. Katz (1986), 19.

15. More recently, on June 28, 2007, the Supreme Court struck down two voluntary plans that were designed to prevent the resegregation of two public schools in Seattle, Washington and Louisville, Kentucky. Even though these plans were not identical, both school used race as assigning some students to schools in order to create a more racially balanced school environment. The Court based its decisions by drawing on the partial use of racial preferences in university admissions as was spelt out in the 1978 case *Regents of the University of California v. Bakke* and *Gutter v. Bollinger*. For a good overview of the Court's decision, see *Parents Involve in Community Schools v. Seattle School District No 1* and *Meredith v. Jefferson County Board of Education*, which "were settled in a joint decision" (Barkan 2008, 49). However, not using race as the primary marker for admission to public school, in the dissenting opinion, Justice Breyer notes:

> it distorts precedent, it misapplies the relevant Constitutional principles, it announces legal rules that will obstruct efforts by the state and local governments to deal effectively with the growing resegregation of public schools, it threatens to resubstitute for present claim a disruptive round of race-related litigation, and it undermines *Brown's* promise of integrated primary and secondary education that local communities have sought to make a reality. (Barkan 2008, 50)

16. These acts were specially aimed at promoting equality of results.

17. Wood (2003), 11.

18. With Executive Order 11246, the president of United Bridge Company, Keith Beach, on August 12, 1985, stated that the company would "recruit and hire qualified minorities and female until such time that the required utilization goals have been met. Should no qualified minorities and female be available, the company will document its efforts to meet goals." See Morris B. Abram, "Affirmative Action: Eair Shakers and Social Engineers" (1986, no. 33). In addition, in the case *Kilgo v. Bowman Transportation Inc.*, the court found that the defendant's hiring practices discriminated against women.

> The court's order demanded that defendant take aggressive and determined steps to seek and recruit qualified women as over-the-road drivers. Reliance on the "old-boy's" network is no longer acceptable. Those women who applied for position and who would have applied had they not be discouraged by attitude of the defendant are entitled to the adoption of a plan that will affirmatively seek out those women who did not have access to these employment opportunities, will actively recruit those overlooked, and will provide remedial action in the form of training and assistance where needed. (Morris 1986., no. 47)

19. The sexual division of labor or the family ethic consigns women as wives and mothers to the private realm, the prearranged cradle of Meg Luxton's "more than a labor of love." As I have pointed out in my other work, this was not just any love, but a love that positioned one woman above all other women and silently weighed her down with domestic, reproductive work. With the disconnection of the private (home) from the public (work), and the removal of middle-and upper-class white women from productive activities, a new definition of the facet of motherhood and its celebrated maternal functions emerged and unfolded within the social signification of the presumptive nuclear family unit. It is in the family unit, women were, in the Marxian sense, maintained as the reserve army of labor for capital to draw on in times of labor shortage. More recently, the new reserve armies of labor are the welfare recipients and immigrants, both legal and illegal. When women work outside the home, most women find jobs that are an extension of the work they do at home. These jobs are mostly located in the "female job ghettos," which are characterized by low-skill, poorly paid work in unsafe or inadequate conditions and with little or no upward mobility. How-

ever, for black women and other women of color, the private-public dichotomy cannot explain their position in the labor force. Starting with slavery, black women, especially, have always been working outside of the home.

20. Feminists, including Shulamith Firestone and Kate Millet, have argued that sexism shaped, for example, racism. See Firestone's *The Dialectic of Sex: The Case for Feminist Revolution* (1970); and Millet's *Sexual Politics* (1970). However, black feminists, including Rose M. Brewer and Evelyn Brooks Higginbotham, have argued that race shapes gender oppression. Higginbotham, for example, writes, "Gender identity is inextricably linked to racial identity . . . In Jim Crow South prior to 1960s . . . little black girls learned to use the bathroom for blacks instead of the bathroom for women." (1996, 185).

21. For more on intersectionality, see Avtar Brah and Ann Phoenix, "Ain't I a Woman? Revisiting Intersectionality" (2004); Evelyn Brooks Higginbotham, "African-American Women's History and the Metalanguage of Race" (1996); Jill Quadagno, *The Color of Welfare: How Racism Undermined the War on Poverty* (1994); Audre Lorde, *Sister Outsider: Essays and Speeches* (1984); Angela Y. Davis, *Women, Race and Class* (1983); and bell hooks, *Ain't I a Woman: Black Woman and Feminism* (1981).

22. Pay equity, at least in principle, promotes equal pay for work of equal value in the United States. This simply means that women must be paid the same as men for doing the same work (equal work). Equal work requires that the work be similar in each component. Equal value means that women will be paid the same as men for doing a different job requiring an equal amount of skill, responsibility, working condition, and effort. However, occupational segregation, in terms gender, continues to exist. In other words, women and men in the labor force continue to work in sex-typical jobs with coworkers of the same sex.

23. To be white and female is to occupy a category that is inescapably tied to the cult of true womanhood. Black women and other women of color, in truth, stand outside the cult of true womanhood. As Kathleen M. Brown notes, white women are embodied in the privileges and virtue of the cult of true womanhood. See Brown, *Good Wives, Nasty Wenches, and Anxious Patriarchs: Gender, Race, and Power in Colonial Virginia* (1996), 2.

24. Myrdal (1962), 49.

25. Bell (1973), 425.

26. See *Griggs v. Duke Power Company*; and *Regents of the University of California v. Bakke*.

27. Higginbotham (1996), 185.

28. See Jill Quadagno, *The Color of Welfare: How Racism Undermined the War on Poverty* (1994); Adolph Reed Jr., "The Underclass as Myth and Symbol: The Poverty of Discourse about Poverty" (1992); and Gertrude Ezorsky, *Racism and Justice: The Case of Affirmative Action* (1991).

29. For a more comprehensive reading on the impact of Hurricane Katrina on blacks in New Orleans, see Sherrow O. Pinder, "Notes on Hurricane Katrina: Rethinking Race, Class, and Power in the United States" (2009).

30. Johnson (1966), 635.

31. Farrar (2005), 372.

32. Burstein (1985), 44.

33. Lloyd L. Gaines, a black man, applied to Missouri's law school but was refused admission because of his race. After both the Boone County Court and the Supreme Court upheld the university's decision not to admit Gaines, the case was taken by Gaines's lawyer, Charles Hamilton Houston, to the United States Supreme Court. On December 12, 1938 the Court ordered the University of Missouri either to accept Gaines or provide a school of equal stature within the state's borders. On March 19, 1939, Gaines disappeared and never attended law school.

34. Dyer (1988), 44.

35. This act "sealed the faith of American city" in terms of racial segregation. In 1939, the Federal Housing Authority's *Underwriting Manual* provided the guidelines

for granting housing loans and clearly used race as the decisive factor: "If a neighborhood is to retain stability, it is necessary that properties shall continued to be occupied by the same social and racial classes" (Duster 1996), 46–47. Also, see George Lipsitz, *The Possessive Investment in Whiteness: How White People Profit From Identity Politics* (1998), 372–74.

36. Fanon (1964), 31.

37. Drake (2003), 59. For other readings on when affirmative action programs were white, see Ira Katznelson, *When Affirmative Action Was White: An Untold History of Racial Inequality in Twentieth Century America* (2005); Karen Brodkin, *How Jews Became White Folks and What That Says About Race in America* (1998); and Herbert Hill, "Race, Ethnicity and Organized Labor: The Opposition to Affirmative Action (1987).

38. Kennedy (1986), 1329 no. 7. I do not mean to imply that black doctors should only treat black patients and vice versa. However, given that many black patients, through no fault of their own, are more comfortable with black and other nonwhite doctors, ending affirmative action in medical school admission have only make matters worse, rather than reducing the racial tensions, in the first place, that have contributed to such a discomfort from black patients.

39. Lowell High School in San Francisco, California is allowed to enroll students from four to nine racialized ethnic groups, with no group representing more than forty to forty five percent of the student population. "Affirmative action for whites" stirs up a big controversy with the decision of Lowell High School to raise the admission standards for Chinese students over other minority as well as white students. For a more comprehensive reading of this issue, see Katherine Seligman, "Ethnic Concerns Cloud Lowell" (1993), A2. The school has a sixty-nine–point admission index. In 1992 and 1993, for example, in order to be admitted, "Chinese students had to score at least sixty six; white, Japanese, Korean, Filipino, American Indian, and other 'non-white' students, fifty-nine; and black and Spanish-surnamed students, fifty-six" (Lau, 1993), 4.

40. See John T. Woolley and Gerhard Peters, *The American Presidency Project*.

41. Kennedy (1986), 1343 n55.

42. Affirmative action also appears in Present Lyndon Johnson's Executive Order 11246, which prohibits discrimination by federal contractors. The order states: "The contractor will take affirmative action to ensure that applicants are employed, and that employees are treated during employment, without regard to their race, color, religion, sex, or national origin."

43. Johnson (1965), 635–40.

44. As early as 1884, in Massachusetts, a law was implemented to protect individuals from religious discrimination when they were seeking employment in the civil service. By 1945, twenty-two states implemented discrimination laws managing civil service employment. Race and religion, which, allowed for open discrimination, were incorporated into these laws by some states. Eventually, antidiscrimination clauses in state contracts with private firms were also frequent. For a more comprehensive reading of the history of American discrimination laws, see Arthur Earl Bonfield, "The Origins and Development of American Fair Employment Legislation" (1967).

45. The Order extended President Dwight D. Eisenhower's Executive Order 10479, which was signed on August 13, 1953. It established the antidiscrimination Committee on Government Contracts, which was based on Executive Order 8802 known as the Fair Employment Act that was signed by President Franklin D. Roosevelt on June 25, 1941 to prevent racial discrimination in the national defense industry.

46. Abram (1986), 1318 no. 22.

47. Johnson (1966), 635.

48. In the case, *Regents of the University of California v. Bakke*, in 1978, Allan Bakke (a white man) sued the University of California, Davis for not admitting him into its medical school. The medical school had set aside sixteen out of its one hundred spots for applicants from marginalized groups. The California Supreme Court ordered the medical school to accept Bakke and disallowed California universities to take race into

consideration when admissions are being made. For a good overview of the case, see Bernard Schwartz, *Behind Bakke: Affirmative Action and the Supreme Court* (1988); and Ronald Dworkin, *A Matter of Principle* (1985), 293–315.

49. Kennedy (1986), 1327–28. In the same case, Justice Lewis Powell stated: "If petitioner's purpose is to assure within its student body some specified percentage of a particular group merely because of its race or ethnic origin, such a preferential purpose must be rejected not as insubstantial but as facially invalid." He proceeded to say: "Preferring members of any one group for no reason other than race or ethnic origins is discrimination for its own sake . . . would hinder rather than further attainment of genuine diversity." Also, see Bernard Schwartz, *Behind Bakke: Affirmative Action and the Supreme Court* (1988).

50. Young (1989), 269.

51. Fiss (1976), 155.

52. Lately, with the implementation of the Personal Responsibility Work Opportunity Reconciliation Act, whose generic term is workfare, the poor are now expected to work outside the home in exchange for their welfare checks. See Sherrow O. Pinder, *From Welfare to Workfare; How Capitalist States Create a Pool of Unskilled Cheap Labor (A Marxist Feminist Social Analysis)* (2007).

53. Young (1989), 269.

54. See Frederick Douglass, *Narrative of the Life of Frederick Douglass, an American Slave* (1982).

55. Johnson (1966), 636. This quote is extracted from a speech that the British Prime Minister Winston Churchill gave on November 10, 1942 at Lord Mayor's luncheon, which was held at the Mansion House in London.

56. hooks (1992), 1.

57. The Equal Protection Clause in the Fourteenth Amendment states: "No State . . . deny to any person within its jurisdiction the equal protect of the law." The clause proved fundamental during Reconstruction to protect blacks from discrimination. However, the southern state ignored the Equal Protection Clause. The right of black men to vote, according to fifteenth amendment, met barriers through state legislation such as the poll tax, the literacy test, and the grandfather clause. In addition to violating the rights of blacks, Japanese rights were violated with the Japanese internment camps. More recently, the United and Strengthening America by Providing Appropriate Tools Require to Intercept and Obstruct Terrorist Act of 2001, commonly referred to as the Patriot Act, implemented by the Bush administration after 9/11, has provisions that provide officials at the airports with unrestrained surveillance power, which, in many cases, targets Muslim Americans.

58. Harris (1993), 1767–68.

59. West (2001), 156. For a more comprehensive understanding of race in America, see Sherrow O. Pinder, *The Politics of Race and Ethnicity in the United States: Americanization, De-Americanization and Racialized Ethnic Groups* (2010), 17–22; and Robert Miles and Rodolfo D. Torres, "Does 'Race' Matter? Transatlantic Perspectives on Racism After 'Race Relations'" (1999).

60. Gates (1992), 147.

61. Fanon (1967), 118.

62. See Shelby Steele, *The Content of our Character: A New Vision of Race in America* (1991); Clarence Thomas, "An Afro American Perspective: Towards a Plain Reading of the Constitution—The Declaration of Independence in Constitutional Interpretation" (1987); and Thomas Sowell, *Civil Rights, Rhetoric or Reality?* (1984).

63. See Martin Luther King's famous speech, "I Have a Dream."

64. Buchanan (2003), 220.

65. First Nations' battles, slave riots, lynching, and race riots are some illustrations of racial strife that presented itself in America.

66. Glazer (1987), 250. In this discussion, "affirmative discrimination," "preferential treatment," and "affirmative racism" are used interchangeable. The underlying meaning of these terms is that whites are disadvantaged by affirmative action. The extent of

white hostility toward affirmative action was demonstrated in a 1977 survey, which found that most whites were opposed to quotas and timetables for blacks in employment and higher education. See Sidney Verba and Garry R. Orren, *Equality in America: The View from the Top* (1985), 63.

67. Young (1989), 267.

68. Hall (1993), 361.

69. In fact, visible display of differences is intolerable. For example, in France, Muslims women are banned from wearing scarves in public.

70. Wilson (1980).

71. See Orlando Patterson, "Affirmative Action, on the Merit System" (1995); Sandra Foster, "Difference and Equality: A Critical Assessment of the Concept of Diversity" (1993); Randall Kennedy, "Persuasion and Distrust: A Comment of the Affirmative Action Debate" (1986); and Martin Luther King Jr., *Why We Can't Wait* (1964).

72. In fact, many whites are attempting to reclassify as blacks and Mexicans to take advantage of affirmative action. This reclassification is referred to as "reverse passing" (Harris 1993, n6).

73. For more on the crisis of whiteness, see Charles Gallagher, "White Reconstruction in the University" (2003).

74. Kennedy (1986), 1342.

75. King (1964), 124.

76. Regents of the University of California (1995).

77. Dworkin (1985), 298.

78. Dworkin (1985), 300.

79. Morrison (1993), 59.

80. Blacks placed into positions that were traditionally held by whites are now looked on as "reverse discrimination." The flagrant difficulties and contradictions of "reverse discrimination" are clearly illustrated in post-apartheid South Africa when, in 1993, "Telkcom, South Africa's national telephone company, with more than 58,000 people, had one black manager. In 1995, as a part of its affirmative action program, the company had decided to employ eighty-three black managers and had decided to recruit and hire more. "More than 5,000 white workers have threatened to strike to protect the new policy. 'It's reverse discrimination' complained A.C. van Wyk, spokesman for the Mine Workers Union of South Africa, a union that still bars blacks from joining." Affirmative action initiatives in South Africa are referred to by its critics as neoapartheid. See Troy Duster, "Individual Fairness, Group Preferences, and the California Strategy" (1996, 43).

81. See *City of Richmond v. J.A. Croson Company*; and *Wygant v. Jackson Board of Education*.

82. See the *New York Time*, "Police Officer Starts to Defend White Men" (1995).

83. Kennedy (1986), 1345.

84. Ahmed (2004).

85. Hage (2005), 186.

86. Hochschild (1995), 55.

87. Lipsitz (1998), 7.

88. Moreton-Robinson (2008), 83.

89. Fanon (1967), 110–11.

90. Wilkins (2000), 38.

91. See Noel Ignatiev, *How the Irish Became White* (1995); Theodore W. Allen, *The Invention of the White Race: Racial Oppression and Social Control* (1994); David R. Roediger, *The Wages of Whiteness: Race and the Making of the American Working Class* (1991); and W. E. B. Du Bois, *Black Reconstruction: An Essay Toward a History of the Part Black Folk Played in the Attempt to Reconstruct Democracy in America, 1860–1880* (1935). Eric Arnesen, "Scholarly Controversy: Whiteness and the Historians' Imagination," cautions that some whiteness studies scholars, using W. E. B. Du Bois' reflection on the "psychological wage" as a foundation for their work, provide "poorly as a new explanation for the old question of why white workers have refused to make common cause

with African Americans" (2001), 3. And posing doubts about the ways in which the "psychological wage" is employed by whiteness studies scholars, starting with David Roediger, to demonstrate the relationship between race and class, Arnesen concludes that whiteness studies scholars "fail to address several critical questions raised by the Du Bois passage: How does this passage function in Du Bois' larger argument about the relationship of black and white worker to one another, and of both to their employee? What assumptions are embedded in the formulation? And finally, what is new here? What does Du Bois' formulation, upon close inspection, actually tells? The answers to these questions cast some doubt on the utility of the concept of 'psychological' wage." Hence, he returns to his question:

> Why white workers have refused to make common cause with their black counterparts? "The theory of laboring class unity," Du Bois explained only a few paragraphs earlier, "rests upon the assumption that laborers, despite internal jealousies, will unite because of their opposition to exploitation by capitalist." The interests of the laboring class and those of the planter class were "diametrically opposed" throwing "white and black labor into one class" and precipitating "a united front for higher wages and better working conditions." (2003, 9–10)

The planter class has to constantly find ways to create a conflict between white and black workers. Whites are made to feel superior and blacks are made to feel inferior. In the end, white workers are advantaged because of their access to white privilege and the opportunism that accompanies it is inescapably the disposition of the "psychological wage."

92. Regents of the University of California (1995).
93. Regents of the University of California (1995).
94. Wilson (1996), A21.
95. Butler (1998), 164–65.
96. D'Souza (1995B), B1.
97. Kennedy (1986), 1332.
98. King (1964), 124.
99. *New York Times* (1995), A11.
100. Barkan (2008), 51.
101. Lorde (1984), 123.
102. The Immigration Act of 1965, signed by President Lyndon Johnson, ended the Immigration Act of 1924 that established "the national origins quota system" aimed at restricting racialized ethnic groups from immigrating to the United States. When America's founding fathers, Benjamin Franklin and Thomas Jefferson argued to "keep the doors of America open" for immigrants, they were thinking only about whites, especially from England. Franklin, for one, asked provocatively, "Why should [America] in the sights of superior being darken its people? Why increase the sons of Africa by planting them in America where we have so fair an opportunity by excluding of Blacks and Tawneys and increasing the lovely whites." His desire was for more "purely white people" because "all Africa is black or tawny; Asia chiefly tawny; America (exclusive of the new comers) wholly so. In Europe, the Spaniards, Italians, French, Russians, and Swedes are generally of what we call a swarthy complexion; as are the Germans also, the Saxons only excepted, who, with the English, make the principle body of white people on the face of the earth. I could wish that their numbers would increase" (1961), 234. Jefferson had a solution for Franklin's desire for increasing the "lovely whites." Jefferson contemplated shipping blacks to the independent black nation of Santo Domingo. See Jefferson, *Notes on the State of Virginia* (1999). The Immigration Act of 1924 was partly premised on the fear that America would have to come to terms with its racial and ethnic homogeneity. Indeed, fear is the byproduct of America's entrenched racism.
103. Abram (1986), 1317.
104. Dyer (1988), 44.

105. The argument is presented that by 2089 America would be largely populated by Hispanic and Asian, which would change the face of America as white.

106. Ward Connerly, an African American businessman, was Chairman of the "Yes on Proposition 209" campaign, which supported the 1996 California Civil Rights Initiative.

107. Regents of the University of California (1995).

108. Barkan (2008), 50.

109. Starting in 1999, California guaranteed admission of the top four percent of every graduating high school class in the state to any one of the University of California institutions; Texas admitted the top ten percent; and Florida the top twenty percent.

110. In November 1999, Governor Jeb Bush's Executive Order 99–281 banned affirmative action in public education, hiring, and contracting.

111. Foster (1993), 122.

112. Dworkin (1985), 304.

113. Foster (1993), 132.

114. For more on interculturalism, see Bhikhu Parekh, "Multiculturalism" (2007); Paul Gilroy, *After Empire: Melancholia or Convivial Culture* (2004); and Avtar Brah, *Cartographies of Diaspora: Contesting Identities* (1996).

115. Foster (1993), 116.

116. Foster (1993), 105.

117. Foster (1993), 111.

118. Gates (1992), 109.

119. Schlesinger (1998), 133.

120. Mills (2003), 45.

121. Myrdal (1963).

122. See Orlando Patterson, "Affirmative Action on the Merit System" (1995), A13.

FOUR

Whiteness and the Problematics of Whiteness Studies

Years ago W. E. B. Du Bois, in *The Souls of Black Folk*, analyzed the process of whiteness that brought about the subordinated position of blacks and other nonwhites in the very question, "How does it feel to be the problem?"[1] To put it differently, the first-wave of "whiteness studies," emanating from W. E. B. Du Bios to Toni Morrison, has named and classified the "problem" as that of whiteness, a system of domination. Bell hooks, for one, has theorized the role of whiteness, as visible, "the mysterious, the strange and the terrible," in structuring the daily experience of blacks and other nonwhites.[2] Eventually, the critique of whiteness, in the 1990s, has evolved within the corpus of the second-wave of "whiteness studies." Ruth Frankenberg, Richard Dyer, David R Roediger, Noel Ignatiev and John Garvey, George Lipsitz, and Mike Hill, among many others, have tried to provide a definition and a framework for the second wave of "whiteness studies."[3]

Before the above mentioned authors became involved in what is now identified as "whiteness studies," Liz MacMillan's article, "Lifting the Veil of Whiteness: Growing Body of Scholarship Challenges Racial Norm," appeared in *The Chronicle of Higher Education* on September 8, 1995. It introduced the term "whiteness studies" for the first time. In the United States, "whiteness studies" has, since then, emerged in many academic disciplines such as history, gender studies, cultural studies, anthropology, film studies, media studies, humor studies, linguistics, art history, rhetoric and communication, material culture, and dance. According to whiteness studies scholars, "to leave whiteness unexamined is to perpetuate a kind of asymmetry that has marred even many critical analyses of racial formation and cultural practices."[4] Lately, the "third wave of whiteness" scholarships are opening up "new line of research and analyses of racisms and racial formation."[5]

Whiteness is at the center of America's institutions and systems, its epistemologies and everyday discourse, and its public history. As such, it must be interrogated in order to resolve its endemic racial issues. To gain new perspectives, whiteness studies scholars have positioned whiteness within an exposed position on white privilege.[6] Yet whiteness remains an area of studies that is characterized by intrinsic contradictions, which remain as one of its most outstanding and meaningful characteristics.[7] Given that whiteness is considered invisible, unmarked, and unnamed, it is somewhat on this basis that the nature of whiteness, as only invisible to those who inhabit it, has been downplayed by many of the literature in "whiteness studies."[8] Its invisibility is, for the most part, its most familiar talked about attribute.[9] Nonetheless, for blacks and other nonwhites, there is nothing invisible about whiteness as it is manifested in the cultural practices of the United States of America. Howard McGary, in "Race and Social Justice," defines practice as "a commonly accepted course of action that may be overtime habitual in nature; a course of action that specifies certain forms of behavior as permissible and other as impermissible, with rewards and penalties assigned accordingly."[10] How whiteness as a cultural practice gains its preeminence must be elucidated; when and how whiteness came into being in America are the elementary questions to pose in order to demystify the cultural practice of whiteness and view its horror with undetached eyes. I have already pointed to the emergence of whiteness in colonial America.

Whiteness is everywhere at work — in the parks, on television, in films, books, magazines, newspapers, on university campuses, in the board rooms of corporations, in the laws, institutions and systems, everyday discourse and language, behaviors and attitudes, on the streets, at the banks, homeownerships, and at the courthouses. People of color, for a long time, knew, to borrow from Langston Hughes's famous saying, "the ways of white folk." W. E. B. Du Bois, in "The Souls of White Folk," gets to the heart of the matter and offers a vision of whiteness that is already visible by the nonwhite "other."[11] Unlike John Paul Sartre's illustration of the impact of "the anti-Semitic consciousness" on anti-Semites,[12] W. E. B. Du Bois acknowledges that when whites become aware of how visible they are to blacks and other nonwhites, they become anxious and "embarrassed,"[13] and "white talk," a "talk that serves to insulate white people from examining their individual and collective role(s) in the perpetuation of racism"[14] often highlights the embarrassment. How can whites recover from this apprehension and embarrassment? Is "whiteness studies" a way to recover from a traumatic realization? Feeling embarrassed and apprehensive can also function as a form of self-centeredness, which returns the white subject "back to itself." Instead of facing the other as the subjective source of their embarrassment and anxiety, they dismiss it and take refuge in their own malaise.[15] Is this reaction, then, symptomatic of the solipsism of whiteness studies scholars?

Whiteness studies scholars such as Michele Fine and her colleagues declare, "We worry that in our desires to create spaces to speak, intellectually or empirically, about whiteness, we may have reified whiteness as a fixed category of experience; that we have allowed it to be treated as a monolith, in the singular, as an 'essential something,'"[16] which allows for the rehegemonizing of whiteness. "Whiteness studies" finds, thus, itself caught up in the caldron of rehegemonizing whiteness has to be prefixed with the word *critical*.[17] Is placing *critical* before "whiteness studies" a way of compensating for the disquiet that has taken over some whiteness studies scholars? Quite often, *critical*, as we very well know, functions as a place where we "deposit our anxiety." Scholars of "whiteness studies" might think, for example, that if they are doing "*critical* whiteness studies rather than [merely] whiteness studies" they can protect themselves from being judged and ridiculed. They cannot be accused of doing "the wrong kind" of whiteness studies. But the word *critical* does not eliminate possibilities. It just describes what "we are doing over here," as incongruent to "them over there."[18]

The task of "whiteness studies" is to explore how whiteness as domination works to reinforce, perpetuation, and maintain white privilege, as well as bring out the effects of that privilege on those who are identified as white. By contesting the privilege that whites accrue, these scholarships purport to describe, unveil, and name white privilege. The name gives its existence to the "thing." By naming, one gives identity. The inexistence of whiteness for whites recedes before its naming. "Whiteness studies" critically engages with whiteness and revolves toward what Judith Butler calls "citational practice," meaning that white privilege is named and confessed.[19] What does it mean then to acknowledge one's privilege? Are our concerns justified when we fear that with this form of acknowledgement, whites are "irrevocably on the wrong sides?"[20] Does confessing one's privilege involve indeed unlearning that privilege? What does one learn, when one learns to see one's whiteness as a form of privilege? In fact, "the process of learning to see," to borrow from Sara Ahmed, is always a project for the privileged,[21] which reminds us of how, at an early age, white children learn "to see" their whiteness and are culturally whitened. Some of the questions asked by white children: "why is she that color? Is she sunburned? Can she change?" are not traditionally the questions asked by whites about themselves. More importantly, these questions show that "white children do not come to 'accept' their whiteness, but consider themselves always already white."[22] Such questions, however absurd as they sound, lead whites to enter adulthood secured in their whiteness. As a result, whites have learned to simply accept themselves as the norm and have not learned to experience themselves as the racialized "other."

Whiteness impacts every aspect of America's daily life, from history, biology, philosophy, and political debate to literature, to name a few. Toni Morrison's *Playing in the Dark: Whiteness and the Literary Imagination* shows how American literature has been oblivious of people of color and carefully safeguarded whites' viewpoints, especially that of white men.[23] Literature, if studied, is white. It teaches "the pedagogy of whiteness," the ways one learns to understand oneself as a white person.[24] In this sense, it is not about how white people experience their whiteness or the representations of whiteness in American society, as is the focus of many whiteness scholars; it is about the normalization of whiteness; literally making white the normative way of being. Whites are inherently tied to structures of domination, which "alert us to deep relation between whiteness and the unconscious and thus of the specificity of dominant subject formation. In Lacanian terms, the discourse of whiteness can be said to function as a condition of dominant subjectivity: It inserts the subject into the symbolic order."[25] The fact that at an early age white children are educated to conduct themselves in accordance to the norms of whiteness is to be found in Ruth Frankenberg's confession: "I have been performing whiteness, and having whiteness performed upon me, since—or actually before—the moment I was born."[26]

Whiteness owes its hegemonic status not to its natural but naturalized status. Does it imply that confessing one's whiteness produces some sort of self-deprecation? Confessing one's whiteness fixes attention on the relations between past and present privilege accrued by whites.[27] Confession, in Richard Terdiman's words, "is the most self-reflective of all the art of memory."[28] If Barry Schwartz and Horst-Alfred Heinrich are correct, recent memory literature promotes an "unprecedented concern for minority dignity and rights,"[29] and whiteness, more recently, is reacting "to the entry of historically marginalized racial and ethnic groups into the political arena and the struggle over social resources."[30] Can we then situate the work of whiteness studies scholars within "memory studies?" It is important to recognize how "whiteness studies," far from the discarding of how whiteness functions in America's past, which has shaped its future on race relations, is pointing to a remembering that is often painful. Remembering is a practice that permits severe breakthrough but also leads to confusion. It is not a quiet act of looking at past practices and events. America's shameful history of whiteness compels a painful act of remembering that permits its mutilated past to make sense of the suffering of the present.[31] We can see, then, that remembering resonates deeply with how Audre Lorde understands poetry as "a vital necessity of our existence [that] forms the light within which we predicate our hopes and dreams toward survival and change, first made into language, then into idea, then into more tangible action."[32] Given that remembering is not outside the realm of history, we are perpetually tied to history, to the task of hearing and remembering what has already been repeatedly articulated.

It is my concern that by centering whiteness as an object of analysis and study, whiteness studies scholars "might have reified [indeed] whiteness as a fixed category of experience" and render "white identity as an essential something,"[33] a predetermined presence, truth, representation, and meaning, standing against erasure. At this juncture, it is useful to introduce the provocative question and ask: why should an emphasis be placed on exposing whiteness, given the danger by undertaking scholarly work on whiteness one might add to practices of "re-centering rather than decentering it, as well as reifying the term and its inhabitants?"[34] It is not surprising that this concern propels Richard Dyer's blood to become "cold at the thought that talking about whiteness could lead to the development of something call 'white studies,'"[35] or "that paying attention to whiteness might lead to white people saying they want to get in touch with their whiteness."[36] We know too well the prevailing whiteness of disciplines at the universities such as philosophy, political science, and anthropology.[37] In the end, the disquietude to confess and name white privilege (citational practice), if it serves to reaffirm the white subject at the core of "discursive and psychic power," to borrow from Robyn Wiegman, "whiteness studies" must inevitably be regarded, to a great degree, with distrust. White privilege must not only be confessed, but one has to unlearn that privilege. It is easy to see from the emphasis being placed on the production of a particular knowledge counting as legitimate that the learning itself is taking place in a culture that sanctions such privilege as a social fact.[38]

The French sociologist Émile Durkheim explains that "a social fact is every way of acting, fixed or not, capable of exercising on the individual an external constraint; or again, every way of acting which is general throughout a given society, while at the same time existing in its own rights independent of its individual manifestations."[39] When Gayatri C. Spivak proposes that "unlearning one's privilege by considering it as one's loss,"[40] she is joined by Richard Dyer who sees the unlearning as necessary "to dislodge [whites] from the position of power."[41] The fact that there is nothing outside of power, no opposition on the part of whiteness to power is in itself a treasured part of that power, because power is not done away with, it is just transformed into another form of dominance. Hence, any doing away with power must first take into consideration the intricacy of power itself. Michel Foucault, in his work on power, as I understand it, warns that "there are no relations of power without resistance."[42] How First Nations, blacks, Chinese, and other racialized, then, are able to resist the white power structure? If disciplinary power functions, as Foucault observes, "according to a double-mode; that of binary and branding (mad/sane; dangerous/harmless; normal/abnormal); . . . of differential distribution (who is; where he must be; how he is to be characterized; how a constant surveillance must be exercised over him in an individual way, etc.),"[43] do nonwhites have the possibility to view themselves differently than as seen by the normalized white gaze that never stops determining and situating them? For sure, an emphasis on Black Nationalism and Black Power, radical leaders such as Malcolm X and Black Muslims, and rioting, for example, did pose a threat to disciplinary power and created some anxiety amongst the power elite. In the end, however, resistance to power, even though it can reallocate power's temperance, is constantly policed and always on trial, which is the true working of disciplinary power itself. Power, according to Judith Butler, must be seen "as forming the subject as well, as providing the very condition on its existence and the trajectory of its desire."[44] It is another way to transform the subject or social being into, what Judith Revel observes as, "a new instrument of control"[45] in such a way that the democratic state would see it as fit to promote multiculturalism and diversity as a perception of individual and collective agency. It is not a surprise, then, that resistance outside of the state apparatus disrupts the power structure at all times.

There are many indeed excellent reasons for whites to critically engage in the study of whiteness, and, certainly, the academy is a strategic location for the political contestation of whiteness because of the whiteness of the academy. However, Karen Brodkin suggests that "studying whiteness should not be academic"[46] because, as a critical intellectual undertaking, it amalgamates with, rather than destabilizes, whiteness. At this point of our reflection, the elemental question that brings all the others in its wake is: What exactly is "whiteness studies"? Who are the beneficiaries of a "self-reflective whiteness"? And, after Sigmund Freud and Frantz Fanon, we can apply their question to "whiteness studies" and ask: "What does 'whiteness studies' want?" Is "self-reflective whiteness" another way of skillfully reiterating, reenacting, and perpetuating the white subject position since for many whites, whiteness, it is assumed, is in some kind of crisis? As Charles Gallagher remarks, "a fundamental transformation" of whiteness is occurring.[47] Is there an actual crisis of whiteness, or an anxiety about whiteness?[48] Is "whiteness studies" relinquishing or appealing to whiteness? Does the Foucauldian notion of power continue to function in "whiteness studies"? In other words, is whiteness dislodged from its deployment and position of power? Is promoting "whiteness studies" another way of legitimizing whites' privilege as a safe space to theorize about whiteness? Is it about the removal of "unearned assets" given to whites? Is it about supplanting white supremacy or, on the contrary, replicating the relentless logic of white supremacy that it wants to displace? To what extent can "whiteness studies" helps us answer these questions? Or, are the issues of "whiteness studies" new ones altogether? Are "old" answers sufficient to address "new" questions? Is whiteness transforming itself, as some scholars have argued, to "an essential something"?[49] Does it demonstrate a political commitment to deinstitute whiteness and produce a post-white identity?

To answer these questions we need to engage with the actual deconstruction of the semantics, metaphysics, and logics of whiteness that have brought alive "whiteness studies" in the first place. Because, if whiteness is transformed into "an essential something" in the face of normalized whiteness, it runs the risk of rehegemonizing itself. "Whiteness studies" cannot free whiteness from its presumptive hegemony since it is within its own structure of power that it is nurtured. Spivak puts it plainly, "The impossible 'no' to a structure which one critiques, yet inhabits intimately is the deconstructive philosophical position and the everyday here and now named [whiteness studies] is a case of it."[50]

My purpose in this chapter is to look at whiteness, explain what "whiteness studies" is, and bring out its complexities. For many whiteness studies scholar, race and whiteness must be examined in order to understand how "whiteness studies" fails to position whites as a raced subject.[51] Given that whiteness "functions as an ontologically neutral category that advances a subject as raceless and unmarked,"[52] the uneasiness about assigning race to whites is augmented because "whiteness seems to banish the troubling asymmetry that is the essence of racism."[53] Even though racism has changed over time, taking on new forms and serving diverse purposes, these changes are essential to what racism is. Racism is an inheritance of America's history, as Alastair Bonnett explains, "and/or/thus as inevitably placed within an untenable position within research on 'racial' oppression or non-White people."[54] In the Marxist sense, inheritance is fundamental for a conceptualization of history. Even though we "make history," for Karl Marx, this *making* is wrought by inheritance. Indeed, as a scholar rightly describes it: "[H]uman beings make their own history, but they do not make it arbitrarily in conditions chosen by themselves, but in conditions always already given and inherent from the past."[55] Racism, as the consequence of assigning race, is translated into racial identity. Racial identity functions as a tool for domination as well as for resistance.[56] Racialized ethnic groups have tried to create lives of their own, but in many cases they are faced with structural and cultural barriers that prevent racial equality. I am referring here to the discriminatory practices that are ever-present in the workplace, the schools, and the criminal justice system.

In chapter 1, I examined how whiteness determined the reprehensible positions of First Nations and blacks, and other racialized ethnic groups in America. I now turn to specific characteristics of whiteness.

SPECIFIC CHARACTERISTICS OF WHITENESS

Like in all Western democracies, in the United States, whiteness is considered the norm. Hence, it is *unmarked* and *unraced*. Its meanings and functions are inextricable from the larger scheme of race making that is centered on the dialogical relationship between the white self (us) and nonwhite "other" (them), fostering, to borrow from Marx and Engels, in *The Communist Manifesto*, "two great hostile camps . . . facing each other." Toni Morrison draws on the sycophantic nature of whiteness constructed and contingent on a nonwhite presence,[57] fashioning itself within a social milieu that is structured by an asymmetrical hierarchy of race, which promotes white superiority. The central task of white superiority, as Oliver Cox also explains, is not that "white is superior to all human beings but to insist that white must be supreme."[58] The behavior of working class whites during the nineteenth century prizes "whiteness to such an extent that instead of joining with black workers, [for example], with whom they shared common interests, [working class whites] adopt a white supremacy vision."[59] It is not a surprise that during slavery, the practice of an annual "muster," where armed whites terrorized slave communities to incite revolts, served to unite whites across class lines.[60] In addition, white supremacist principles and practices united poor whites in "the hood of the Ku Klux Klan (KKK) and sophisticated scholars in robes in the hall of academia."[61] It is the systematic racism operating on the basis of skin color that establishes a system of racial hierarchy that places whites above blacks and other nonwhites. In fact, there is nothing for whiteness to feel superior about. What it does is to impress on the white self a presumptive view of itself as superior and, as a result, falls prey to its own conceitedness. This conceitedness is, at best, illustrated in Harper Lee's *To Kill a Mocking Bird*. Mayella Ewell, "a thick-bodied girl accustomed to strenuous labor,"[62] has nothing to feel superior about, except for her white skin privilege; she lives behind "the town garbage dump in what was once a Negro cabin."[63] Mayella Ewell, by publicly using the word *nigger* to refer to "a respectable Negro" Tom Robison who is on trial for the alleged raping of her, performs the conceitedness of whiteness that she seeks.

In "Racializing Babylon: Settler Whiteness and the 'New Racism,'" Penelope Ingram draws our attention to another appreciation of whiteness as the norm. By analyzing white settler texts such as *David Malouf's Remembering Babylon*, Ingram alleges that whiteness is not portrayed as normalized and unmarked. In fact, whiteness is raced. Her desire to move away from the argumentation that presents whiteness as the norm is significant. She writes, whiteness, in *Remembering Babylon*, "is a part of a general valorization of racial and cultural difference which far from benefiting indigenous and racial others through a respect for difference, confirms instead to ideologies of what Pierre-André Taguieff and Etienne Balibar have called the 'new racism,'"[64] a transition from nature (biological) to nurture (cultural).

In fact, the "new" racism is not understated, un-institutional, and unguided by nonracial practices that maintain white supremacy. On the contrary, the "new" racism is made visible through discourses and practices that are racial and are inherent in terms of multiculturalism, diversity, and culturalism.[65] Cultural differences are encoded, made universal, and constrained within a distinctive culturalism, which is not only obstructive but in fact immobilizing because, paradoxically, the much racialized aspect that culturalism purports to obliterate is maintained. Once again, race as a signifying practice is reiterated. Hence, it is not a surprise that racist logics continue to be reproduced. In fact, the "new" racism, which is coded within a cultural logic, where *culture* is required to assume an artificial consistency and functions as a substitute for *race*, does not depend on racial cataloging that, in the past had, for example, created a compendium of ill treatments toward nonwhites, i.e., the allocation of First Nations (Native Americans) to Indian Reservations, the implementation of Jim Crow South, the Chinese Exclusion Act, the Immigrant Act of 1924, Tydings-McDuffe Act of 1934, and Japanese American Internment. Today, it is apparent that "we" — a "we" that considers itself to be "different" from the "them" — can talk about a group of people as having a deficient culture and label "them" as the "underclass," even though the term "underclass" is itself a racist term.[66] One of the main connotations of the "underclass" puts the blame on poor people for their poverty. "The significance of poverty," writes J. Donald Moon, "is not just the suffering it involves, though that is obviously important, but the fact that it represents an undeserved exile from society."[67] What is just as disconcerting as the "underclass" is the consideration of Muslims nowadays as terrorists. From this assimilation, racism, in the form of racial profiling, ensues. For nonwhites, the "new" racism is no less terrorizing than the "old" racism because both racisms position nonwhites as the object of racial discrimination.

Given that racial discrimination is not experienced by whites, there is no essential reason why racism would mean a great deal for many whites. Despite what Alice McIntyre refers to as "white talk," which protects whites from probing their individual and collective role in the upholding of racism,[68] —whiteness allocates everybody a position in the relations of racism.[69] Given that whiteness remains invisible to those who inhabit it and are inhabited by it, racism should logically remain invisible to those who cannot experience it. As a matter of fact, many whites frequently allege, unaware of their "white talk," that racism has nothing to do with them because they are not racist. Even though many whites' understanding of whiteness most often ignore their white skin privilege,[70] it is a conundrum for whites to assert that whiteness has nothing to do with them.[71] In a word, "whites," as Linda Martín Alcoff explains, "cannot disavow whiteness. The way one learns to experience one's self as white still operates to confer privilege to whites in numerous and significant ways."[72] Whiteness, in this sense, is not always created and upheld through obvious benefits, it is also imbedded in the discursive and nondiscursive practices that shape and maintain whiteness.

Racial differences create and define the racialized subject positions. The focus on culturalism sets the stage for the comparison and measurement of the dualistic concept of whiteness (civilized) and nonwhiteness (uncivilized) within which the latter is reduced to a disturbing alterity, and is characterized by what David Theo Goldberg describes as "the weight of race."[73] The proverbial *weight* on the shoulders of the beleaguered populations such as First Nations, blacks, Chinese, Mexicans, and other people of color becomes so heavy indeed that the signifier for racial otherness ultimately comes to denote "racial defects."[74] The historical legacy of racial otherness amalgamates all racialized groups in America, even though racial meanings are disputed both within and between groups. In the end, the process of racial othering, prevailing in every facet of communal existence, takes its toll on nonwhites and on American society as a whole.

Given that blacks and other nonwhites lack the properties granted through white identity, they have a peculiar existence. They are trapped in a janus-faced identity, "two souls, two thoughts, two unreconciled striving, two warring ideals in one dark body"[75] as W. E. B. Du Bois describes in *The Souls of Black Folk*; or, as Fanon puts it, "two frames of reference,"[76] one individual, one racial; having an existence that is maintained by its lack of whiteness and by being the illustration of what whiteness is not. A master for understanding this peculiar inkling that nonwhites experience is Fanon's *Black Skin, White Masks*. In this formulation, *black skin* represents the oppression that nonwhites endure because of the hermeneutics of racial inferiority; and the *white mask* compensates for their alleged inferiority by becoming the screen separating the white self from the nonwhite "other." Given that the racialized body is the medium through which the significance of race unfolds and plays out, the truth is that nonwhites cannot escape America's practice of, what Diana Fuss labels "physical identity formation."[77] Consequently, nonwhites are forever confronted by a "peculiar sensation," as W. E. B. Du Bois names it, a symptom of the double consciousness, "an absence of true self-consciousness,"[78] permitting a nonwhite person to see himself or herself "through the revelation of the other world,"[79] defined by whiteness, and, as a consequent, "always looking at one's self through the eyes of others."[80] "Not only must" a nonwhite person be nonwhite but he or she must be nonwhite in relations to whites.[81]

The absolute exteriority, the very alterity of nonwhiteness unsettles whiteness. Fanon makes elaborate use of the association of blackness with fear. The white child pointing to a black person cries out, "Look a Negro . . . mama, see the Negro! I'm frightened."[82] The failure of non-whites to live the options offer by whiteness—"turn white or disappear"[83] becomes paramount. Differences, stemming from race, for example, will not be alleviated any time soon. I suppose, this was what Stuart Hall had in mind when he asserted that the ability "to live" with the constitutive character of difference, even though difference is an imperialist ideology[84] "is the coming question of the twenty first century."[85] Race, then, becomes the central signifier shaping nonwhiteness as an alterity fixed in its difference—gender, sexual, class, age, religious, ethnicity, and physical and mental abilities. To put it differently, it is the imagery of race that is salient because "race in itself—in so far as it is anything in itself—refers to some intrinsically insignificant geographical/ physical differences between people,"[86] which is regrettable and, as such, propels and motivates us to be "against race."[87] In fact, it is partly for this reason that Anthony Appiah hopes that race "was sunk without a trace"[88] because not anything handed down from the past could continue to keep race alive if we did not continually reformulate and reritualize it to fit our own terrain. If races live on today, it can do so only because we persist on creating and recreating it in our everyday life, keep on validating it, and accordingly continue to need a concept that will permit us to make sense, not of what our ancestors did then, but of what we choose to do at the present.[89]

We cannot deny that race in the United States, as a sociohistorical or cultural practice that defines social experience, cannot be avoided. Even though Paul Gilroy in *Between Campo: Nations, Culture, and the Allure of Race*, is hopeful that we move beyond race—which does not mean the disappearance of race—and collapse all forms of differences, stemming from racialization, in order to construct new possibilities, (such as a collective space that encourages a form of hybridity and constitutes a multifaceted and complex subject), the difficulty remains how to proceed in the face of normalized whiteness as an ongoing process. Yet within the framework of normalized whiteness, the concept of "the liminality of whiteness" has suggested that not all whites experience whiteness in the same manner. Scholars have pointed to the internal hierarchy of whiteness and concluded that not all whites are "equally" white.[90] In fact, as we will see later, when whiteness is both unmarked and othered, it appears as impracticable to deconstruct. Hence, its normality is upheld. It is to "the liminality of whiteness" that I now turn.

THE LIMINALITY OF WHITENESS

As a part of the distinctive hermeneutics of whiteness, many whiteness studies scholars have demonstrated that there is a social distinction among whites. Even though all whites have the same white skin, incorporation, adaptation, and enhancement into the "white club" are not guaranteed for all whites. Whites who are poor may experience deprivation, stigmatization, and subjugation, which interlock to define their status as dissimilar to upper-class whites. Neil Foley, in *The White Scourge: Mexicans, Blacks, and Poor Whites in Texas Cotton Culture,* explains how being a poor white person reduces the benefits of being white. He points to "the ways in which 'whiteness' itself fissured along race and class."[91] Given that whiteness, for Foley, "also comes increasingly to mean a particular kind of white person,"[92] the prefatory observation is that "not all whites, in other words, [are] equally white."[93] Poor whites, because of their status as lower class, occupy the space of otherness. They are the poor "white trash," experiencing, as Brannon Costello's describes, "something other than privilege and social power,"[94] the "otherness" of "whiteness within," the liminality of whiteness. The poor "white trash," by allowing the reconfiguration of white privilege into an intricate distinctiveness of underprivileged based on class orientation, undercuts the notion of a hegemonic, self-sufficient white identity and presents what Matthew F. Jacobson describes as "the full complexities of whiteness in its vicissitudes."[95] The poor "white trash," "[is] not quite white," but is in the process of "becoming white," that is, to borrow from Richard Dyer, "the natural, inevitable, ordinary way of being human."[96]

Granted, nonwhites are raced; whites are simply human. Nonwhites, on the other hand, "overdetermined from without," as Fanon explains it, are "slave not of the 'idea' that others have of [them] but of [their] own appearance" as raced bodies.[97] By assigning race to whites, the cultural production of whiteness and its dominance functions, to use the words of Audre Lorde, as a "mythical norm."[98] Race is, for the most part, associated with nonwhiteness, and whiteness, for the most part, as "whiteness studies" postulates, remains an unmentioned racial identity unless it juxtaposes itself against racialized ethnicities.[99] Barbara J. Fields's clearheaded conclusion according to which race is associated with identity declares that "whiteness seems to banish the troubling asymmetry that is the essence of racism"[100] is without any doubt fundamental. In America, racism, as an obligatory and dependable assignment of race, which operates homogonously is emaciated into racial identity of which whites are not assigned.[101] In the absence of racism, racial distinctiveness is devoid of meaning.[102] In this sense, it is not the presence of purposeful physical differences that create race as a concept, but the social responses of such differences as socially significant,[103] which, to a large extent, depends on what Michael Omi and Howard Winant term "racial formation" as "the sociohistorical process by which racial categories are created, inhabited, transformed, and destroyed,"[104] and its ongoing dynamics. In this sense, then, race must be viewed as an organizing principle of social relations that shape nonwhites' identity at all levels of their lives, and depends on a larger process, which is racialization. To define racism as ideological without taking into account the structural dynamic of power and how it works is to limit its orientation is detrimental. Taking from Judge Potter Stewart on his definition of *obscenity* in terms of pornography, in the case *Jacobellis v. Ohio*, "I know it when I see it," the same can be said of racism, "we" know it when "we" "see" it. And, as John Berger reminds us, "seeing comes before words." However, "the relations between what we see and what we know is never settled."[105] Racism is never a finished and settled process.

Earlier, I pointed to the dangers of substituting race for racism. While proven this substituting as being unhelpful, one of the greatest concerns is the preeminence of racial antagonism in America. In spite of very particularistic terms such as colorblindness and post-racial, which are now part of the discourse adopted in the media and scholarly works to defend the indefensible argument according to which America has moved beyond race (post-racial), a thoughtful work that has made this argument a non sequitur is professor Cornel West's work, *Race Matters*. Race "matters so much," West tells us, "that it has become almost impossible for one to think outside of 'racial' categories"[106] and decontextualize or a-historicize the formation of race and racial thinking in the United States. The essential point, here, is that the power of race thinking has continued to be one of the most crippling forces in America's race relations, and the absurdity of denying that racism still exists is beyond comprehension. Examples of such denials are embedded in familiar statements such as: "I have nothing against Mexicans, but . . . " "Some of my best friends are black, but   " It is regrettable that these types of discourses and conversational practices maintain and reproduce the cultural hegemony of racism that advertently authorizes these kinds of discourses.

In the United States, access to authorized whiteness was regulated through the color line to conceal whites from the presence of nonwhites. Abraham Lincoln, in 1862, in a meeting with Negroes at the White House, voiced his feeling about the need to separate blacks and other nonwhites from whites. As is cited by Marvin D. Jones, Lincoln claimed: "You and we are different races . . . This physical difference is a great disadvantage to us both, as I think your race suffer very greatly, many of them by living among us, while ours suffer from your presence."[107] Following in Lincoln's lead, to cure whites from the presence of blacks and other nonwhites, Thomas Jefferson proposed a form of "ethnic cleansing" and suggested that blacks, for example, should be shipped to an "all black country."[108] Indian Reservations, black ghettoes, and China-towns, for example, were created partly to confine nonwhites with their respective races and, more importantly, to make them socially invisible. These racialized communities function as a liminal space where nonwhiteness can be articulated and unremittingly performed.

Matt Wray, *Not Quite White: White Trash and the Boundaries of White-ness*, is an important point of entry in understanding how the poor whites, or what he terms "white trash," are a direct threat to the "symbolic and social order" of authorized whiteness. Given that it is primarily how whites experience their whiteness,[109] a "white trash" is looked on as an object "of contempt for transgressing a racial order that [is] rapidly losing its semblance of naturalness."[110] In fact, the term "white trash" illustrates the "clash and swirl of these two words."[111] White and trash, occupying the interstices between the "self" and the "other" and coexisting to inform the liminality of whiteness is not without implications. "White trash," according to Matt Wray, "reveals itself as an expression of fundamental tensions and deep structural antinomies: Between the sacred and the profane, purity and impurity, morality and immorality, cleanliness and dirt . . . white trash names a kind of disturbing liminality,"[112] which is best illustrated in 1964 when Dr. Martin Luther King warns that America "should also be rescuing a large stratum of the forgotten white poor."[113] In the end, white provides for the differentiation of people that liminal whiteness targets from other type of "trash" who are completely understood to be nonwhites.

Because of gender configuration in society, where women are situated differently from men, are white women, then, in a liminal position because they are separated from white men? Are white lesbians and gays liminal whites? White lesbians and gays do experience the stigma of oppression even though they appear to be part of the very whiteness that oppresses them. Notwithstanding the perniciousness of celebrated homosexuality in a homophobic society, white lesbians occupy an infinitely more precarious subject position than that of white homosexual men. In *The Second Sex*, Simone de Beauvoir reminds us that "a man never begins by presenting himself as an individual of a certain sex. It goes without saying that he is a man."[114] The self-evident truth of maleness explains that white homosexual men may feel resentful. To put it differently, given that patriarchy's tendency overdetermines the privilege and entitlements bestow on white men, white gay men, for the most part, expect to be protected and privileged because of their gender inscription as male. Without warning, the inaptness of their sexuality puts them in tangible danger. The more pressing question, then, is whether whiteness as a signifier can be resignified because of its liminality? What does liminality of whiteness say about nonwhiteness? In terms of racial discrimination, poor whites or white homosexuals are still better off than nonwhites because they do not experience racial discrimination.[115] Nonwhites cannot escape from their racialized bodies, which structure their daily experiences. They are, for the most part, situated on the fringe of a white power structure, making it hard for them to free themselves from such constrictions. As a matter of fact, to be a poor white person does not mean that he or she is positioned in a space of "post-whiteness,"[116] which is unlike a panoptical space that is relentlessly monitored, surveiled, and policed that nonwhiteness triggers.

While the liminality of whiteness masquerades white skin privilege, it is a position of avoidance and comes from the pressure to conform to "cultural whitening," the way one is socialized and constructed to understand oneself as white. However, cultural whitening, to a great degree, does not stand apart from the exterior inscription of white skin. For whites, an identity marker such as class, in this case, is masked behind the white skin. A poor white person, then, must learn the attitudes and behaviors that are tied to whiteness as a fundamental defining signifier of white superiority and a white identity. Eric Arnesen rightfully draws our attention to the synchronizing of whiteness and panoptic power. He writes: "Whiteness is, variously, a metaphor for power, a proxy for racially distributed material benefits, a synonym for 'white supremacy,' an epistemological stance defined by power, a position of invisibility or ignorance, and a set of beliefs about racial 'Others,' and oneself that can be rejected through 'treason' to a racial category."[117] And poor whites, "with nothing but whiteness," are more than willing to hold on to their "property rights in whiteness."[118] Whiteness, visually inscribed upon the body, confers upon all whites a collective sense of entitlement and authority over blacks and other nonwhites. This entitlement is a part of the Foucauldian disciplinary power embedded within the dualistic division "between the normal and abnormal,"[119] the insider and outsider, functioning on a particularistic principle of white privilege.[120] White privilege purposely or involuntarily benefits all whites. For this reason, we cannot put on an equal footing the hierarchy among whites and the racist structure that separates whites and nonwhites.

Unlike blacks and other nonwhites whose class position is always assumed as inferior to their white counterparts, poor whites can avoid social stigmatization by shifting their social and cultural *habitus* and pass for middle-class whites. Race, as physically marked, makes such liminality impossible. For the most part, race gets configured and reconfigured as a powerful stratifying practice in the United States of America. In the end, the liminality of whiteness only serves to produce a new kind of white identity that is consistent with the logic of colorblindness and fails to engage with the problematics of whiteness as a form of property that guarantees aesthetic and psychological rewards to whites. To sum it up, all whites do not need to inhabit the same class and social position to reap the advantages that accompany white privilege. This simple fact brings us to the way in which the poor "white trash" is conceptualized in purely economic term, when class, in this sense, is not simply about economics but encompasses a materiality that is psychologically and culturally determined to position poor whites above nonwhites. Steph Lawlor, a feminist ethnographer, gets to the heart of the issue when she writes: "The inequalities of a class society do not end with economics: indeed, economic may not necessarily be the most meaningful way to talk about class." [121] Given that America's class system is distinctively racialized, in that, blacks and other nonwhites' class position is often assumed as lower class, whiteness is largely what fashions and molds the class that an individual occupies in the United States. It is precisely for this reason that that there is a dire need for a reconceptualization of the study of class that will bear in mind the many ways in which whiteness operates to create class consciousness. [122]

THE CRISIS OF WHITENESS

Whiteness, as a concept, is assumed to be in some kind of "crisis." Claus Offe understands the crisis as "a process in which the structure of the system is called into question." [123] Charles Gallagher, in "White Racial Formation: Into the Twenty-First Century," also suggests that "a fundamental transformation" of whiteness is in the works. In a study that he conducted with university students, he noted that the bulk of white students "have come to understand themselves and their interests as white," and have demonstrated that whiteness is in some kind of crisis. [124] This assumed crisis of whiteness has, in part, summoned the desire to protect whiteness against forces such as *multiculturalism* and *diversity* that are imagined as threats to America's cultural homogeneity. America's cultural homogeneity, I have argued elsewhere, is based on whiteness. [125] Given its ideological significance, whiteness "functions in such a way that it 'recruits' subjects among individuals (it recruits them all) or transforms the individual into subjects." [126]

Indeed, in America, the overt celebration of a "white identity" is widely construed as a part of the political discourse, which, more recently, is associated with the Tea Party movement. It emerged in 2009 and comprises mostly politically sophisticated, well-educated white, middle class Republicans. [127] And, even though many of these conventional whites are indignant by what they see as "reverse racism," there are other seemingly threats to whiteness. For example, an African American was elected president of the United States in 2009; a Latina woman was inaugurated as a Supreme Court judge in 2009; and an Asian American woman, Elaine L. Chao, was selected as the president and chief executive officer of United Way of America in 1992 (a position that had belonged to white men since its formation in 1887). The confirmation of African American, Clarence Thomas, as the Supreme Court Justice in 1991 contributed also to the idea of a crisis that threatened whiteness's pride of place. [128] However, if we understand how power works, as Trinh T. Min-ha understands it, power "has to be shared . . . so that its effects may continue to circulate; but it will be shared only partly, with much cautions, and on the condition that the share is *given*, not taken." [129] In other words, concessions, in the form of visible representation of individuals from marginalized groups into high profile positions is fundamental for keeping the power structure in place. This is what Professor Louis F. Mirón calls the "moral exercise of power."[130] Even though whites, especially men (because, in their minds, affirmative action and quotas prevent white males to continue gaining and holding on to positions of power), still disproportionally inhabit these positions. On the other hand, because of affirmative action, employers, for example, have to take seriously applicants for positions based on qualifications other than whiteness and maleness. As I have shown in chapter 3, we can see the tremendously anxiety that this is causing white men to assert their supremacy.

Gallagher, in "White Racial Formation" draws our attention to the identity crisis facing white students by such remarks: "blacks can point to the middle passage and slavery; Japanese and Chinese can speak of internment and forced labor, respectively." However, whiteness, as an identity, has not "any real social or political import."[131] Is whiteness at present a cultural liability? Henri Giroux, the cultural critic, reaches the following conclusion that a white identity "leaves youths no critical lens, vocabulary, or social imaginary through which they can see themselves as creating oppositional space to fight for equality and justice."[132] As a result, some white youths are adopting an aesthetic practice of black self-empowerment, including dress, hairstyle, and music, which give whiteness some kind of meaning by appropriating signs that are considered "black"?[133] In fact, it is "hip" for whites, nowadays, especially in urban environment, to "act black," or perform "blackness." "Blackness" is equated with a certain kind of racial particularly that make blacks "authentically blacks" (for example, there is a "black way" of singing and dancing), and "this putative authenticity screams out for recognition."[134] Ultimately, "blackness" becomes a form for the "commodification of otherness."[135] It serves as a form of social control that reproduces whiteness as absolute and intact.

These white youths are examples of "wiggers," a pejorative slang that is used to describe white kids reflecting stereotypes of African Americans. Are these white kids another example of the "white Negro" who Norman Mailer describes in his celebratory essay, "The White Negro: Superficial Reflections on the Hipster?" Mailer defines the "white Negro," as a form of racial mimicry of black culture,[136] especially in Hip-Hop cultures, which stands for the new discrete variation of African American culture.[137] Indeed, as the cultural critic Kobena Mercer has indicated, the "white Negro" is like a "photographic negative, . . . an inverted image of otherness, in which attributes devalorised by the dominant culture [are] simply revalorised or hypervalorised as emblems of alienation and otherness, a kind of strategic self-othering in relation to the dominant cultural norms."[138] What ambivalence arises when white subject appropriates signs from the other side of the "morphological equation"? In fact, the white Negro "encodes an antagonistic subject position on the part of the white subject in relation to the normative codes of [whiteness]."[139] However, race still confers on the white Negro bona fide privileges; their marginality is different because it is based on a conscious choice and is not forced on them by a racist society.[140] This form of "race trading" is temporary and should not be taken at face value merely whiteness cannot be transcended because of "race trading." In the end, whiteness continues to remain unmarked and invisible.

"Whiteness studies" makes that which is unseen visible.[141] Visibility is not what the African American philosopher Arnold Farr terms "racialized consciousness," which is seemingly shaped by "racist social structures"[142] and is therefore likely to "perpetuate a form of racism unintentionally."[143] It draws instead on how being white is a guarantor for impeccable privileges given to white people. Can "whiteness studies" reconfigures whiteness as a tool for promoting antiracist, antisexist, anticlassist, and antihomophobic projects? Can it move away from the hegemonic discourse operating within relations of power that is the architect of a particular kind of knowledge that is reliant, context-bound, and historically precise? Michel Foucault and, following his footsteps, Judith Butler's configuration of power allows us to understand that whiteness studies scholars cannot be outside the milieu of power. Given that power frames the subject as well as provides "the very condition on its existence and the trajectory of its desires,"[144] power, in a real sense, is what whiteness depends on for its every day preservation and continuation. Any opposition on the part of whiteness studies scholars to power is in itself a cherished part of that power.

THE ESTABLISHMENT OF "WHITENESS STUDIES" IN AMERICA

In the 1990s, the concept of whiteness emerged as a category of analysis in literary criticism and cultural studies.[145] Since then, as I have mentioned earlier, in many other disciplines as diverse as history, gender studies, political science, film studies, media studies, humor studies, linguistics, art history, rhetoric and communication, material culture, and dance scholars, focusing on whiteness as a concept for analysis, have been lumped together under the opportune label of "whiteness studies."[146] There is an exponential growing body of influential, academic literature that focuses on whiteness in powerful ways.[147] The need to examine whiteness, to promote critical analysis of race and racial meanings in the United States is viewed as essential. Roediger, whose work on whiteness is essential, explicates that "whiteness studies" is neither new nor a "white thing."[148] As we have seen, African Americans, from W. E. B. Du Bois to Toni Morrison, have been influential in locating whiteness presumptive hegemony even before the existence of the second wave of "whiteness studies." Du Bois saw the "public and psycho-logical wage," or "the wages of whiteness," as operating to bar any form of class solidarity between poor whites and nonwhites; and Morrison's *Playing in the Dark: Whiteness and the Literary Imagination* drew our atten-tion to the normalization of whiteness in American literature.[149] Also, authors writing from other racialized positions have focused on white-ness.[150] In other words, the second wave of "whiteness studies" is not new in naming whiteness, "as an essential something,"[151] and in engag-ing "in a process of redefinition, reclassifying and dedifferentiating that which always and already exists."[152] Consequently, it "has been forced into rearticulations, rerepresentations, reinterpretations of the meaning of race, and perforce, of whiteness."[153] It is partly for this reason that "whiteness studies" can be looked on, to borrow from the anthropologist James Snead, as a "cultural contagion. Contagion (being con plus tangere equals 'touching together'), involves an actual process of contact between people, rather than a qualitative of metaphoric value."[154] Since "white-ness studies" is a contagion that "seems to have already made absolute the barriers of its own spread,"[155] it gives the impression that it has decreased in popularity in academic institutions. Roediger, for one, flogs "whiteness studies," in the United States, for not producing any journals, professional associations, book series or a program call critical whiteness studies in American universities.[156] In the same vein, Vron Ware and Les Back claim that "there is no unity of purpose binding this field togeth-er"[157] and "yet, despite its modest proportions, it is at times castigated as if it sits atop the academic food chain, begging to be brought down to size."[158] In addition, the labor historian Eric Arneson, in "A Paler Shade of White," asserts that "after a decade of growing popularity, whiteness studies . . . remains a vague and intellectually incoherent enterprise."[159] Last but not least, the widely read *New York Times Magazine* depicts "whiteness studies" as the most recent academic craze.[160] Nonetheless, whiteness has continued its unparalleled trajectory or fate as unmarked. Specific ways of how whiteness can be denormalized and stripped of its presumptive hegemony is discussed in chapter five.

Whiteness, being at the center of American institutions and systems, must be interrogated in order to resolve the issue of white privilege to which it gives attention. In order to gain new perspectives, "whiteness studies" would need to reposition itself within the field of research on white privilege in such a way that enables the racial subjugation of non-whites to be acknowledged.[161] Most whites remain naively clueless as to how nonwhites experience the effects of whiteness in their daily lives. In April 1997, "The Making and Unmaking of Whiteness" conference at the University of California, Berkeley participated in an (overdue) effort of "examining and naming the terrain of whiteness."[162] In the same year, *The Minnesota Review* published a special issue on whiteness. On August 12–16, 2000, at the Annual Meeting of the American Sociological Association in Washington, DC, a section was devoted to "the current status of whiteness." Many books and articles on "whiteness studies" have been published since then, such as, Aileen Moreton-Robinson, "Writing off Treaties: White Possession in the United States Critical Whiteness Studies Literature" (2008); Steve Garner, *Whiteness: An Introduction* (2007); John Tehranian, *Whitewashed: America's Invisible Middle Eastern Minority* (2008); Matt Wray, *Not Quite White: White Trash and the Boundaries of Whiteness* (2006); Birgit Brander Rasmussen et al. eds., *The Making and Unmaking of Whiteness* (2001); and David R. Roediger, *The Wages of Whiteness: Race and the Making of the American Working Class* (1991).

RETHINKING WHITENESS STUDIES

On the basis that whiteness studies scholars are able to put into practice whiteness as a lived experience, Hooks writes:

> Many white folks active in antiracist struggle today are able to ac- knowledge that all whites (as well as everyone else within white su- premacist culture) have learned to over-value "whiteness" even as they simultaneously learn to devalue [nonwhiteness]. They understand the need, at least intellectually, to alter their thinking. Central to the pro- cess of unlearning white supremacist attitudes and values is the decon- struction of the category "whiteness."[163]

Hooks' remark begs the question: Does the deconstruction of whiteness advance an essentialist approach to race? If the answer is yes, as I suspect it is, then "whiteness studies," in and of itself, relies on essentialist ideas about race.

"Whiteness studies" literature, with few exceptions,[164] has been in- clined to defend an "uncritical, a-historical, common-sense, perspective on the meaning of whiteness."[165] Whiteness in terms of how whites live their lives and "think of themselves, of power, and of pleasures,"[166] as Eric Arnesen puts it, "has become hip."[167] More recently, there has been a will to reorient whiteness as an attempt to "reconceptualize whiteness as a flexible set of social and symbolic boundaries that give shape, meaning, and power to the social category white."[168] Hence, a lot of emphasis has been placed by many whiteness studies scholars on groups, including Irish, Jews, and white immigrants, whose claims to whiteness had been similarly contested.[169] Also, the undisputable presence of hybridity, which stands as an impure and inauthentic identity has been interpreted by some scholars as potentially undermining whiteness.[170]

Implicit in "whiteness studies" is the commitment of whiteness schol- ars to racial justice, antiracist projects, and a more humane society. In- deed, these commitments would restore a more positive view of white- ness in nonwhites' imagination. However, are these commitments about making antiracists feel good because now, "these progressive whites," to use Ruth Frankenberg's phrase, can be provided with a genealogy. In fact, if whiteness it not located within the paradigmatic framework of structural racism, for example, "this leaves progressive whites apparently without any genealogy."[171] In this sense, the role of "whiteness studies" to provide *only* "progressive whites" with such a genealogy makes "whiteness studies," not about decentering the white subject but about recentering the white subject. Hence, the burden of racism — racial profiling, police brutality, poor housing, minimal achievements, poverty, racial harassment — are projected on the nonprogressive whites. Lately, racism has been conceived as a form of ignorance and lack of exposure to nonwhite people. This is like concluding that the violence perpetrated toward women, for example, is conducted by primitive, uncivilized, and backward men.

Whiteness and its primary trajectories can be traced either "as an agent in the history of class struggle"[172] or "as an individual and diverse 'lived experience.'"[173] Frankenberg suggests that "naming whiteness and white people helps dislodge the claims of both to rightful dominance."[174] In this sense, naming whiteness reminds us only too clearly that is not exactly from the voices of the marginalized; it is from the pinnacle of whiteness. Naming of whiteness is primarily for the "other" and outside of the self.[175] It is from voices coming from the high point of whiteness, the norm that always authorizes the powerful to speak for the powerless silenced "other."[176] Since "whiteness studies" engenders and privileges the effects of that naming, would the renaming of whiteness work? It is Frankenberg's hope, nonetheless, that "by examining and naming the terrain of whiteness, it may . . . be possible to generate or work toward antiracist forms of whiteness, or at least towards antiracist strategies for reworking the terrain of whiteness."[177] Even though George Lipsitz suggests that an antiracist white person is hopeless in holding fast to Frankenberg's vision,[178] Roediger holds fast to Frankenberg's expectation by repositioning the class struggle as an antiracist project. His historical account of white racial formation describes, with allurement, the political outlook of "whiteness studies" by imagining for whites a political identity outside the equation of power and privilege associated with white skin.[179]

Indeed, if "whiteness studies" remains disconnected from antiracist practice, it will likely generate scholarships that are unconnected from any thought of its political implications.[180] Antiracism is not the nonappearance of racism; it is a commitment to the liberal notion of equality and justice for all citizens of a democratic polity. Even though the narrative of self that characterizes the foundational level of memoir is thus relentlessly undermined by the site of the lived experiences expressed in such texts, Jane Lazarre's formation of *Beyond the Whiteness of Whiteness: Memoir of a White Mother of Black Sons* helps us to think how memoir and "white studies" can amalgamate in ways that are definitely antiracist and responsive to many ways in which structures of race shape and inform our personal relations and daily experiences.[181] How can whites confront race privilege and achieve the conditions of creating a nonracist space within a racist space? Can antiracists reconstitute themselves as symbolically nonwhite, disempowered and marginalized? Does this kind of reconstituting create a space for overcoming whiteness notwithstanding its alleged nature of being, its metaphysical status? These questions are taken up in chapter five. Given the history of whiteness, "whiteness studies" would have to become an antiracist project aimed at, as Peter McLaren puts it, "emptying the armory of binary logic"[182] and, at the same time, provide a space that can serve as a facilitator for whiteness to shed its presumptive hegemony. It is only then that cultural norms that maintain whiteness despotic position can be challenged. In other words, whiteness "as the natural, ordinary, inevitable way of being human,"[183] has to be discarded.

Some whiteness scholars wish to triumph over white privilege by abolishing whiteness all together.[184] It is a desirable goal but an impracticable one because without changing the very structure of power, it is impossible for whites to transcend their whiteness and, therefore, give up the privileges that come with it. The deconstruction of whiteness is a good starting point in order to put forward a critique of whiteness. However, as we see in chapter five, in order for us to reinscribe an alternative form of whiteness, one of the essential objectives would be first to denormalize whiteness. In other words, whiteness can no longer "be taken as the ubiquitous paradigm, simultaneously center and boundary."[185] Thinking about whiteness as no longer unmarked and as escaping centrality is itself impossible. Whiteness continues to be a structural position maintaining white privilege. On this basis, Ian F. Haney López, in *White by Law: The Legal Construction of Race*, helps us to understand that whites are increasingly more mindful of their whiteness.[186] Since "whiteness studies" does not free whiteness from its presumptive hegemony, the task at hand remains how to denormalize whiteness. A denormalized whiteness is primordial if we are to move beyond whiteness in an effort to construct a post-white identity.

The Marxist pronouncement to change the world is not simply to understand it, gets to the heart of "whiteness studies" as an effective critique of whiteness. By way of a detour, Monique Wittig's summation about women "abstracting themselves from the definition of women, which is imposed upon them," the same can be said of whites, "abstracting themselves from the definition" of whiteness and white privilege. Like blacks, for example, who are seen as blacks, whites are seen as white because they are whites; they are constituted that way.[187] In the end, Michel Foucault's crucial insight about power, which will "categorize the individual, mark him by his own individuality, attach him to his own identity, impose a law of truth on him which he must recognize and which others have to recognize in him,"[188] is at the heart of "abstracting" from white privilege. Is this "abstracting procedure" enough? In the presence of normalized whiteness, it is impossible for whites not to benefit from white privilege. White privilege coupled with entitlement has become the hallmark of most whites' expectations and, as a consequence, many of them believe that they are entitled to jobs and promotions. It is only when whiteness is denormalized that whites can feel less entitled and anxious. How to begin the process of denormalizing whiteness is examined in chapter five.

NOTES

1. This inquisition into whiteness was already explored in 1860, when William J. Wilson asked in his essay "What Shall We Do with the White People?" (1999).

2. hooks (1992), 166. W. E. B. Du Bois in *Black Reconstruction in America, 1860–1890* (1935), draws our attention to the "psychological wage" of whiteness. Other scholars who wrote about the terrifying nature of whiteness include Ida B. Wells-Barnett, *Southern Horrors Lynch Laws in All Its Phases* (1892) and *The Red Record: Tabulated Statistics and Alleged Causes of Lynching in the United States* (1895); W. E. B. Du Bois, *The Soul of Black Folks* (2003); Richard Wright, *Black Boy* (1935); James Baldwin, *The Price of the Ticket* (1995); Ralph Ellison, "Change the Joke and Slip the Joke" (1958); and Stokely Carmichael and Charles V. Hamilton, *Black Power: The Politics of Liberation in America* (1967).

3. For other works on "whiteness studies," see the *Minnesota Review* (1996); Michele Fine et al., *Off White: Readings on Race, Power, and Society* (1997); Henry Louis Gates and Anthony Appiah, *The White Issue: A Special Issue of Transition* (1998).

4. Frankenberg (1997): 1. Although "whiteness may be a new subject of study," there is a tradition of anthropological research that is relevant to its examination." See John Hartigan Jr., "Establishing the Fact of Whiteness" (1999), 193.

5. Twine and Gallagher (2008), 6.

6. Bonnett (1996), 147.

7. Hill (2004), 16.

8. See Ruth Frankenberg, *White Women, Race Matters: The Social Construction of Whiteness* (1993); Richard Dyer, *White* (1997).

9. Keating (1995), 905.

10. McGary (1999), 83.

11. If we turn our attention to Marxist thought in terms of the ruling class and the working class, or in Paulo Freire's conceptualization, in *Pedagogy of the Oppressed*, in which he focuses on the oppressor and the oppressed, it is the latter, according to Marx and Freire, that is equipped with a clear and legitimate insight into the operation and workings of the social order. In other words, oppression has gifted the oppressed with a "second sight," as W. E. B. Du Bois puts in *The Souls of Black Folk*. A good example is the ability of blacks and other nonwhites to see whiteness without being observed. See bell hooks, "Representing Whiteness in the Black Imagination," in *Black Looks: Race and Representation* (1992). On the one hand, the dominant group is rarely in touch with certain realities of their social situation.

12. See Homi Bhabha, "What Does the Black Man Want?" (1987), 119.

13. Du Bois (1969), 29. This embarrassment is transferred into an anxiety and, as Du Bois recognizes, it makes whites furious. Bell hooks' *Black Looks: Race and Representation*, tells us of how surprised her students were to learn that blacks and other non-

whites critically evaluate whites. For hooks, her students' amazement that the gaze of nonwhites is directed toward whites "is an expression of racism." (1992), 167.

14. McIntyre (1997), 31.

15. Ahmed (2004).

16. Fine et al. (1997), 9.

17. Roediger (2002), 15.

18. Ahmed (2004).

19. For Michel Foucault, in *The History of Sexuality: An Introduction*, confession is a form of disciplinary practice. He Writes: "When one confesses one goes about telling, with the greatest precision, whatever it is most difficult to tell" (1981), 59. In addition, he suggests that confession promotes "a different kind of pleasure, the pleasure of knowing that truth, of discovering and exposing it, the fascination of seeing and telling it, of captivating and capturing others by it" (71). However, in terms of confessing whiteness, I am afraid that this confession is leading in the direction of recentering instead of decentering whiteness. For a matrix of similar concerns about whiteness, see Alastair Bonnett, "From the Crisis of Whiteness to Western Supremacy" (2005); Sara Ahmed, "Declaration of Whiteness: The Non-Performativity of Antiracism" (2004); Robyn Wiegman, "Witnessing Whiteness: Articulating Race and the "Politics of Style" (2004); and Linda Martín Alcoff, "What Should White People Do?" (1998).

20. Alcoff (1998), 8.

21. Ahmed (2004).

22. Seshadri-Crooks (1998), 358.

23. Morrison (1993), 5.

24. Costello (2004), 208.

25. Seshadri-Crooks (1998), 358.

26. Frankenberg (1996), 4. Rebecca Aanerud points to the need for white children to "perform their whiteness differently." She draws our attention to "white antiracist mothering" by taking from Sara Ruddick's conceptualization of "maternal thinking" and Patricia Hill Collins concept of "mother work." See Aanerud, "The Legacy of White Supremacy and the Challenge of White Antiracist Mothering" (2007).

27. For a list of these unearned privileges accruing to white, see Peggy McIntosh, "White Privilege: Unpacking the Invisible Knapsack" (2007); and Ruth Frankenberg, *White Women, Race Matters: The Social Construction of Whiteness* (1993).

28. Terdiman (1989), 27.

29. Schwartz and Heinrich (2004), 116.

30. Gallagher (1997), 10.

31. Bhabha (1987), 123.

32. Lorde (1984), 36.

33. Fine et al. (1997), 9.

34. Frankenberg (1997), 1.

35. Dyer (1997), 10.

36. Dyer (1997), 10.

37. See George Yancy, *What White Looks Like: African-American Philosophers on the Whiteness Questions* (2004b); and Charles W. Mills, *Blackness Visible: Essays on Philosophy and Race* (1998).

38. Wiegman (2004).

39. Durkheim (1964), 13.

40. Spivak (1995), 4.

41. Dyer (1997), 2.

42. Foucault (1980), 142.

43. Foucault (1977), 199.

44. Butler (1997b), 2.

45. Revel (2009), 51.

46. Brodkin (2004).

47. Gallagher (1997).

48. Michael Omi speaks to this anxiety. See "Racialization in the Post-Civil Rights Era" (1996); Karyn D. McKinney, "I Fell 'Whiteness' When I Hear People Blaming Whites: Whiteness as Cultural Victimization" (2003); Michele Fine, "Witnessing Whiteness" (1997).

49. See Michael Omi, "Racialization in the Post-Civil Rights Era" (1996); and Charles Gallagher, "White Racial Formation: Into the Twenty-First Century" (1997).

50. Spivak (1991), 172.

51. See Damien Riggs, "We Don't Talk about Race Anymore: Power, Privilege and Critical Whiteness Studies" (2004).

52. Seshadri-Crooks (1998), 353.

53. Fields (2001), 49. Also, see Scott L. Malcomson, *One Drop of Blood: The American Misadventure of Race*, where he points out that from the beginning in America, "the people, who, by general consensus, had races . . . were nonwhites" (2000).

54. Bonnett (1996), 147.

55. Ahmed (2007), 154.

56. Fields (2001), 49.

57. Also, see W. E. B. Du Bois, *The Souls of Black Folk* (2003); Rebecca Aanerud, "Fictions of Whiteness: Speaking the Name of Whiteness in U.S. Literature" (1997); Dana Nelson, *The World in Black and White: Reading "Race" in American Literature 1638–1882* (1994).

58. Cox (1948), 336.

59. Also, see Matthew F. Jacobson, *Whiteness of a Different Color: European Immigrants and the Alchemy of Race* (1998); Noel Ignatiev, *How the Irish Became White* (1995). Becoming white was contingent on sharing the benefits whites derived from racial exploitation. There are various forms of racial exploitation that First Nations, blacks, Chinese, and other racialized groups have experienced. See Charles W. Mills, "Racial Exploitation and the Wages of Whiteness" (2004), 44–45.

60. Roediger (1998), 336.

61. Dyson (1999), 220. Racist ideology was instrumental in Hitler and the Nazi's attempts at completely getting rid of Jews in Germany. See George M. Fredrickson, *Racism a Short History*, (2002), 5.

62. Lee, 179.

63. Lee, 179.

64. Ingram (2001), 157.

65. Many scholars have shown their outright contempt for multiculturalism. They have viewed it as a threat to America's cultural homogeneity that is based on whiteness. This is why Nathan Glazer can muse that "we are all multiculturalists now." See Samuel Huntington, *Who Are We? The Challenges to America's National Identity* (2004); Arthur M. Schlesinger Jr., *The Disuniting of America: Reflections on a Multicultural Society* (1998); Nathan Glazer, *We Are All Multiculturalists Now* (1997); Dinesh D'Souza, *Illiberal Education: The Politics of Race and Sex on Campus* (1991).

66. See Herbert Gans, "Deconstructing the Underclass" (2007).

67. Moon (1988), 29.

68. McIntyre (1997), 31.

69. Frankenberg (1993), 6.

70. In Paul Kivel, *Uprooted Racism*, Kivel was conducting a workshop on racism.

> A white, Christian woman stood up and said "I'm not really white because I'm not part of the white male power structure that perpetuates racism." Next a white gay man stood up and said, "you have to be straight to have the privilege of being white." A white, straight, working class man from a poor family then said, "I've got it just as hard as any person of color." Finally, a straight white middle class man said, "I'm not white, I'm Italian." My African-American co-worker turned to me and asked, "Where are all the white people that was just here a minute ago?" Of course I replied, "Don't ask me, I'm not white, I'm Jewish." (1995, 8)

71. Frankenberg (1993), 6.
72. Alcoff (1998), 17.
73. Goldberg (2009), 8.
74. Fanon (1967), 112.
75. Du Bois (2003), 5.
76. Fanon (1967), 110.
77. Fuss (1994), 22.
78. Owen (2007), 111.
79. Du Bois (2003), 5.
80. Du Bois (2003), 5.
81. Fanon (1967), 110.
82. Fanon (1967), 112.
83. Fanon (1967), 100.
84. See Edward W. Said, *Culture and Imperialism* (1993) and *Orientalism* (1978), in which he points out that central to the ideology of difference is the construction of the oppositional binary of the Orient and the Occident. The Occident, *in Culture and Imperialism*, has become, what Said labels as the "authority of the observer," which provides for a cultural discourse that is built around notions of difference, deeming European as superior and non-European as inferior. Frantz Fanon elaborates on this inferiority that the person of color feels, which is haunted by an unconscious desire to *feel* whiteness, to be white. He writes: "Out of the blackest part of my soul . . . surges this desire to be suddenly white . . . Who but a white woman can do this for me? By loving me she proves that I am worthy of white love. I am loved like a white man. I am a white man . . . I marry white culture, white beauty, white whiteness" (Fanon 1967, 63). Taking from Richard Dyer that "the idea of whites as both themselves dead as bringer of death" (1997, 210) the desire for whiteness, to use George Lipsitz's words, "the possessive investment in whiteness" (1998, 7) as a way of life, in many important ways, is the marked of death. Given that race is marked on the body, which is seen as epidermal aberration, cultural whitening, as a form of honorable whiteness, or borrowing the embellishments of whiteness, is not enough.
85. Hall (1993), 361. W. E. B. Du Bois, in *The Souls of Black Folks*, had predicted that the problem of twentieth century would be the problem of the color line. Is the color line still a problem? Turning my attention to Howard Winant's attempt, in *The New Politics of Race: Globalism, Difference*, to contemplate this question, he declares with confident that the color line "is certainty not," a problem at present (2004, 31). Indeed, if the color line is a metonym for the racial divide, the color line has not disappeared and instead has shown its ugly face in urban ghettoes and super ghettoes, the prison systems, and urban schools.
86. Dyer (1997), 1.
87. See Paul Gilroy, *Against Race: Imagining Political Culture Beyond the Color Line*. Gilroy draws our attention to the uniqueness of post-apartheid South Africa's race relation, which he describes as a transformation of race. For this reason, Gilroy is hopefully that if race can be transformed in South Africa, "the one place on earth where its salience for politics and government could not be denied, the one location where state-sponsored racial identities were openly and positively conducted into the core of a modern civic culture and social relations, then surely it could be changed anywhere" (2000a: 27). Inspired by Gilroy's provocative summation, I am tempted to ask the question: Is it race that is being transformed or whiteness, to some extent, that has undergone some challenges? I turn to Tony Simoes da Silva's "Redeeming Self: The Business of Whiteness in Post-Apartheid South African Writing," where he writes: "In South Africa, this disinvestment from Whiteness allows narrators to free themselves from its weight as signified within the rigid strictures of apartheid. Even on the odd occasions where it is assumed as the clear sign of privilege and power that it was, and remains, whiteness is interpellated in an uncannily self-cancelling act. I am White and ineradicably guilty; I need all the help and understanding I can get" (2008, 8–9). As I see it, South Africa has become an appropriate location for looking at the current

positioning of whiteness, which for sure is overwhelmingly inflected by race and racial implications.

88. Appiah (1985).

89. Fields (1990), 118.

90. Other terms that are used to describe the liminality of whiteness includes "consanguine whites"; "provisional and probationary whites"; "not-yet-white"; "off white"; "not bright white"; and "not quite white" (Arnesen 2001, 16).

91. Foley (1997), 5.

92. Foley (1997), 5.

93. Foley (1997), 5. Also see, Brannon Costello, "Poor White Trash, Great White Hope: Race, Class and the (De)Construction of Whiteness in Lewis Norton's *Wolfe Whistle*" (2004).

94. Costello (2004), 209.

95. Jacobson (1998), 18.

96. Dyer (1988), 44.

97. Fanon (1967), 116.

98. Lorde (1984), 116.

99. For good discussions of white racial identity, see Andrew Hacker's *Two Nations: Black and White, Separate, Hostile, Unequal* (2003); and David Roediger's *Towards the Abolition of Whiteness: Essays on Race, Politics, and Working Class History* (1994), and *The Wages of Whiteness: Race and the Making of the American Working Class* (1991).

100. Fields (2001), 49.

101. Laws, including the one-drop rule, were in place to determine legally whether one was black. In the nineteenth Century, in the South, there were many trails to determine a person's racial identity. In some instances, a person would go to court to claim his/her whiteness. The Abbey Guy's trial is illustrative.

102. See W. E. B. Du Bois, *The Souls of Black Folk* (2003). Du Bois' metaphoric construction of *the veil* as the representation of race relations in America, operating at a personal and institutional level of social interaction, fully demonstrates the theory of racism. Du Bois is doubtful that *the veil* would ever be lifted as is demonstrated proper in his masterwork *Black Reconstruction in American*. Also, on the theory of race and racism, see Cornel West, *Race* Matters (2001); Charles W. Mills, *The Racial Contract* (1997); Frantz Fanon, *Black Skin, White Masks* (1967).

103. Van de Berghe (1967), 11.

104. Omi and Winant (1994), 55.

105. Berger (1990), 7.

106. West (2001), 156.

107. Jones (1997), 82.

108. See Thomas Jefferson, "Notes on the State of Virginia" (1999).

109. Wray (2006), 2.

110. Hartigan (1999b), 28.

111. Morrison (1989), 123.

112. Wray (2006), 2.

113. King (1964), 138.

114. Beauvoir (1964), 15. For a good overview of "The Rights of Man," how men were treated, see the Declaration of Independence that was written by Thomas Jefferson. "We hold these truths to be self-evident that all men are created equal, that they are endowed with by their Creator with certain unalienable Rights, that among these are life, liberty and the pursuit of happiness." Given that the United States was portrayed as white, all men never meant nonwhite men; and equality never meant equal opportunities, treatment, and results for all men. *Plessy v. Ferguson* is a case in point. "The rights of man," as Toni Morrison explains, are "permanently allied with another seductive concept: the hierarchy of race" (1993, 38).

115. While racism was legally defined, racial discrimination was not legally defined. "The Failure to provide a legal definition of this term is at the core of the United States Supreme Court's conclusion over the implementation of Affirmative Action." Conse-

quently, programs designed to create opportunities for blacks and other people of color so that they can seek the same socioeconomic advancement as whites constitute the form of racial discrimination that has historically been practiced against them. In addition, it "violates the equal protection clause and Titles VI and VII of the 1964 Civil Rights Act." See J. Owen Smith, "The United States Supreme Court's Human Rights Violation in the University of Michigan Case" (2005, 120–21). The US Supreme Court first made such a ruling in *Regents of the University of California v. Bakke* in 1978. Since then it has made a number of such rulings, including *City of Richmond v. J. A. Croson Company* and *Gratz v. Bollinger*. In other words, the Supreme Court is interpreting race-based remedies to address America's history of racial discrimination that disadvantaged blacks and other nonwhites. A notable exception is *Grutter v. Bollinger*. In the case, the Court's majority ruling, which was written by Justice Sandra Day O'Connor held that diversity was central to the American dream and the legitimacy of the dominant class. As I have already discussed in chapter three, while the entire debates about reevaluating the federal government's policy on affirmative action in California, for example, is problematic in itself, it lacks a sense of history and consequently fails to take into account America's discriminatory past.

116. Yancy (2004a), 7.

117. Arnesen (2001), 9.

118. See Derrick A Bell, Tracy Higgins, and Sung-Hee Suh, "Racial Reflections: Dialogues in the Direction of Liberation" (1997, 107–108); Cheryl I. Harris, "Whiteness as Property" (1993).

119. Foucault (1977), 304.

120. For a more in-depth reading on white privilege, see Peggy McIntosh, "White Privilege: Unpacking the Invisible Knapsack" (2007).

121. Lawlor (1999), 4.

122. See David Roediger, *The Wages of Whiteness: Race and the Making of the American Working Class* (1991).

123. Offe (1984), 36.

124. Gallagher (1997), 7. Alastair Bonnett, "From the Crisis of Whiteness to Western Supremacy," synchronically views this crisis of whiteness "as a movement of disruption and challenge to white supremacy" and "the end of white economic control over global markets" (2004, 9). Bonnett, quoting extensively from Charles H. Pearson's *National Life and Character*, first published in 1893, he writes:

> The day will come, and perhaps is not so far distance, when the European observer will look round to see the globe girdled with a continuous zone of the black and yellow race, no longer too weak for aggression or under tutelage, but independent, or practically so, in government, monopolising the trade of their own regions, and circumventing the industry of the Europeans; when Chinamen and the native of the Hindostan, the states of Central and South America, by that time predominantly Indian . . . are represented by fleets in the European seas, invited to international conferences and welcome as allies in quarrels of the civilized world. The citizens of these countries would then be taken up into the social relations of the white races, will throng the English turf or the salons of Paris, and would be admitted to inter-marriage. It is idle to say that if all this should come to past our pride of place will not be humiliated . . . We shall awake to find ourselves elbowed and hustled, and perhaps even thrust aside by peoples whom we looked down upon as servile and thought of us as bound always to minister our needs. The solitary consolation will be that the changes have been inevitable. (2004, 10).

This inevitable end of white supremacy is, partly for this reason, whiteness, Bonnett points out, "is being reinvented, as well as sustained, as the cornerstone of 'global racism' well into the twenty-first century" (2004, 8) As a global colonizing force, whiteness continues to operate systematically and unconsciously (Bailey and Zita 2007, 7).

125. See Sherrow O. Pinder, *The Politics of Race and Ethnicity in the United States: Americanization, De-Americanization and Racialized Ethnic Groups* (2010).

126. Althusser (1971), 163.

127. The Tea Partiers have openly retaliated against the Obama administration. They have protested several Federal laws, including the Emergency Economic Stabilization Act of 2008; the American Recovery and Reinvestment Act of 2009; and the Health Care Reform Bill of 2010. Michel Martin, on MPR news, April 10, 2010, has reported that the Tea Partiers have accused the Obama administration as "too worried about black people and the poor." Yet, according to a survey by "a conservative media group," the Tea Partiers are "dismayed of being tagged as racist."

128. The image of the wounded white male, lost in a society that no longer values him, was given its most dramatic articulation in the 1993 film *Falling Down*, where Bill Foster, a white male, played by Michael Douglas, lost his job as defense Engineer and is also divorce. Foster goes on violent rampages in Los Angeles. He comes into contact with gluttonous Korean shop owners and Hispanic gangsters, which cast a shadow against the America he used to know. A certain kind of nostalgia to return to the America he once knew envelopes him, which, in his mind, legitimizes his violent retaliation against the balkanization of America, which Arthur Schlesinger has horrendously deprecated as the "disuniting of America," directed at the owner of a Korean shop. More recently, in the midst of the Obama administration, many whites, calling for "taking the country back" and "returning the American government to the American people," echoes Douglas's presumption that white is what America is; notwhite, and the stereotypes quickly gather in, is what America is becoming. However, if at present homogenous white America no longer exists, it is because, in spite of the presence of a racially and culturally heterogeneous population—First Nations, blacks, and other nonwhite groups, the United States, at the very beginning, was constituted as a culturally homogeneous nation.

129. Min-ha (1990), 134

130. Mirón (1999), 85.

131. Gallagher (1997), 8.

132. Giroux (1997), 296.

133. Mercer (1994), 339.

134. Appiah (1994), 133.

135. hooks (1992), 61.

136. Mailer (1957), 278. However, according to Gary T. Marx, the phrase "the white Negro" was popularized by Norman Mailer and, in fact, did not originate from him. For several centuries, in the West Indies, the term has been deployed "to describe white men who have become submerged among their Negro servants and concubines." See Gary T. Marx, "The White Negro and the Negro White" (1967), 169 no. 3.

137. For a more comprehensive reading of how and why white youths appropriate signs that are considered "black," see Pamela Perry, *Shades of White: White Kids and Racial Identities in High School* (2002).

138. Mercer (2002), 197.

139. Mercer (1991), 432–33. William Upski Wimsatt, in *Bomb the Suburbs*, draws our attention to another possibility where, for example, the rap audience will be mostly whites as is the case in many jazz clubs (2008), 21.

140. In Jane Lazarre, *Beyond the Whiteness of Whiteness: Memoir of a White Mother of Black Sons*, her "crossing over" or "passing over" to blackness is quite different. She draws our attention to the tensions between having a white skin and rejecting whiteness as her social identity. According to Lazarre, her social identity, as an "honorary black," is "hidden" by her white skin.

141. Ahmed (2004).

142. Farr (2004), 144.

143. Farr (2004), 145.

144. Butler (1997a), 2.

145. See Toni Morrison, *Playing in the Dark: Whiteness and the Literary Imagination* (1993); Rebecca Aanerud, "Fictions of Whiteness: Speaking the Names of Whiteness in US Literature" (1997); Valerie Babb, *Whiteness Visible: The Meaning of Whiteness in American Literature and Culture* (1998); Shelley Fisher Fishkin, "Interrogating 'Whiteness,' Complicating 'Blackness': Remapping American Culture" (1995); David Roediger, *Black on White: Black Writers and What It Means to Be White* (1998); and Crispin Sartwell, *Act Like You Know: African American Autobiography and White Identity* (1998). In addition, "Whiteness studies" is international in its scope. See Aileen Moreton-Robinson et al., *Transnational Whiteness Matters* (2008).

146. Fishkin (1995), 442.

147. See Charles Gallagher "White Reconstruction in the University" (2003); Richard Dyer, *White* (1997); Ruth Frankenberg, "Introduction: Local Whiteness, Localizing Whiteness" (1997); and David R. Roediger, *The Wages of Whiteness: Race and the Making of the American Working Class* (1991).

148. Roediger (2002), 19.

149. Morrison's *Playing in the Dark: Whiteness and the Literary Imagination* cautions us that American writings, including Poe, Melville, and Twain, make use of "the African-ist character . . . to limn out and enforce the invention and implication of whiteness" (1992, 52). She draws our attention to the dialogic relationship between whiteness and blackness. Also, see W. E. B. Du Bois, *The Souls of Black Folk* (2003).

150. See George Yancy, *What White Looks Like: African-American Philosophers on the Whiteness Questions* (2004b); Samina Najmi and Rajini Srikanth, *White Women in Racialized Spaces: Imaginative Transformation and Ethical Action in Literature* (2002); Mike Hill, *Whiteness A Critical Reader* (1997); Linda Martin Alcoff, "What Should White People Do?" (1998); Cheryl I. Harris, "Whiteness as Property" (1993); Michele Fine et al., *Off White: Readings on Race, Power, and Society* (1997); and Richard Delgado and Jean Stefanic, *Critical White Studies: Looking Behind the Mirror* (1997).

151. Fine et al. (1997), 9.

152. Alexander (2004), 652.

153. Winant (1997), 40.

154. Snead (1990), 245.

155. Snead (1990), 245.

156. See David Roediger, "Whiteness and Its Complications" (2006), 6–8.

157. Ware and Back (2000), 6.

158. Roediger (2006), 8.

159. Arnesen (2002), 34.

160. See Margaret Talbot, "Getting Credit for Being White" (1997).

161. Bonnett (1996), 146.

162. In Australia, conferences on "whiteness studies" include "Historicising Whiteness: Transnational Perspectives on the Construction of an Identity" (2006); "Reorienting Whiteness" (2008); in the United Kingdom, "New Territories in Critical Whiteness Studies" (2010); in the United States, "Critical Whiteness Studies Symposium" (2010).

163. hooks (1992), 12.

164. See Alastair Bonnett, "From the Crisis of Whiteness to Western Supremacy" (2005); Robyn Wiegman, "Whiteness Studies and the Paradox of Particularity" (1999); Frank Towers, "Projecting Whiteness: Race, and the State of Labor History" (1998); Eric Arnesen, "Scholarly Controversy: Whiteness and The Historians' Imagination" (2001); Sara Ahmed, "Declaration of Whiteness: The Non-Performativity of Antiracism" (2004).

165. Bonnett (1996), 146.

166. Roediger (1993), 132.

167. Arnesen (2001), 3.

168. Wray (2006), 6.

169. See, for example, David Roediger, *Working Towards Whiteness: How America's Immigrants Became White, The Strange Journey from Ellis Island to the Suburbs* (2005);

Karen Brodkin, *How Jews Became White Folks and What That Says About Race in America* (1998); Matthew Frye Jacobson, *Whiteness of a Different Color: European Immigrants and the Alchemy of Race* (1998); Noel Ignatiev, *How the Irish Became White* (1995). Also, in Texas, in the early twentieth century, Mexicans were seen as "almost white." See Stanley Crouch, *The All-American Skin Game, or the Décor of Race* (1996).

170. For a different reading of hybridity produced by immigration, exile, or existence in the borderlands, and how it can sometimes silence one emergent identity, see Marine Hong Kingston, *The Woman Warrior: Memoirs of a Girlhood among Ghosts* (1976); Gloria E. Analdúa, *Borderlands La Frontera: The New Mestiza* (1987). For Analdúa, "to survive the Borderlands, you live *sin fronteras* [without borders]/be a crossroads" (1997), 135. Also, Hamid Nafficy is dubious about the cultural politics of hybridity. See Nafficy, *The Making of Exile Cultures: Iranian Television in Los Angeles* (1993).

171. Frankenberg (1993), 232.

172. See David R. Roediger, *The Wages of Whiteness: Race and the Making of the American Working Class* (1991); Neil Foley, *The White Scourge: Mexicans, Blacks, and Poor Whites in Texas Cotton Culture* (1997); Noel Ignatiev, *How the Irish Became White* (1995); and Matthew F. Jacobson, *Whiteness of a Different Color: European Immigrants and the Alchemy of Race* (1998).

173. Bonnett (1996), 146. Also, see Charles Gallagher, "White Reconstruction in the University," (1995); Ruth Frankenberg, *White Women, Race Matters: The Social Construction of Whiteness* (1993); and Richard Dyer, *White* (1997).

174. Frankenberg (1993), 234.

175. Rai (1998), 95.

176. This unacknowledged privilege assigned to whiteness has always been a problem for post-colonial theorists. Something absolutely imperative is the indignity of speaking for the "other." See Linda Martín Alcoff, "The Problem of Speaking for Others" (1995); Anthony Appiah, "But Would That Sill Be Me? Notes on Gender, Race, Ethnicity as a Source of Identity" (1990); Edward Said, *The Politics of Dispossession: The Struggle for Palestinian Self Determination, 1969–1994* (1994); Gayatri C. Spivak, "Can the Subaltern Speak?" (1988).

177. Frankenberg (1993): 7.

178. See George Lipsitz, *The Possessive Investment in Whiteness How White People Profit From Identity Politics* (1998).

179. Roediger (1991).

180. Rasmussen et al. (2001), 14.

181. Lazarre (1996).

182. McLaren (2001), 417–18.

183. Dyer (1988), 44.

184. See Noel Ignatiev and John Garvey, *Race Traitor* (1996); David R. Roediger, *Towards the Abolition of Whiteness: Essays on Race, Politics, Working Class History* (1994).

185. Ferguson (1990), 10.

186. Haney López (1996), 3.

187. Wittig (1992), 11.

188. Brown (1995), 28–29.

FIVE

The Quandary of Antiracist Whiteness

In the United States, whiteness determines the positioning of nonwhites (them) as devalued and whites (us) as valued. Seemingly, we cannot move beyond this dichotomy that separates "them" from "us" because it is this very dichotomy that determines and maintains the ultimate conditions of whites and nonwhites. Since the "them" is signified as dissimilar from the "us," it is in this instant of differentiation that domination, in the form of white supremacy, is produced and propagated. It is for good reason that professor Charles Mills speaks for many when he views whiteness as "a political commitment to white supremacy."[1] White supremacy, that is, the intertwining axis of power, spatial position, and history, has provided the paradigm for racial indifference and has remained evident in every day practice. However impeded by the hooks and smears of white privilege, a good starting point for rethinking white supremacy is presented by "antiracist whiteness," whites working in the direction of antiracist strategies that counter America's racism and its multidimensional forms of oppression. In fact, there are several grassroots organizations working to combat racism. The Institutes for the Healing of Racism, for example, holds seminars and dialogues in more than one hundred and fifty cities in the United States.[2]

It is socially and culturally unacceptable nowadays to be overtly supremacist. White supremacy (as is expressed for example, by the Tea Party movement) is veiled behind an intellectualized and "disinfected" discourse. The social and cultural taboos that surround racist discourses represent a radical break from the past where plain ignorance and sheer violence were the hallmarks of the Ku Klux Klan.[3] The transformation from de jure to de facto white supremacy is documented and explained by W. E. B. Du Bois, in "The Souls of White Folk," in which he refers to white supremacy as "the new religion of whiteness."[4] However, the shift in white supremacy has to do with the fact that whiteness has been severely fractured by the racial conflicts of the post-civil rights era. Ever since the 1960s, racial discourse has been unable to articulate and justify why blacks and other nonwhites should be excluded from accessing the public good, job opportunities, and university admissions. Therefore, it has been forced into "rearticulations, representations, reinterpretations of race, and perforce of whiteness."[5] Terms such as colorblindness, post-racial, and race neutrality have surfaced in order to assert and mimic the systemic standard of state-sponsored white hegemony. Since white supremacy remains pathological, we have to analyze and reveal it for what it truly is. It is an obligation that we all share, especially whites.[6]

The endemic relationship that equates domination to white identity is important to understand. These days, antiracist whiteness has reconfigured white identity to be racialized.[7] I have already pointed to the dangers of assigning race to whites and substituting race for racism. Nonetheless, antiracist whiteness, in some cases, by the reoperationalizing of "consciousness-raising" or "awareness-training" forms of antiracism,[8] have made quite extraordinary efforts for whites, above all, to come to terms with their whiteness and seemingly move beyond it and work to fight racism and its multidimensional forms of oppression.[9] Antiracist whiteness, in its desire to denounce racism and its multifaceted forms of inequality, shows us that whiteness has not disentangled itself from white supremacy. Taking into consideration America's racist traditions of upholding white supremacy in the face of its professed creed of liberty, equality, and freedom for all Americans,[10] we need to redirect our attention to the actuality that antiracist whiteness is trapped within the trimmings of normalized whiteness.

What it means to be outside the construction of whiteness offers important incites for blacks and other nonwhites to be aware of the "ways of white folk," which, in important ways, intrigues W. E. B. Du Bois. He writes: "I know many souls that toss and whirl pass, but none there are that intrigue me than the Souls of White Folk. Of them I am singularly clairvoyant. I see in and through them . . . I see these souls undressed from the back and the side. I see the working of their entrails. I know their thoughts and they know that I know. This knowledge makes them embarrassed, now and furious."[11] In this sense, whiteness is already seen and observed by the nonwhite "other." In *Black Looks: Race and Representation*, bell hooks characterizes this sensibility by drawing closely on the representation of whiteness in blacks and other nonwhites' imagination. Subsequently, the problematic of antiracist whiteness is how to deal with the inherent contradiction of "what whiteness wants" and what whiteness "is,"[12] which is what I dub as the quandary of antiracist whiteness.

Analyzing the range and reach of whiteness is necessary if we are to conceive of the concept of the white self and subjectivity, and how this conception has impacted the nonwhite "other." Hence, placing whiteness "front and center of the analysis in order to subject it to the kind of scrutiny that rouses it off [as] unmarked" and unraced is paramount.[13] And since blacks and other nonwhites are therefore the dual agents of a "white racial unconsciousness," the need for self-reflective activity, or, generally speaking, subjectivity, on the part of whites is a good starting point for freeing whiteness of its presumptive hegemony. As a matter of fact, whiteness cannot be magically unmarked without taking into consideration whiteness as a system of domination and how whites themselves are invested in such a system. Hence, we need to think of practicable ways in which we can gradually work to free it of its domination.

As we have seen in chapter 4, scholars, working within a "whiteness studies" framework, are moving toward antiracist forms of whiteness or, at least, toward antiracist approaches for a "different" form of whiteness, where whiteness is named. In engaging with "citational practice," as a process that names, confesses, privileges, and the prototypical form of mnemonic performance, the question can be put simply: Why would whites renounce their hold on privilege and entitlement? What propels whites toward an antiracist practice? Do antiracist projects denormalize whiteness? Given that whiteness is about the power to exclude the "other" from privilege based on what Michel Foucault calls the "technologies of the self,"[14] the question ensues: Are antiracist projects equipped to relinquish the privilege that comes with whiteness? It is not unusual that antiracists who have devoted their lives to the dismantling of white privilege would experience a forged unity with blacks and other nonwhites, living with the *weight* of race and racism. In fact, white privilege is never given up; it is just transformed into another form of power, which becomes difficult to extricate. Denial of such privilege, then, is an extension of what Eduardo Bonilla-Silva calls colorblind racism,[15] which works to maintain white privilege and allows for the justification that whites are "the deserving" and nonwhites are "the undeserving" of such privilege. Hence, job recruitment, hiring, promotion, access to the best schools and universities, and residing in affluent neighborhoods are habitually reserved for whites. Nevertheless, we do not have to be colorblind to be blinded by the pervasiveness of racism. And even though white identities are heterogeneous—antiracists, poor whites, racists, and so on—colorblind racism allows for the redefinition of a white identity that does not renounce white entitlement. Entitlement is a symptom of whiteness, and what colorblind racism does is to promote, for example, the notion that race-conscious affirmative action programs discriminate against whites.

As I see it, when whites persistently denounce whiteness, what whites are actually denouncing is a constructed and constructing self that is shaped and constituted by the very whiteness that they are denouncing. Does the denunciation, then, create some kind of existentialist crisis for antiracists because they are still a part of the privilege group that benefits from whiteness? If Michel Foucault is right about power as not just repressing nonwhites through the racist structures that are in place, but also simultaneously producing the forms, promises, and privileges of white subjectivities,[16] then Gayatri C. Spivak's conclusion about relocating the subject from the *center* to the *margin* is important for meaningfully denouncing white privilege. It is only then, that the critical gaze from the "other" to the self can be realized; the self can now undergo critical scrutiny.[17]

Indeed, by exposing the reliance on the *center* and *margin*, deconstructionalism has provided a definite critical practice and intellectual atmosphere that has facilitated and encouraged scholars to start interrogating the *center* of race relations. Professor Cornel West warns that in order to understand America's race problem it is not helpful to start with people of color but the historical rootedness of whiteness that serves to disadvantage blacks and other people of color.[18] Given that whiteness "has been elevated to the status of 'independent variable,' one that scientists use to predict other outcomes,"[19] antiracist projects, taking to task white identity as their central theme, are relevant starting points to think about white supremacy. However, focusing on whiteness as an identity and retracting from whiteness as domination is not productive for any attempts aim at denormalizing whiteness.

Significantly, however, antiracist whiteness has helped us to understand Toni Morrison's assertion, in *Playing in the Dark: Whiteness and the Literary Imagination*, that sums up this rotation as "an effort to avert the critical gaze from the racial object to the racial subject, from the described and the imagined to the describers and imaginers."[20] When the gaze is shifted from the "other" to the self, whites would be able to reinvent themselves by means of self-reflection and counter-hegemonic actions. However, it is becoming increasingly clear that this depreciatory gaze has to be broadened to include nonwhites as they internalize whiteness. Hence, it is fundamental that we interrogate its ontological domination.[21] How to insert a different gaze and conceive of it as not simply a reversal of the hegemonic gaze but as another kind of exchange represents a real challenge. "Whiteness studies" and antiracist struggles have been working to redirect the gaze from the nonwhite "other" to the white "self."

Antiracist struggles require that whites acknowledge their whiteness and the benefits that accompany it. Part of the privilege has been the fact that whites rarely think of their whiteness. When whites are asked what it means to be white, many whites confess that they have not thought about it. As one white student puts it, "You really don't think about [whiteness] that much, at least I don't . . . There is always a feeling of comfort."[22] For many whites, whiteness becomes definable only when its endemic privilege is threatened to be lost. A concrete example presents itself with working class whites articulating their whiteness when they feel that blacks and other nonwhites are taking their jobs.[23] Clearly, whites are more mindful of their whiteness when they assumed that some kind of a threat to their being is manifesting itself.[24] However, when whites, working within the prototype of an antiracist whiteness, acknowledge their whiteness, their acknowledgement "cumulates, paradoxically, in the production of the saintly white person, the responsible white person, the politically accountable white subject." Once again, what we are seeing is that this form of self-glorification associates whites with honorable righteousness.[25] However, whiteness is most relentless when it remains invisible, something that many whites take for granted. Whiteness, as invisible to most whites, held sway, until the recent rise of "whiteness studies."

In this chapter, I want to show that while it is understandable that the individual choices of a few whites embarking on antiracist whiteness remain important for fighting racism and its multifaceted forms of inequality, it is not enough to transform the normative practices of domination and subordination; whiteness continues to be normalized. And because whiteness is the norm, people of color, for the most part, have to assimilate whiteness. As a result, they internalize whiteness, that is, they commit to the centrality of whiteness and endorse its ways of being and knowing. Hence, for whiteness to be freed of its hegemony, it would have to be denormalized, stripped of its normality. In thinking about how to denormalize whiteness, as a start, anxious whiteness would have to be transformed into secure whiteness, a new form of white consciousness that is freed from whites' feelings of superiority. When whiteness becomes anxious, it urges whites to assert their feelings of superiority; and once again the hegemony of whiteness is at work, upholding whites' superiority. Whites would need to constantly work to reinvent themselves through self reflection and counter hegemonic actions, aiming at challenging and opposing all forms of domination and oppression. It is only when whiteness is freed from its anxiety that whiteness can begin the process of denormalization, which would allow us to move beyond the current form of whiteness and inaugurate a post-white identity.

In the following section, I examine antiracist forms of whiteness and their significance for denormalizing whiteness. Given that whiteness is associated with domination, are antiracist forms of whiteness recentering or decentering whiteness? Aren't these projects precisely fostering the idea that whiteness is infested with complexities and ends up focusing on whiteness as identity? Whites' attempt at forging antiracist positions for themselves does not alleviate the accruing privilege that accompanies their white skin. Charles Gallagher, for one, argues that "apart from the benefits that accrue to whites because of their skin color no single metanarrative of whiteness exists."[26] Ruth Frankenberg joins Gallagher by concluding that "whiteness as a site of privilege is not absolute but rather cross cutting by a range of other axes of relative advantage and subordination; these do not erase race privilege but rather modify it."[27] While deemphasizing the epistemological and ontological status of whiteness as a system of domination, both Gallagher and Frankenberg speak about white privilege, and fail to truly come to terms with the ontological nature of racism and whites' involvement with racist systems and structures. Whites' failure to take into account the materiality of racism and white privilege and its impact on individuals and groups that are outside the stricture of whiteness is one of the many difficulties that antiracists face. When whites do this, they are experiencing a "double consciousness," which is the legacy of whiteness on the one hand and white antiracist identity on the other hand, each pulling them into two opposite directions. It is partly for this reason that these seemingly antithetical extremities, whiteness (domination) and white identity (antiracist) need to be interrogated first separately, then together. And while it is important for members of the dominant group to accommodate the interests of the nondominant groups, this is not sufficient to denormalize whiteness.

Many scholars have written endless about discrimination that is race-based. The point is how to do away with racism. Given that the full eradication of racism would require relocating and transforming the power structure that is in place, which currently seems impossible, antiracists are employing several strategies that work against racism and its multidimensional forms of oppression. However, in the face of normalized whiteness, antiracist projects are not enough to decenter whiteness and free it of its normalization. To further consider these concerns, we will now turn our focus on antiracist struggles as practiced by whites.

ANTIRACIST STRUGGLES AND WHITENESS

In thinking about the arrangement and accomplishments of antiracist struggles, I think that we must start by examining the antiracist struggles of blacks and other people of color. Blacks, for example, in diverse and contrasting ways, have always been involved in antiracist projects that challenge racism[28] —from black abolitionists, including David Walker, Henry Highland Garnet, Fredrick Douglas, and Sojourner Truth, Ida B. Wells; black nationalists, including Marcus Garvey, W. E. B. Du Bois, and Malcolm X; civil rights leaders and activists, including Mary McLeod Bethune, Medgar Wiley Evers, A. Phillip Randolph, Dr. Martin Luther King, James L. Farmer, Jesse Jackson, Roy Emile Alfredo Innis, James H. Meridith, and Al Sharpton. More recently, antiracist struggles have embraced a model that names whiteness and white privilege. Black feminist scholars, including Audre Lorde and bell hooks, have made whiteness the center of analysis in order to advance antiracist projects. Whites coming to terms with their whiteness and recognizing the privilege that accompanies it, in some ways, can materialize into a self-destructive paralysis of white guilt. How does one account for such an observation?

In a handout by the Center for the Study of White American Culture, one could read the following:

> While minority cultures have struggled to obtain power, white Americans must struggle to share the power we have. While minority cultures have struggled to retain their autonomy, white Americans must struggle to make our culture exist without dominating other cultures. We need to develop a public discussion of issues that apply uniquely to us as white Americans in a multicultural America.[29]

From the preceding statement, it is clear that *cultures* belong to racialized ethnic groups. More importantly, the statement fails to incorporate all the ambiguities that are embedded within the nondominant cultures and assign them an essential signifier, which denies them, to borrow from Diana Fuss, "the very radicality of difference."[30] The writers of this handout aim to pilot an antiracist intervention that relies on a faulty understanding of minority cultures. While white American culture denotes dominance and a white identity is accepted to "speak for itself," white American culture "is proffered to convey the material relations and social structures that reproduce white privilege and racism in this country, quite apart from what individual whites may feel, think, and perceive."[31] To sum it up, antiracists are still members of the dominant culture.

The handout leaves intact the durability of whiteness as a system of domination that functions to subordinate racialized groups such as First Nations, blacks, Chinese, and Mexicans, and whiteness is viewed as unproblematic and is not subject to the regular processes of confrontation and modification that have characterized the situated subjectivities of racialized ethnic groups. In this sense, the handout merely dismisses the racialization process in America. When we problematize whiteness and conceive of it as a system of domination, whites have to come "out as white," as professor Helen Charles puts it, because "it is negatively exhausting teaching" whites "what is like to be black," for example,[32] and embark on a greater need for restorative, sacrificial, and deferential action that is the converse of white guilt.

Given that one of the tasks at hand for antiracist whiteness is to enable whites to confront and try to eliminate racism, however ineffectively and inconsequentially, does antiracist whiteness make whites "self-conscious and critical" of their privilege? "Self-conscious," as Sara Ahmed points out, "has its own genealogy; its own condition of emergence. A self-conscious subject is one that turns its gaze toward itself and that might manage itself, or reflect upon itself, or even turn itself into a project. Yet we have to be aware that such a self-conscious subject, for the most part, is not exempted from the uproar of social life and, thus, does have the time and resources to be a "self."[33] In other words, there is a discernable discrimination at work here so that the issue of who gets to be a "self," a way of being and knowing, is overwhelmingly determined by gender, class, ethnicity, physical and or mental abilities and inabilities, sexuality, and, ultimately, by race as the primordial signifier. Hence, talking about whiteness and white privilege as "an essential something,"[34] a development that replicates the gaze back on itself, or, as Sara Ahmed puts it, "as that which gives itself to itself,"[35] is an important issue that continues to resurface. In the end, even if whites become "self-conscious and critical," it does not end, at least not entirely, the privilege and entitlements that whites accumulate whether it is at a conscious or unconscious level. In the end, antiracist whiteness is not about denormalizing whiteness. It facilitates whites to secure a privilege location in such a debate. Their white identities allow them to be, as Alastair Bonnett explains it, "passive observers, of being altruistically motivated, of knowing that their 'racial' identity might be reviled and lambasted but never actually made slippery, torn open, or, indeed, abolished."[36]

Talking about white privilege with other whites and not attending to it by, for example, regularly mingling with blacks and other nonwhites at a personal level make sure that white privilege remains invisible to whites.[37] In fact, it is not a secret that blindness to First Nations, blacks and other racialized groups has been, from the beginning of America's formation, studiously incorporated into whites' ways of lives so that it was easy for whites to render nonwhites invisible to them. Whiteness expresses itself without any contemplation of nonwhiteness.[38] Thus, for any antiracist project to be effective, it needs to engage in works that reach out to marginalized individuals and groups. If the imperative for antiracist projects is confronting the norm rather than accommodating the marginal, we are faced with the problematic of how power determines what the norm is and what assumptions and structures are available that determines a comfortable norm.[39]

When whites are outside of their comfort zone and come into contact with people of color, it is a dramatic and frightening experience because race is fashioned into a fake construct (or what Judith Butler describes as a "proper object"), race becomes a "mundane sort of violence"[40] that is physiological because it imprints onto the white self the "truth" of the nonwhite "other." A subscription to the reality of race is Frantz Fanon's account in *Black Skin, White Masks* of a little white boy's use of language to ensnare blacks and other people of color in the realm of corporeality. "Look a Negro . . . mama, see the Negro! I'm frightened."[41] While blacks and other people of color, for the most part, occupy a fixed racialized position, the materiality of the racialized body—"the fact of blackness"—conjures up anxiety in whiteness.

To actually engage antiracist whiteness it would require whites "to undertake both painful and difficult personal reflection and constant attention to thought and action,"[42] i.e., the daily behavior of whites—from making choices where to live, work, and socialize; the kinds of partner that they choose for intimate relationships; voting and the election of local, state, and national officials; membership in groups and organizations; being aware of prejudiced actions like holding on tightly to one's purse, or crossing the street whenever you see a nonwhite man, for example; publicly denouncing racism and other form of inequalities at the expense of assimilating "otherness" as a fundamental constituent of the self; speaking out when discriminatory actions are carried out in your presence; disrupting racist stereotypes and jokes; being actual witnesses to race-based social anguish; to constantly engage, in a positive way, with race related social issues—are important for whites to come out of their comfort zone. In fact, for antiracists, racial injustices can only be felt personally if the people who experience such discrimination are their children and lovers, personal friends, pastors, and neighbors. In other words, whites, as Joe Feagin explains it, would "personally [have to] feel some of the pain that comes from being enmesh in the racist conditions central to the lives of the oppressed other."[43] It is only then that antiracist whiteness can embrace an "ethic of accountability" as the foundation for a new sensibility that truly commits itself to resisting white privilege and entitlements. In short, whites would need to feel immediate solidarity with those who are discriminated against because of their race.

Antiracist whiteness has to "perform new relations with the subjectivities, the ideologies, and the material legacies of those historical relations"[44] because they work to disadvantage nonwhites. For David R. Roediger, the relocation of class struggles in "the making of the American working class" is an antiracist project.[45] The process of relocating "has the power to deconstruct practices of racism and make possible" an antiracist whiteness as a critical intervention.[46] In fact, when whites are willing and able to convert their lived experience into awareness and to use the already acquired awareness as a process to uncover new understanding of whiteness, whites can participate rigorously in dialogues as a process of learning and knowing.

Are antiracist projects equipped to relinquish the privilege that comes with whiteness? White privilege is never given up; it is just transformed into another form, which becomes difficult for privilege to extricate from positions of power. As I have mentioned before, it is clear that when whites denounce whiteness, what they are actually denouncing is a part of themselves. Does this act of denunciation create some kind of existentialist crisis? Why should antiracist whiteness be accountable for revealing the very core of whiteness as the vehicle for whites to be viewed as the agents of knowledge and enlightenment that sustain the Eurocentric world view; the admixture of the histories of trauma and terror that it perpetuated toward the nonwhite "other" and from which it had protected itself against; the aggressive essentials that make it anxious; its troubled form of a presumptive power, that is, the violence and terror it inflicts in an effort to remain hegemonic. Trying to fathom the unfathomable focus of antiracist whiteness on drawing attention to whites' "possessive investment in whiteness,"[47] let us cut through the meandering and ask: why should antiracist whiteness take on and reexpose white privilege? However, taking on and reexposing white privilege is not moving toward an alternative form of whiteness. Whiteness remains normalized.

Whites, for the most part, are reluctant to discuss their investments in whiteness and its connection to white supremacy.[48] It would make sense, then, for many antiracists to repress the extent to which they gain from white privilege. Repression, in this milieu, functions as a defense mechanism to protect their perception of the self from an overwhelming trauma that may threaten the possessive white self from ontological disturbance.[49] For this reason, we can make sense of George Lipsitz's assertion that an antiracist white subject is impossible, given whites' "possessive investment in whiteness,"[50] which functions "socio-discursively through subjectivity" and the relationship between power, knowledge production, agency, and privilege that whites profit from.[51] To this extent, it is easy for antiracists to extricate themselves from racism because they are not the perpetuators of racist programs and policies. As a matter of fact, white entitlement allows for many whites to frequently allege that racism has nothing to do with them because they are not racist. However, it is much harder for whites to assert that whiteness has nothing to do with them.

Antiracist whiteness is important because it allows for whites to recognize and acknowledge the ways in which America's cultural practice reinscribes white supremacy.[52] It is not a secret that some liberal, leftist, or progressive whites have joined in the common cause with people of color to fight slavery, racism, and other forms of America's oppressive racial practices. They have empathized and identified with blacks and other people of color and sometimes go as far as denouncing their whiteness to embrace "honorary blackness," for example. Jane Lazarre, in her book *Beyond the Whiteness of Whiteness: Memoir of a White Mother of Black Sons*, reveals that she is no longer white. She simply states (or, maybe not so simply), "I am no longer white. However, I may appear to others, I am a person of color now."[53] We can understand, then, why Vron Ware and Les Back would be in agreement with Lazarre, as they put it, "for finding the will and the courage to change oneself from a white person to a not-white person"[54] because "as long as you think you're white, there's no hope for you."[55] However, given that one's subjectivity is entirely steeped in the practice of speaking from the position of one's situatedness, the practice of speaking as a white person does not entail a disconnection from the constituted white self. In fact, as a way of revealing the position from which whites speak as whites, whiteness, in this case, is revisiblized against the milieu of an unseen blackness.

Like the "white Negro," Lazarre encodes an antagonistic subject position in relations to the code of cultural whiteness, the way one is socialized and constructed to experience oneself as white. And even though, with hard work and perseverance, one can unlearn cultural whiteness, that is, taking on whatever whiteness is not and assimilate blackness, for example, because Lazarre is identifiably white, her white skin confers on her bona fide privilege. In this sense, one can oppose racial inequality, be a part of the antiracist struggles to end racism, and so on, yet continues "to possess all the privileges and 'pleasures' of whiteness."[56] Hence, any suggestion that the category "white Negro" provides for the disengagement of whiteness as domination only serves to discard the significance and scope of white skin privilege.

Due to the fact that whiteness remains unmarked, deconstructing whiteness, that is, how it functions "as a mythical norm," wholesome and pure, is necessary for any antiracist project.[57] Given that antiracist whiteness are linked to antiracist projects, politics, and pedagogies, I think that antiracist whiteness, however troublesome it may be for denormalizing whiteness, does position itself in ways that are definitely important, especially on college and university campuses. Higher institutions of learning, for the most part, are organized to advance the interests of the dominant group. By opening a theoretical space for teachers and students to think about their whiteness, a clearer picture is drawn that outlines how whiteness understood as a strategy of power rather than an essential identity has been constituted and wrought within a culture that is racist. Hence, antiracist whiteness can promote some kind of connection in thinking about the kind of responsibilities whites might presume for being a member of such a culture in which they are accorded white privilege largely at the expense of blacks, First Nations, Mexicans, Chinese, and other racialized groups.[58] Talking about whiteness, a *normal* part of American society, without providing some hope for its denormalization is not enough. It is only when whiteness is denormalized that we can, as Peter McLaren writes, "Choose against whiteness," which, rightfully so, "is the hope and promise of the future."[59]

Bell hooks' writings in the 1990s clearly allow us to reflect on antiracist ideology and practice. She acknowledges that, because we live in a white supremacist culture, we have learned to overvalue whiteness and simultaneously learn to devalue nonwhiteness. Antiracists, for example, are aware of the need, at least intellectually, to rework their thinking,[60] and one of the goals of antiracist projects is to make whiteness visible, through language and discourse, for those for whom it has been invisible. However, we need to take heed to Sara Ahmed's warning that "putting whiteness into speech, as an object to be spoken about, however critical, is not an antiracist action."[61] Given that white antiracists are, for the most part, flawed because they are "raven with supremacist pretensions and extensions,"[62] we are provoked to ask the question, what then entail truly antiracist projects? As a response, those that are truly willing to challenge racism have to foster identities that "perform differently, embodying new forms of responsiveness, or developing new habits"[63] that goes against normalized whiteness. Given that whites "have been performing whiteness, and have whiteness performed upon [them]," even before birth,[64] "white antiracist" parenting is deemed as essential. As Rebecca Aanerud explains it, "White antiracist [parenting] calls upon white [parents] to challenge and resist the reproduction of racialized power structures that materially benefit their white children."[65] Because the ability of blacks, First Nations, Mexicans, and other nonwhites to parent was and continued to be policed, antiracist parenting plus raced-based empowerment for nonwhite parenting might be helpful in combating racism and its multifaceted forms of oppressions.

Antiracist scholars have developed "white awareness training method" where whites can deal with their racism so that, as Judith H. Katz puts it in her now classic book, *White Awareness: Handbook for Anti-Racism Training*, "all people can be free. It is through this process of self-examination, change, and action that we will someday liberate our society and our self."[66] The Doris Marshall Institute located in Toronto, Canada, in its antiracist efforts, as appeared in an article titled "Maintaining the Tensions of Anti-Racist Education," insists "that white people take responsibility for confronting racism and assist white people in this when necessary."[67] In fact, when whites are talking openly about racism, they are looked on as these "saintly whites" and, once again, "whiteness is equated with moral rectitude."[68] However, it is important for whites to "deal" with their racism. Given that whites, for the most part, are given the space, resources, and credits for sponsoring antiracist projects, the question, however, where do blacks and other nonwhites fit into the antiracism archetype of whites working toward challenging racism, becomes a pressing one.

Blacks and other nonwhites shared a common bond because of racism. Racism is embedded in the social, institutional, and discursive structures. It reproduces the social order and perpetually shapes the lived experiences of people of color. Within the multifaceted metric of power and racial hierarchy, more recently, concepts such as model minority and honorary whiteness have surfaced, which only serve to create conflicts within and amongst racialized ethnic groups, and to promote a false consciousness that there is a "declining significance of race" and "the end of racism." Although *racism* is a white problem, it demands a multiracial solution where not just whites but blacks, Chinese, First Nations, Mexicans, and other racialized ethnic groups have to join in the struggle to work against racist systems, strategies, institutions, epistemologies, practice, and goals.[69] In post 9/11 America, the amounts of transparently racist rhetoric, policies, and laws that are surfacing are great cause for distress. For instance, the Patriot Act (the United and Strengthening America by Providing Appropriate Tools Require to Intercept and Obstruct Terrorist Act of 2001), has given officials at the airports, for example, the license to racially profile Muslim Americans. Instead of relieving whites of their accountability, more important, then, is to examine "the impact of racism on those who perpetuate it."[70]

In returning to the question: are antiracist projects forms of denormalizing whiteness? as I have pointed out in the previous chapter, in analyzing "whiteness studies," we can see clearly that the Foucauldian understanding of power has not disappeared. The same can be said about antiracist projects as leaving the center of white privilege intact. In the end, antiracist whiteness cannot be understood as, racialized consciousness, which is shaped by the social structures that are in place, disadvantaging blacks and other people of color. To put differently, these structures are instrumental in producing racist discourse, practices, and the maintenance of whiteness presumptive hegemony. Hence, given the ontological superiority of the white subject, well-meaning whites, without the slightest discomfort with their racism, "may perpetuate a form of racism unintentionally."[71] For example, when whites make comments (white talk) such as "You speak so well for a black person," or "You should be good at math because you are Chinese," "the inevitable charter of benevolence racism" is surfaced.[72] In addition, the delineation of racism is best illustrated when whites declare: "We" like Mexican Americans but "We" think that they should all go back to Mexico because they are a threat to American cultural identity.[73] "We" are not racist. "We" are just nationalists. Since whites are the beneficiary of racism, what can be assumed about whites that oppose racism and work toward the elimination of it? We have to be alert to the fact that whites working toward promoting antiracist projects of justice and equality does not signal that racism has disappeared. In some ways, antiracist projects are complicit in reproducing the same hegemonic structure of racism that it seemingly wants to dismantle. The difficulty with antiracists is that, for many, "thinking white," is still a cherished ideal inscribed within normalized whiteness. The task at hand, then, is not only about promoting antiracist whiteness, but to work to develop ways in which whiteness is no longer constrained by its normalization.

Since whiteness is normalized through social and institutional practices that occur in daily interaction, in reality whites renouncing their whiteness is a clear form of white privilege. Conversely, nonwhiteness is an external corporeal textuality that is marked and cannot be renounced. It is, somewhat, for the reason that Henri Giroux begs whites "to learn to live with their whiteness."[74] However, whites learning "to live with their whiteness" would require a different kind of whiteness; a whiteness that is seen in a positive light. For this, and all the other reasons that I have discussed earlier, there are many challenges that would present themselves if we were to denormalize whiteness and strip it of its domination. Whiteness cannot, and will not, be unmarked because of the changes in attitudes of a few progressive whites, taking up antiracist work so that they can join in the fight for equality rights, liberty, and freedom for all citizens of a democratic polity.

The belief that if we move beyond race and embrace the normal Enlightenment principles of equality, rationality, and objectivity, racism would magically disappear cannot be taking seriously. What is seriously exposed in this uncritical thinking is that moving beyond race does not mean that race has disappeared. It is just transformed into another oppressive process like colorblindness and, as such, it becomes all right to attack programs such as affirmative action and reinforce anti-immigration measures to hamstring the "undesirables" from entering the United States. Colorblindness allows whites, because of their privilege status, to universalize this colorblind experience—not having to antagonize about racial discrimination because of their skin color—to utilize this experience as normative for all social relations. In the end, colorblindness further reveals the reality of race in America which, as I have already argued, is not settling down soon. Any obliviousness to race must be seen for what it is; it is a huge part of the privilege that whites accrue. And when David Roediger concludes that "gender—indeed heterosexism—combined with class could overcome race"[75] he, apparently, overlooks how whiteness has shaped identities including race, class, gender, ethnicity, sexuality, and mental and physical abilities.

WHITENESS AND A WHITE IDENTITY

Feminists have helpfully problematized the conception of a monolithic white identity by drawing on issues of gender, sexuality, ethnicity, age, geography, physical and mental disabilities, and class. Many theorists, for whom class is at the center of their analysis, have argued that class, for the most part, goes unnoticed, dismissed, and not theorized. However, in the analysis of whiteness, it would be a mistake for us to center our attention on class. White workers often identify as white rather than as workers because it is through their whiteness that they have prescribed access to social, economical, political, and psychological benefits. Class-consciousness, for the most part, is buried deep within white identity. Although most whites hold little or no real power, all they can claim is their excessive privileged white identity that promotes white supremacy.[76] The ruling class, through the systems, institutions, and power, works to unite white workers to their whiteness. White identity, such as "white trash," gains a new status and prompts discussions about the liminality of whiteness, or the "otherness" of "whiteness within." It leads to the critical reconfiguration of white privilege into an intricate distinction of underprivileged based on class orientation. Poor whites are unrelentingly compared to the few upwardly mobile blacks and other non-whites.[77] In this sense, in accordance with whiteness, poor whites are provided with the trimmings of agency, which allows for the rehegemonizing of whiteness and a white identity under the logic of *class*.

In addition, poor whites, for the most part, have nothing else to hold on to but their "possessive investment in whiteness," and this might be the reason why they wear their supremacy more pretentiously than other whites. In fact, working class whites usually cherish whiteness to such a degree that instead of joining together with other workers with whom they share economic interests, they prefer to downplay their working class status and endorse a white supremacist vision that compels them to shun their nonwhite fellow workers.[78] Shunning working class blacks and other nonwhites further connects them to their whiteness. This does not mean that whites and nonwhites of the same economic class share a common fate. In fact, many whites are willing to construct and maintain a social and symbolic gap with nonwhites, which nonwhites unfittingly, if not pathologically, experience. When nonwhites moved into a white neighborhood, which then becomes racially integrated, in many cases, "white flight" from those neighborhoods are visible.[79] According to Joe R. Feagin, "Since at least the 1970s, many whites have moved away from large cities with growing populations of blacks, Asian, and Latino Americans to whiter suburban and exurban areas or into guarded-gated communities in those cities."[80]

Even though whiteness is in operation everywhere—at work, in schools, colleges and universities, at the airports; in the parks, stores media, films, banks, and courtrooms, boardrooms, and on the streets— literally and symbolically, whiteness remains powerfully unmarked. Hence, whites are able to secure materials and social gains just by being white. At the same time, as Peggy McIntosh explains, "whites are carefully taught not to recognize white privilege."[81] Their blindness to their privilege is accompanied by white entitlement, which constantly redirects resources, such as employment, education, and housing loans from nonwhites to whites. In the end, seeing whiteness as invisible is the indication of willful blindness. In fact, there is nothing invisible, for example, about racial profiling, black ghettoes and super ghettoes marred by social death and its occupants reduced to "bare life"; the prisons crowed with blacks and Mexicans; and a high rate of high school dropouts of blacks, Mexicans, and First Nations.

Granted, the recognition of whiteness is not only about having white skin. Its meanings and status are unrelentingly reinforced through institutional and systemic arrangements of whiteness as the norms. Therefore, it is fundamental to examine the complexity of the various ways in which nonwhites have internalized whiteness. Internalized whiteness brings about two simultaneous processes: the split between whiteness as power and privilege (structural) and nonwhites' daily experience of whiteness (personal); and it serves as an impasse between nonwhiteness and whiteness locked in a symbiotic relationship of subordination (nonwhiteness) and domination (whiteness). And while people of color, for the most part, are wrought by the preeminence of whiteness, seeking to reduce nonwhiteness to its own category and principle of white dominance as a form of colonized violence, nonwhiteness is constantly shaped and re-shaped by a dominant white identity. Hence, nonwhites are trapped within the dialectic of performing whiteness on the one hand and resist-ing whiteness on the other hand. For the most part, however, whiteness has been internalized by the nonwhite "other."[82] It is to internalized whiteness that I, in brief, now turn.

INTERNALIZED WHITENESS

W. E. B. Du Bois first asked what it is about whiteness that one might want to retrieve toward it.[83] In a culture that normalizes whiteness as an ontological neutral category and upholds the white subject as raceless, whiteness is seen as natural. That which is natural is inevitably normal. Individuals, belonging to groups outside of whiteness, are raced, abnor-mal, and unnatural. For the most part, they have tried to hold on to the "natural, ordinary, inevitable way of being human,"[84] by assimilating the norms, values, and expectations of whiteness. Because whiteness remains a concept based on power relations that foster white domination and nonwhite subordination, whiteness denies legitimacy to those groups that have been assigned as nonwhite. Hence, what we dismissed are these facts: First Nations Reservation and black ghettoes and super ghet-toes are marked by increasing crime and poverty. I have already point to the fact that these, and other racialized ethnic enclaves, are America's internal colonies. Internal colonialism makes available an effective entry point for analyzing racial subjugation in the United States through the invocation of a colonial model, which reproduces whiteness as domina-tion and nonwhiteness as subordination.

Given that whiteness authorizes and controls nonwhites' identifica-tion process, blacks and other nonwhites, in some cases, have expressed ambivalence toward their constructed blackness, First Nationness, Chi-neseness, or Mexicanness. During the 2004 presidential election, for ex-ample, many Mexican Americans aligned themselves with white elites of the Republican Party and distanced themselves from black Americans.[85] Starting in 1964, with the presidential campaign, the party moved away from the once-sought after black voters and focused on the white voters. Feagin notes, "Today, the party is antagonistic to key issues of concern to black Americans."[86] However, it is not surprising that Mexican Americans would want to join with the Republicans in the shunning of blacks. This is exactly how internalized whiteness works. Those who are not white would, at any costs, align themselves with whites and con-sciously or unconsciously accept the standards of whiteness.[87] Echoing W. E. B. Du Bois, James Baldwin's "My Dungeon Shook: Letter to my Nephew on the One Hundredth Anniversary of the Emancipation," reminds us opportunely that "there is no reason for [nonwhites] to become like white people, and there is no basis whatsoever for their impertinent assumption that they must accept you."[88] Partly for this reason, discourses such as *model minorities* and *honorary whiteness* are used as a disciplinary device against people of color who perform their racial identity in such a way that threatens to shatter the power structure. Nonwhites assimilating whiteness illustrates, in an exemplary manner, how whiteness projects its anxiety of being disavowed.

I will rely on Fanon's reading and rereading of the colonizer (oppressor) and the colonized (oppressed) model of inequality to account for the aforementioned case scenario. While opening up newly insightful analysis of how racial oppression is structured, Fanon allows us to see how the oppressed (nonwhites) becomes the diabolic "other" in relations to whiteness, which for the constructed "other," the implications of otherness is an "implicit knowledge," as fanon calls it.[89] In other words, blacks and other people of color continuously are made aware of their condition as the "other" through this "implicit knowledge" of otherness, which is played out in the dialectic of inferiority (nonwhites) and superiority (whites). And even though some scholars have suggested that this dichotomization is obsolete, we continue to see the symbiotic relations between the oppressor and the oppressed as two acknowledged opposite. More importantly, the "double-consciousness" through which blacks and other people of color experience themselves is essential in this context.[90] It is through the oppressor-and-oppressed-model that whiteness is internalized, and it is therefore through this model that blacks and other nonwhites determine and shape their sense of themselves.

Even though whiteness, in some cases, is regarded with fear, suspicion, and anger, the attraction to whiteness has afflicted people of color who recognize the privileges that whiteness automatically prescribe. They identify with whiteness because they understand that it is the key to social recognition and approval. However, identification is an ongoing process and is never settled because it is persistently constituted and reconstituted by the tenacity of the white gaze that does not see blacks and other nonwhites as equal to themselves. Hence, it is important for whites to position themselves as "different" from people of color. Whites project what Diana Fuss explains as identification's "alienation effect" onto people of color who are "enjoined to identify and to dis-identify simultaneously with whites, to assimilate but not to incorporate, to approximate but not to displace."[91] The "other" is never able to escape from the abyss of otherness and unconsciously conform to the very standards of normalized whiteness from which they feel rejected. Maya Angelou envisions this forced adaptation "as evil threats to the well-being and real identities of people within their sub-national group."[92] The process of internalizing whiteness can only be brought to an end if whiteness is denormalized and stripped of its power. While denormalizing whiteness cannot happen in a vacuum, it needs the inside support of the whites to change systems and structures that identify with whiteness. However, denormalizing whiteness does not mean that there would be an immediate overthrow of the existing power relations. Whiteness would have to constantly work to decenter itself.

These days, membership into what I call "the white club" has extended itself to include individuals who are invested with honorary whiteness. This social club is unquestionably exclusive and closed to blacks and other nonwhites unless they have absorbed "the ways of white folk" and embraced a kind of racial etiquette that enables them to perform whiteness. Would saying "no" to this club membership help in the denormalization of whiteness? Nonwhites saying no to honorary whiteness, for the most part, would deter them from reaping the so-called benefits of honorary whiteness. This is another reason why whiteness would have to be denormalized.

In the following section, I want to look at how to start the process of denormalizing whiteness and bring about an alternative form of whiteness. However, for whites to embrace any kind of self-reflection, "self-marking" is important. As is observed by Judith Butler, "To mark oneself is to take account, to give account, and hence, implicitly, to answer to a charge of [white supremacy] and seek exoneration." And even though "self-marking" proffers an "unmediated presentation of self as a 'legitimating move,'"[93] such as process, flawed as it is, retains a necessity for moving toward the deconstructing, in the post-structuralist sense, of white supremacy. Given that white supremacy is an expression of *anxious whiteness*—a whiteness that is apprehensive about its narcissism, insensitivity, privilege, and conceitedness—which constantly has to assert its dominance, by depriving people of color their right to self-definition and self-determination, I want to show that the first task for denormalizing whiteness is to transform the anxious whiteness into a secure whiteness. But first, white supremacy must be recognized, examined, analyzed, and challenged.

DENORMALIZING WHITENESS

Is the *Race Traitor*, a white person who refuses to be white and move "inexorably toward a place that lies beyond the homelands of power and the ghastly structures of 'thinking white,'"[94] leading to some form of denormalized whiteness couched in a post-white ontology—as is projected by the new abolitionists of whiteness?[95] One of the main goals of the new abolitionists, including Noel Ignatiev and John Garvey, David R. Roediger, and Vron Ware and Les Back, is to get rid of whiteness. Their motto as, Noel Ignatiev and John Garvey put it: "Treason to whiteness is loyalty to humanity."[96] In fact, the new abolitionists make use of Paul

Gilroy's plead, in his book *Between Camps: Nations, Culture and the Allure of Race*, to move beyond race, transcend race thinking, and move in the direction of what Gilroy calls "planetary humanism" where people of color, (especially blacks) and whites can advance toward a "raceless democracy."[97] However, appealing this might sound, all this appears to be is that *Race Traitor* is attacking the very notion of race and racial identities by assigning race to whites, which is a huge problem in itself, as I have argued elsewhere in this book.[98] The argument that "white people are raced just like men are gendered"[99] points to the transformation of a white identity, which is centered on race. Given that whites have not gone through the process of racialization,[100] whites, creating an identity centered on race, sadly so, fail to take into account race and racism as two separate but interlocking systems that oppress people of color. And to ignore this fact is to redouble the hegemony of whiteness. Because of the practice of whiteness in subjugating people of color, refusing to be white, or "choose against whiteness," is not enough.[101]

In thinking about ways to denormalize whiteness, the first challenge is to reposition whiteness in a way that it refrains from defining and constructing the "other" as inferior, but participates in reconstituting a form of whiteness that is no longer synonymous with white superiority and its corollary anxiety. In looking back at "how the Irish became white,"[102] one can see that the acquisition of a white identity was simultaneously comforting and source of anxiety. To make sure the Irish were finally on the right side of the color line, they had to reassert their white identity by separating themselves from blacks and other people of color.[103] It is important, then, to fashion new ways in which whites can take an ontological break from their whiteness, challenge the anxiety and achieve, in the much cited words of Rodieger, "the withering way of [normalized] whiteness."[104] Is there a need for a counterhegemonic understanding of white ontology? How do whites disconnect from their position of normalized whiteness? How can we denaturalize the naturalness of whiteness? Whites would have to "confront the ready potential of speaking or acting in ways that are based on or slide into arrogance, moralizing, self-congratulation, liberal politics, appropriation, careerism or rhetoric" in order to denaturalize whiteness.[105] Is disrupting the norms of whiteness another way of denaturalizing and repositioned normalized whiteness? What comes to mind is black popular culture, which is steadily being reconfigured through music, dance, dress, and the language of rap and hip-hop as defiant of white social norms. Given that black popular culture carries the signifier black, to further investigate this point, I have to ask: Do whites have a place in black popular culture? What happens when whites appropriate signs from black popular culture?

White youth are adopting marker from black popular culture, including verbal communication, dress, hair style, and music.[106] In the course of "honorary blackness," this "act" of "passing," whiteness is redefined because it goes up against the cultural codes of whiteness. However, this does not mean that whiteness, as domination, has transformed itself. [107] And even though this form of passing simply obscures a ubiquitous system of advantage and racial socialization where whites can affirm their dominance, that is, their rights-claims to cross, with ease, cultural borders,[108] this form of willful "passing," does it signal that whiteness is in some kind of crisis, forcing whites to take a break from their whiteness and assimilate blackness, for example? In fact, for some white youths, assimilating blackness has become hip. The problem with this form of "race trading," even though it is hopeful for challenging, even superficially, the operative norms of whiteness, is not a sufficient cause or even a necessary pointer that whiteness is forced into to the process of decentering itself. Further, the fact that these whites can retrieve back to their white identity signals the power of whiteness and its application. Therefore, how to move "inexorably toward a place that lies beyond the homelands of color and ghastly strictures of thinking white," to borrow from Ware and Les Back, is paramount.[109] However, it is important for whites "to feel good about themselves as White people. All too often Whites deny their whiteness because they feel that being White is negative."[110]

Belonging to the dominant group grants social and cultural capital to its member. As I have already shown, whiteness appears as deficient and responds to its deficiency through the racial hierarchy by asserting its privilege; it is repeatedly, as Richard Dyer suggests, exposed for its "emptiness, absence, [and] denial."[111] Since "whiteness is nothing but oppressive and false," whiteness must increasingly pursue a horrifying effort to construct an identity based on what it is not.[112] Judging from this, there is nothing for whites to feel superior about. We can see why some whites, nonetheless, failing to take into account their social reality as whites, would want to denounce whiteness and refuse to be white[113] and work to solve the problem of racism as thoroughly ideological. Indeed, whites are always the problem solvers and blacks and other non-whites are always the problem. W. E. B. Du Bois' "How does it feel to be the problem," is a recurring theme within normalized whiteness. For sure, the attitudinal changes of some whites about race and racism do not signal the dismantling of white supremacy. In fact, the way racism works among antiracists or the new abolitionist of whiteness is that they want to construct and create new subjectivities and subject positions that are not infused with racism, which is no doubt illusory and impossible because of the ontological nature of racism. When blacks, for instance, are equated with race, and they are agitating in the name of the *race*, it is a direct outcome of racism.

Given that whiteness is entrenched in a decidedly expressed social structure and system of meaning that secure and promote white privilege, how can whites become independent of whiteness without being trapped within its ontological specificity as a system of domination? Is the rethinking of white privilege enough? In Peggy McIntosh's "White Privilege: Unpacking the Invisible Knapsack," for example, where she acknowledges and names the many unearned privileges that accrue to whites, how can whites separate themselves from these privileges? Notwithstanding the fact that not all whites are racists and some have chosen to go against normative whiteness by living out seemingly oppositional white identities, we cannot simply abandon the saliency of white skin and how it functions to position whites, regardless of gender, sexuality, class, mental and physical abilities, or national origins, as separate from racialized ethnic groups for privilege in spite of the intension of any particular white person.[114] In looking back at antiracist whiteness, it lays bare indeed that it does not signal an end to white privilege. In the face of normalized whiteness, white cannot "simply opt out of systems of privilege"[115] and "escape whiteness."[116] Hence, in order for whiteness to beginning the process of denormalization, we would have to take into account the historical process that worked to construct, define, reinforce, perpetuate, and maintain whiteness where whites were, and continue to be, automatically marked with privilege unlike racialized ethnic groups who were considered as inferior and undeserving of these rights. In other words, white rights are intimately intertwined with denying people of color their rights. Whiteness, then, as a system in place was constituted, and continues to be constituted, by the domination of blacks, First Nations, and other racialized ethnic groups. It is already the norm and cannot be made otherwise in a society that is premised on white domination. And given that whiteness, to borrow Noel Ignatiev's phase, is a "two-sided process,"[117] in that, those who have internalized whiteness and those who "feel whiteness," the converse of not being the "other," the arduous process of the oppressor and oppressed asymmetric activity of promoting white supremacy has to be examined and transgressively erupted.

In light of the preceding observation, for a denormalized whiteness to emerge, the reorientation of the practice of white supremacy is necessary. According to recent articles that were published by *Newsweek* and *Business Week*, white men feel that they are under attack because business offices that were completely white are now focusing on diversity.[118] As I have shown in chapter three, when whites feel threatened by social changes, white supremacy is heightened. The task at hand, then, is how to transform white supremacy into white security so that whites can become more secure in their whiteness.

W. E. B. Du Bois points out, "The discovery of personal whiteness among the worlds' people is a very modern thing."[119] In fact, if whiteness as domination is to be effective, its true nature had to be concealed. With assistance from the intersection of the various laws, systems, and structures that position whiteness, both symbolically and literally, as the norm, wholesome and pure, whiteness maintains its dominance.[120] Since

changes in the laws and their interpretations, for example, do not necessary result in social transformation of white supremacist views and values, white supremacy must be identified, investigated, analyzed, contested, and transformed. I think, then, we have to start by exposing the
myth of white supremacy as ontologically bare, epistemologically decep-
tive, and ethically destructive in the way that it advances as mainstream
consensus, whites as superior in contrast to nonwhites as inferior.[121]

If we are to embrace the liberal ethos that we are all equal as human
beings, a kind of humility would have to take the place of white supremacy. Seeing that humility, as Pablo Freire so aptly demonstrates, "does
not flourish in people's insecurities,"[122] but in one that is more secure in
its identity, the task at hand is to transform the anxious and undesirable
whiteness into its opposite, that is, a whiteness that feels secure about
itself. Whites, feeling secure in their whiteness would allow for what
Henri Giroux calls an "oppositional space"[123] aimed at the liberation of
whiteness from its "emptiness, absence, [and] denial."[124] Whiteness as
performative in the Austin's sense, as doing what it sets out to do, which,
in this case, is to grant privilege to whites, denormalized whiteness
would perform differently. It is only then that whites would have the
courage to "[break] out of a white identity . . . and embark on a daily
process of choosing against [normalized] whiteness."[125] As long as
whiteness in its current form exists, I would follow Noel Ignatiev and
John Garvey in acknowledging that "all movements against racism are
doomed to fail."[126]

White supremacy, in some cases, can lead to whites' self-loathing and
hatred, as I have already drawn on what is brought to life in Ruth Frankenberg's dialogues with some white women,[127] where whiteness is
viewed as deficient and repeatedly exposed for its "emptiness."[128] For
these white women, nonwhite culture is better than their own. It is more
"interesting," "natural," and "spiritual." Because of white women's privileged position within the racial hierarchy, it permits dichotomized thinking of self and "other," which has created anxiety about whiteness.[129]
Whites' identification, in this respect, "carries an ontological and epistemological valence, such that the question "who or what am I?" becomes a
question of being and knowing, a question of desire."[130] What does a
white person want?

Because of whiteness as terrorizing as well as brutalizing, all too often
whites reject their whiteness because they feel that being white is negative. It is essential for whites to embrace their whiteness and feel good
about being white.[131] In fact, when cleansed of its racist implication, a
positive white self-identification can work to delegitimize white preeminence. It is only then that whites can truly be able to come to terms with
nonwhites as equally able to access the available resources that would
allow for the promotion and preservation of a just society. There would
no longer be a need for whites to be reactionary and on the defensive,

which provide a fertile soil for white supremacy to flourish and grow. Secure whiteness would, for the most part, propel whites to want to embrace projects that work against white supremacy.

When practitioners of "diversity awareness" try to find ways to train educators, workers, and managers to become aware of how whites should be privileged no more than any other groups, they seems to be offering their mostly white clients the outlook of restructuring their white identity in a critical and positive manner.[132] However, practitioners have to be careful not to rehegemonize whiteness. When whites celebrate their whiteness and associate it with beauty and acceptance, they are engaging in a self-reflective political act, the dispelling of whiteness as is seen and experience by the "other" as terrifying and dominating. In some cases, the liberal rational construction of the white self is replaced by a more multifaceted self, a self that is now a critical agent that is unbounded so that is can embrace the otherness within the self. This post-white self would be more sensitized to the fact that race still matters in the America.

The dehegemonized position of whiteness would create a shift, not in the way that Gayatri C. Spivak envisions the white self as "the subject position of the other,"[133] reproducing whiteness as the necessary "other" to the fixed homogeneity of an inverted nonwhite "self," but as a "self," becoming self-conscious. Such an alternative subject position of the "self" is important for the reconstructing of a post-white self, as a critical and ethical self, which would work to reconstitute a post-white identity. This enhances, rightfully so, the following question: What would the post-white identity look like? In the following section, I want to look briefly at the post-white identity.

THE POST-WHITE IDENTITY

Denormalizing whiteness is a way of rethinking and rearticulting an alternative form of antiracist whiteness that would work to reconstitute a post-white identity. And since the denormalizing of whiteness is an ongoing process, rather than the post-white identity positing itself external to America's racialized process and practice, a self-reflective whiteness would now be embraced by whites. Given that whiteness is maintained by a series of expressively recursive acts, in this case, the government's antidiscrimination measures, a post-white identity would have to constantly work to decenter itself from such a practice. In fact, within the concept of "white fetishism,"[134] there is a form of hierarchical thinking about the "other" in relation to the self, which allows for the denial of human dignity to people of color and the rights to be humanly different from whites. I have shown in chapter one, how First Nations, blacks, and other nonwhites were constructed as subhuman as opposed to white humans.

The question then is whether the new location of whiteness as "denor-malizing" can reconstitute a post-white identity. Can this new identity be more of a reflective position, a delicate balance between the white self and the nonwhite "other?" In *Memory, History, Forgetting*, Paul Ricoeur's argument that even though the self and the "other" have been "estranged from each other," they can very well complement each other is appeal-ing.[135] Can we, then, construct a "self-other" from this idea? I think that we would have to be careful that this new "self-other" is not heading in the direction of a "third-self," that is, a merging of the self and "other" to create a complex hybrid identity. For sure, the third-self would enable a movement beyond bounded identities and binary oppositions of white-ness and nonwhiteness; however, again we have to be careful about the third-self, being positioned between the two identities, self and "other," as a form of liminality, an in-between sameness and difference. "I am the same, but yet I am different" is what Fanon reveals as the doubling of identity, functioning as a narcissistic manifestation of the self in the "oth-er."

Spivak, for strategic reasons, has prescribed that the very status of the "self" should be reinscribed into the "other"[136] or, as it should be, that whites should assimilate blackness, for example.[137] When Frantz Fanon, in *The Wretched of the Earth*, calls for destroying the area of the Algerian frontier that the settler (whites) occupied so that they seizes to be two separate spaces, one for the settler (whites) and one for the native (non-whites), this was partly what he had in mind. Can the "self" be trans-formed into the "other"? As I see it, reinscribing the self as the "other" without addressing power relations, where the very basis of our subjec-tivities are entwined, would be a disaster. I suppose that what is more important is not a third-self, but a post-white self that is freed from a "double consciousness" which, in this case, is the twoness, self and "oth-er," in a single subjectivity. A post-white self would work against the binary opposition of the white self and the nonwhite "other" in which the very status of the white self is already dehegemonized. Yet we have to be careful that this post-white self is not appropriated in such a way that denormalized whiteness does not retrieve back to whiteness and be-comes the refractory signifier of defeat and deficiency, creating this new form of white identification where is all right, then, for whites to now identifying themselves as marginalized and the new oppressed group.[138] And even though, many mainstream thinkers view the government's antidiscrimination measures, as I have shown in chapter three, as repel-lents for white males' power position, and the deficiency and the down-fall of white supremacy, this is false. Paul C. Taylor reminds us that it was John Dewey in the "Introduction to Selected Poems of Claude McKay," who confessed that white supremacy allows for whites, espe-cially white men, to express a "humiliated sympathy."[139] We see this clearly in the new discourse on "reverse racism," where whites feel victimized.

A post-white identity would work to deflect from the assumption that whiteness is in some kind of "crisis," which emanates from a "me-too-ism" perspective of white victimhood and lays claims to minority status: "I am a white male" and "I am now the minority." And even though the "I," with its expected solipsistic tendency, effectively induces and makes obligatory hidden signs of race and gender superiority, by its very nature it racializes and genderizes. When the white male names himself as raced and gendered, this annunciation points into the direction of claiming minority status, which Judith Butler, in an extraordinary way, labels "a willful act of self-reduction."[140] And since self-reduction works against dismantling white supremacy, what needs to take its place is self-reflection. It is only then can anxious whiteness be transformed into secured whiteness. When anxious whiteness is transformed into white security, a new pedagogy of white subject position will be grounded in the notion of whiteness not as victimization but as celebration. Whites would be able to develop a new ethics, that is, the courage to denounce a whiteness that is anxious in order to announce a secure whiteness, or, to borrow from Fanon's terms, the "being for [self]" to "beings for [others]" that allows for positive self-presentation of post-white identity. It is my hope that a post-white identity would find comfort in its ontological vocation to act upon and embrace a world where a dialogical encounter with "otherness," of the "other" and well as the self is celebrated. Given that knowledge of the self, the other, and society is socially and institutionally produced and constituted, a post-white identity is always a work in progress. It has to work to continuously decentering itself.

NOTES

1. Mills (1997), 126–27.
2. Feagin (2006), 256. Other organizations in the United States working to contour racism include: People's Institute for Survival and Beyond, White Panther Party, Think Again, and Antiracist Action.
3. Cornel West has highlighted three white supremacist logics: the Judeo-Christian racist logics, the scientific racist logics, and the psychosexual story of Ham, son of Noah who, in failing to cover Noah's nakedness, had his offspring blackened by God. For a more comprehensive overview, of how white supremacist discourses are guided by the construction of whiteness, see West's *Keeping Faith: Philosophy and Race in America* (1993). More recently, white supremacy also has entered the digital age by customizing Internet technology and digital media in ways that are "innovative, sophisticated, and cunning" (Daniels 2009, 4). Hate speeches, disguise as promoting and celebrating the rights of white supremacist, are, in some cases, protected under the First Amendment. For critical race theorists, the first amendment, providing provision for hate speech to be protected successfully supports "conscious and unconscious racists—Nazis and liberals alike—with a constitutional right to be racist" (Daniels 2009, 161). In addition, for a comprehensive account on "cyber racism," see Les Back, "Ar-

yans Reading Adorno: Cyper-Culture and the Twenty-First-Century Racism" (2002), 632.

4. Du Bois (1969), 30.

5. Winant (1997), 40.

6. Lipsitz (1998), 19.

7. Helen Charles, "Whiteness–The Relevance of Politically Coloring the 'Non,'" observes that when white is discussed as a racial identity in postcolonial texts, "it is a challenge and a sign of change" (1992, 31) and centers "around notions of belonging and exclusion, benevolence and responsibility, and complicity" as is shown in Karen Blixen's *Out of Africa*. See Tony Simoes da Silva, "Redeeming Self: The Business of Whiteness in Post-Apartheid South African Writing" (2004). However, in America, racial identity is applied to blacks and other people of color. Whites have been socialized of not thinking of themselves in racial terms, which serve as a powerful differentiated process that communicates to whites a view of themselves as unlike racialized groups who are look on as inferior. In chapter four I have already discussed the problematics of assigning race to whites. Also, see Barbara J. Fields, "Whiteness, Racism, and Identity" (2001). However, in the face of normalized whiteness, whiteness studies scholars are bent on assigning racial identity to whites.

8. See Judith Katz, *White Awareness: Handbook for Anti-Racism Training* (2003).

9. See David R. Roediger, *Colored White: Transcending the Racial Past* (2002); Matthew F. Jacobson, *Whiteness of a Different Color: European Immigrants and the Alchemy of Race* (1998); Noel Ignatiev and John Garvey, *Race Traitor* (1996); and Ruth Frankenberg, *White Women, Race Matters: The Social Construction of Whiteness* (1993).

10. In *The Racial Contract*, Professor Charles Mills make a compelling case for why blacks and other nonwhites were excluded from this creed. The feminist theorist Carol Pateman, in *The Sexual Contract*, by drawing on the family ethic, has shown why women were excluded from the American creed that has its roots in John Locke's "law of nature," which is based on the social rules of mutuality. In exemplifying this point, she writes: "Locke assumes that marriage and the family exist in a natural state and he also argues that the attributes of individuals are sexually differentiated; only men have the characteristics of free and equal beings. Women are naturally subordinate to men and the order of nature is reflected in the structure of conjugal relations" (1988, 52).

11. Du Bois (1969), 29.

12. Hill (1997), 3.

13. Fine et al. (1997), 8.

14. Foucault (1988), 18.

15. See Eduardo Bonilla-Silva, "Color-Blind Racism" (2007); and *Racism Without Racists: Color-Blind Racism and the Persistence of Racial Inequality in the United States* (2006).

16. Michel Foucault, *Power/Knowledge: Selected Writings and Interviews, 1972–1977* (1980); *Disciplining and Punish* (1977); and *The History of Sexuality* (1978).

17. Spivak (1990), 30. Also, see Toni Morrison's *Playing in the Dark: Whiteness and the Literary Imagination* (1993).

18. West (1992), 24.

19. Fine (1997), 58.

20. Morrison (1993), 90. Also, see Michele Fine, "Witnessing Whiteness" (1997); and Ruth Frankenberg, *White Women, Race Matters: The Social Construction of Whiteness* (1993).

21. Yancy (2004), 10.

22. McKinney and Feagin (2003), 235. However, Charles Gallagher, in "White Reconstruction in the University," shows that whites are increasing become conscious of their whiteness (2003).

23. Fine (1997), 63.

24. Haney López (1993), 3. When whites are outnumbered in a multicultural setting, whites suddenly claim their whiteness in the form of their superiority over people of

color. In Karyn D. McKinney, "I fell 'Whiteness' When I Hear People Blaming Whites: Whiteness as Cultural Victimization," she draws our attention to the confession of one of her white students that she interviewed for her study. The student was at an amusement park with her parents and, according to her, no one spoke English. "I have never been so annoyed . . . I am definitely very ethnocentric in that I think that my culture and my ways are the best," the student admitted (2003, 50–51). This is a good illustration of commonsense racism where "nationalist" is being substituted for racist. Also, on whiteness as entitlement, see Peggy McIntosh, "White Privilege: Unpacking the Invisible Knapsack" (2007); Charles Gallagher, "White Reconstruction in the University" (2003). Ruth Frankenberg, *White Women, Race Matters: The Social Construction of Whiteness*, show how white women exult their privilege position and promote dichotomous thinking about self and "other" (1993).

25. Butler (1995a), 443.

26. Gallagher (2000), 80.

27. Frankenberg (2001), 76.

28. As a way of combating racism, many blacks, for example, have expressed their pride in being black and wholeheartedly embraced the idea that black is beautiful.

29. Frankenberg (1997), 18.

30. Fuss (1989), 12.

31. Hartigan (1998a), 184.

32. Charles (1992), 33.

33. Ahmed (2004).

34. Fine et al. (1997), 9.

35. Ahmed (2004).

36. Bonnett (1999), 204.

37. See Sara Ahmed, "Declaration of Whiteness: The Non-Performativity of Antiracism" (2004); Barbara J. Fields, "Whiteness, Racism, and Identity" (2001); Rebecca Aanerud, "Fictions of Whiteness: Speaking the Name of Whiteness in U.S. Literature" (1997); Toni Morrison, *Playing in the Dark: Whiteness and the Literary Imagination* (1993); bell hooks, *Black Looks: Race and Representation* (1992); and Helen Charles, "Whiteness: The Relevance of Politically Coloring the 'Non'" (1992).

38. See James Baldwin's path breaking work, "Notes of a Native Son," in *Collective Essays* (1998).

39. Rasmussen et al. (2001), 13.

40. Butler (1994), 6.

41. Fanon (1967), 112.

42. Hill (2008), 10.

43. Feagan (2000), 255.

44. Harris (1999), 184.

45. Roediger (1991).

46. hooks (1992), 346.

47. See George Lipsitz, *The Possessive Investment in Whiteness: How White People Profit From Identity Politics* (1998); and "The Possessive Investment in Whiteness: Racialized Social Democracy and the 'White' Problem in American Studies" (1995).

48. See George Yancy, "Introduction: Fragments of a Social Ontology of Whiteness (2004a); and Charles W. Mills, "Racial Exploitation and the Wages of Whiteness" (2004).

49. Moreton-Robinson (2008), 85.

50. Lipsitz (1998), 7.

51. Moreton-Robinson (2008), 85–86.

52. hooks (1992), 346.

53. Lazarre (1996), 135.

54. Ware and Back (2002), 160.

55. Ware and Back (2002), 28. This quote also appeared in David R. Roediger's *Black on White: Black Writers and What it Means to be White*, who was quoting James Baldwin (1998), 22.

56. Arnesen (2001), 15.
57. Lorde (1984), 116.
58. Giroux (1997), 314.
59. McLaren (1999), 11.
60. hooks (1992), 12.
61. Ahmed (2004).
62. Alcoff (1998), 6.
63. Aanerud (2007), 20.
64. Aanerud (2007), 20. Also, see Ruth Frankenberg, "'When We Are Capable of Stopping, We Begin to See': Being White, Seeing Whiteness" (1996).
65. Aanerud (2007), 20.
66. Katz (2003), 10.
67. Bonnett (1999), 206.
68. Butler (1995a), 443.
69. Aanerud (2007), 33–34.
70. Morrison (1992), 11.
71. Farr (2004), 145.
72. Prashad (2001), 4.
73. See Samuel P. Huntington, *Who Are We? The Challenges to America's National Identity* (2004).
74. Giroux (1997), 299.
75. Roediger (1994), 158.
76. Harris (1993), 1760. Also, see Matthew F. Jacobson, *Whiteness of a Different Color: European Immigrants and the Alchemy of Race* (1998); Noel Ignatiev, *How the Irish Became White* (1995); and David R. Roediger, *The Wages of Whiteness: Race and the Making of the American Working Class* (1991).
77. The economic plights of poor whites are often blamed on illegal immigrants (who most often are nonwhite), too many handouts directed at minorities (social programs), and affirmative action programs. Rarely are macroeconomic policies of the government examined and deemed responsible for the situation in which the poor find themselves.
78. Roediger (1991), 190.
79. A good illustration of "white flight" from neighborhoods that are racially integrated is depicted in the documentary, *Why Can't We Live Together*. In the film, a number of whites are interviewed about their decision to move from a formally all-white suburb in Chicago to another all-white remote town. One mother explains that this town is "'a good place to race children [because] live is back to family and playing all day.' Because there are no people of color, particularly African American, living nearby, she doesn't have to worry about 'her kids walking into the street and getting shot by gangs'" (Aanerud 2007, 21).
80. Feagin (2006), 238.
81. McIntosh (2007), 177.
82. On the other hand, black nationalists have reacted to whiteness by incorporating the language, values, traditions, and culture of Africa through Pan-Africanism. Through the Universal Negro Improvement Association, led by Marcus Garvey, many blacks were mobilized to deal with American racism.
83. W. E. B. Du Bois (1969), 30.
84. Dyer (1988), 44.
85. Twine and Gallagher (2008), 19.
86. Feagin (2006), 238–39.
87. See Paulo Freire, *The Pedagogy of the Oppressed* (2003); and Franz Fanon, *Black Skin, White Masks* (1967); and *The Wretched of the Earth* (1963).
88. Baldwin (1995), 8.
89. Fanon (1967), 111.
90. Du Bois (2003).
91. Fuss (1994), 24.

92. Huntington (2004), 4.

93. Butler (1995a), 442–43.

94. Ware and Back (2002), 9. Also, see Noel Ignatiev and John Garvey, *Race Traitor* (1996); and David R. Roediger, *Towards the Abolition of Whiteness: Essays on Race, Politics, and Working Class History* (1994); and *The Wages of Whiteness: Race and the Making of the American Working Class* (1991).

95. The new abolitionists have argued that whiteness was invented simultaneously with the development of and rise of capitalism. This view is found in the works of critical legal theorists and radical historians. Their reading and rereading of American histories of reading and writing engage with what is viewed as the "Race Traitor," that is, the working to abolish whiteness. This involves whites rejecting their privileges and working to end white supremacy.

96. Ignatiev and Garvey (1996), 10.

97. Gilroy (2000b).

98. See chapter 4, "Whiteness and the Problemnatics of 'Whiteness Studies.'"

99. Frankenberg (1993), 1.

100. For a more comprehensive account on the racialization process in America, see Michael Omi and Howard Winant, *Racial Formation in the United States from the 1960s to the 1990s* (1994).

101. McLaren (1999), 11.

102. According to Noel Ignatiev, the Irish immigrants in the United States were often referred to as "niggers turned inside out," and in Britain, Carlyle referred to them as "the white Negroes." Blacks, at that time, were referred to as "smoked Irish" (1995, 41). Comparing the Irish with blacks deemed the Irish as black as well. It is clear that the metaphoric guideline is at work here, in that, in spite of the physical difference between Irish and blacks, it is the sameness that is confirmed, made visible, and insisted on.

103. Hence, this process of becoming white is wholly immanent to bearing in mind, knowing (acquired by experience) and, above all, to being made evident in the literal and cultural forms of whiteness. Alternative subject positions and opposing devise of whiteness would have to be reemployed.

104. Roediger (1994), 13.

105. Chater (1994), 100.

106. Mercer (1994), 339.

107. At North Newton Junior-Senior High School, a white school (two of the 850 students are black), located in Morocco, Indiana, several female students calling themselves the "Free to Be Me" group, identify with the Hip-Hop culture by having hair that are dreadlocks and wearing baggy jeans and combat boots. In order to preserve the accepted code of whiteness, these girls have experienced both physical and psychological violence from many of their peers at school. Several of the girls from the "Free to Be Me" group were talking about the experience of "race trading" on the Montel Williams show, a black-hosted TV talk show. See Linda Martín Alcoff, "What Should White People Do?" (1998, 16). The "Free to Be Me" group, functioning as a problematic and disrupting presence for whiteness, does not mean that whiteness as cultural practice has been denormalized.

108. See Henri Giroux, "Rewriting the Discourse of Racial Identity: Toward a Pedagogy and Politics of Whiteness" (1997).

109. Ware and Back (2001), 9.

110. Katz (2003), 145.

111. Dyer (1988), 44.

112. Roediger (1991), 13.

113. See Noel Ignatiev and John Garvey, *Race Traitor* (1996).

114. It is also true for men. Even though they might have unlearned their sexism and constantly works on not to be sexist, they, indeed, continue to benefit from patriarchy's horrible predispositions.

115. Taylor (2004), 237.

116. McLaren (1999), 39.

117. Ignatiev (1995), 59.

118. Gallagher (2003), 302

119. W. E. B. Du Bois (1969), 29–30.

120. bell hooks, in *Black Looks: Race and Representation*, has already drawn our attention to the terrifying nature of whiteness in blacks' imagination (1992, 170). Blacks and
other nonwhites have been taught to fear the unfathomable dismay of whiteness.

121. McLaren (1999), 34.

122. Freire (1998), 40.

123. Giroux (1997).

124. Dyer (1988), 44.

125. Haney López (1996), 193.

126. Ignatiev and Garvey (1996), 10.

127. See Ruth Frankenberg, *White Women, Race Matters: The Social Construction of
Whiteness* (1993).

128. Dyer (1988), 44.

129. A further investigation of white anxiety is seen in the way "whiteness studies"
scholars have articulated the relationship between white skin privilege and racism.
Annalee Newitz and Matt Wray, for example, note: "Perhaps white trash can also
provide a corrective to what has been called a 'vulgar multiculturalist' assumption
that whiteness must always equal terror and racism. It is our wish that 'white trash'
and *White Trash* [the volume that we edited] start to lay the groundwork for a form of
white identity that is comfortable with multiculturalism, and with which multiculturalism is comfortable as well" (1997, 5). This desire to point to the variations within
whiteness, I think, is the kind of critique that ends up producing an essentialized and
racist discourse that fails to take racial discrimination into account.

130. Lauretis (2002), 54.

131. Katz (2003), 145.

132. Frankenberg (1997), 18.

133. Spivak (1990). In terms of the racialization process that is at work, Spivak's
position is clearly strategic. Noel Ignatiev and John Garvey, in *Race Traitor*, make the
similar observation that whites should "assimilate" blackness, for example. They
noted: "When whites reject their racial identity, they take a big step towards becoming
human. But may that step not entail, for many, some engagement with blackness,
perhaps even an identification as 'black'? Recent experience, in the country and elsewhere would indicate that it does" (1996, 115). This is one way that whites can escape
from their whiteness. However, this escaping remains problematic. It underestimates
and disregards whiteness normality. Hence, for Jane Lazarre, in her book *Beyond the
Whiteness of Whiteness*, in order to understand the "blackness of blackness," it "would
have to be accompanied by a willingness to explore whiteness" (1996, 22). But exploring is not enough. Whiteness would have to be denormalized.

134. For a more comprehensive reading on white fetishism, see Ghassan Hage,
"White Self-Racialization as Identity Fetishism: Capitalism and the Experience of Colonial Whiteness" (2005).

135. Ricoeur (2004), 95.

136. See Gayatri C. Spivak, *The Post-Colonial Critic: Interview, Strategies, Dialogues*
(1990).

137. See Vron Ware and Les Back, *Out of Whiteness: Color, Politics and Culture* (2002),
159–60; and Noel Ignatiev and John Garvey, *Race Traitor* (1996).

138. In fact, this form of white identification is another feature of the property rights
of whites in their whiteness because to be oppressed is to experience the difficulties
that accompany the oppression.

139. Taylor (2004), 227.

140. Butler (1995a), 443.

Conclusion: Reflections

Whiteness is a production that habitually obscures its origin[1] and histori-cal specificity.[2] Hence, to reestablish the genealogy of whiteness and the development of racism in America, one must begin with the analysis of indentured servitude. Even though the economic conditions of inden-tured servants were the same, skin-color, hair, and other phenotypical distinctions served as anchors to peg differences, and placed people into racial categories, which became instrumental for the hegemonic project of whiteness. Even though there is a dialogic relation between whiteness and nonwhiteness, what Simone de Beauvoir has observed about the manner in which women are "defined and differentiated with reference to man and not he with reference to her," the same can be said of non-whiteness and whiteness: nonwhiteness is defined in its relation to white-ness. In this sense, nonwhiteness "is the incidental, the inessential as opposed to the essential."[3] Blacks and other people of color were a separat-ate "natural kind" and inferior to whites in the "Great Chain of Being." In other words, in the United States, the naturalization of nonwhites' inferi-ority is fundamental to the understanding of the ontological genesis of racism as a symptom of whiteness.

Whiteness, giving rise to and is premised on white supremacy, sets itself up as the essential, normal, and superior as opposite to nonwhite-ness, the inessential, abnormal, and inferior. In other words, this opposi-tional, binary logic by means of its genealogy, move forward, establishes, maintains, supports, and perpetuates that whites are necessarily superior and, thus, functions in such a way as to marginalize nonwhites. It is precisely for this reason that for all of America's vaunted progress, en-lightened practice, and democratic institutions, the inferior ("them") and the superior ("us") model continues to be a signifying practice. More recently, in post 9/11 America, people who look Middle Eastern are viewed and treated as the "them." Since the "them" is perceived as racial-ly and culturally different from the "us," it is in this instant of demarca-tion that domination in the form of whiteness is fashioned and dissemi-nated.

Blacks and First Nations were deemed uncivilized, deficient, and lack-ing in human qualities and, as such, deserving of discriminatory treat-ment under indentured servitude. Slavery, symptomatic of America's ra-cism and characteristically appealed to the dictate of white supremacy, continued to merely systematize in law and cultural practice, the inferior-

161

ity of blacks and, most crucially, established them as property. Besides laws and ideology to keep blacks subservient, an effort was made to exclude them from other spheres of American life. Religious texts, for instance, were used to show that the inferior position of blacks and other nonwhites was determined in heaven and would be to their advantage on earth. These texts were invented by white men such as to justify the natural inferiority of blacks and other nonwhites, and to explain the cruel fate imposed on them as natural.[4]

In fact, in the slave society, the slaves and their masters were united by a shared need, which, in this case, was economic. Yet the master never made a point of expressing how important slave labor was for him to accumulate profits. He had in his power, through laws and cultural practice, ways of keeping the slaves dependent on him, and he constantly worked to instill upon the slaves their inferior status. We are, by now, familiar with the savage conditions, for the most part, that most slaves endured. Even though, slavery ended for apparent reasons that I will not discuss here, and the constitutional amendments granted equal rights, at least in theory, to ex-slaves, it was important for states to implement law that would deter blacks of such rights and reinvoke whites' claim to superiority. None offered a more concise example than the Jim Crow laws. How whiteness works, then, as domination and the consequences of that domination on racialized ethnic groups become overriding.

While whiteness as domination is homogeneous, white identity remains heterogeneous and fractured by the simultaneous practice, for example, of racists and antiracists. It is important for antiracists to work to combat racism and its multidimensional forms of oppression. However, if antiracist action is to have any effectiveness, contemporary racism, in its multifaceted forms and the internal function of the logics by which it is vindicated and rationalized, must be attended to. Such a concept as "reverse racism" is therefore imminently questionable. While "reverse racism," willfully erases the facts of whiteness and white privilege, it is an actual defense of white male entitlement, obliterating the very nature of white supremacy and how much it impacts the lives of racialized ethnic groups. As the victims of white preeminence, nonwhites are more sensitive to its effects and, thus, more likely to detect and name it. The contagious influence of race and racial thinking, which emerged and continues to pervade American life represents, I think, the greatest challenge that the United States will continue to face in the future.

The election of Barack Obama has mostly led to the idea that the American society has finally reached its post-racial phase. America, declaring itself as post-racial, reflects what Slavoj Žižek has to say about post-ideological that "the denial of ideology only provides the ultimate proof that we are embedded in ideology."[5] The same can be said of race in America. America is entrenched in race and racial thinking. Extending Žižek's approach, in terms of thinking about race in America, is essential to decisively scrutinize how racial ideology works as a form of power in the construction of racial domination. The painful truth is that blacks and other nonwhites continue to be racially profiled. It is no wonder that the anthropologist Jane H. Hill, citing Gloria Ladson-Billing, writes, "Your race is what you are when the cops pull you over at two o'clock in the morning."[6] In the rawest form, as Diana Fuss remarks, "Race remains an important site of intense political contestation"[7] and an influential force in societal relations. Post-racial America, then, is another one of those myths that constructs and shapes the reality and obsession with race that it purports to dispel. However, if America is post-racial, the task would be how to reconstitute *race* outside the system of normalized whiteness and put post-raciality into practice. Given that the ontology status of race is transformed into an irregular representation, that is, whites are now assigned *race*, even though America is supposed to be post-racial, how do these assumptions inform the discourse on race? Because of America's racialization process, how do we address whites as raced, taking on social visibility and meanings that are not related to the regulatory practices of whiteness and its unambiguous institutionalization of racism, structuring, organizing, reinforcing, and maintaining the unequal status of blacks and other nonwhites? Since these regulatory practices, in effect, appeal to racial commonsense as a technique of legitimate power that works in the interest of whiteness, we must challenge or overturn the contradictions and strength of these representations.[8] Race, I think would indeed disappear, or take on new meanings, when whiteness is disrupted, displaced, cracked open, fractured, deposed, and eventually stripped of its presumptive hegemony. As way of freeing ourselves from claims of whites as raced, which is resultant of anxious whiteness, to denormalize whiteness, as is expressed in a differentiating need for an oppositional whiteness, is a commitment that we should all share, especially whites.

As a matter of fact, race-based discrimination is an everyday fact of life for blacks and other people of color. Even though colorblind discourse has tried to suppress the visible appearance of race, race, as physically visible, represents a decisive category for blacks and other people of color's existence.[9] It is indeed the most "explosive issue in American life"[10] because it continuously mediates, shapes, and structures social relations. Race, indeed, is America's single most perplexing problem, but the perplexing problem of race is that few of us have any idea what race is.[11] Like gender for Judith Butler, "a fictive construction through the compulsory ordering of attributes into coherent gender sequence,"[12] race can be viewed in similar construction such that it materializes as prearranged, natural, and indisputable. We think we *see* race when we come across certain physical differences among people such as skin color, eye shape, hair texture, and other phenotypical distinctions. What we in fact *see* are the learned social meanings, the stereotypes, or "controlling images" that have been linked to those physical features by the ideology of race and racial thinking, and the historical inheritance it has imprinted on us. I have already pointed to how, historically, in the United States, skin-color determined who were marked by race. Race and race ideology are consonant with their historical development and continue to epitomize contemporary sociocultural realities for blacks and other nonwhites. Race is marked on the body and it is repeatedly reenacted or resignified. In spite of the arguments according to which America is experiencing a "declining significance of race," and is witnessing "the end of racism" or, more recently, that America has moved beyond race (post-racial), it does not mean that race, as a meaningful concept for the twenty-first century, has disappeared.

Countless examples of racial antagonism can be found in the contemporary United States. For instance a Harvard undergraduate student Stephanie Grace declared in 2010, in an e-mail exchange with one of her peers, that African Americans might be genetically inferior to whites. Other noteworthy occurrences of blatant racism are racial profiling of Muslim Americans; the arrest of professor Louis Gates of Harvard University in 2009; the racist controversy that showed its ugly face with the nomination of Sonia Sotomayor as Supreme Court judge in 2009; a noose was found hanging on the office door of the African American professor Modonna Constantine at Columbia University; and nooses were found hanging in the school yard of Jena High School in Jena, Louisiana in 2006; the unjustifiable jailing of Bryonn Bain, a Harvard Law Student, in 2003; the shooting and killing of Amadau Diallo by white police officers in 1999; the murder of James Byrd in Jasper Texas in 1998; the sodomizing of Abner Louima with a plunger by white police officers in New York City and the burning alive of Garnett Paul Johnson in 1997; the beating of Rodney King by white police officers in 1991. The list is too long to be cited exhaustively but the preceding examples show that *race* is indeed not settling down any time soon. Professor Cornel West's *Race Matters*, active in inscribing an extraordinarily rich analysis on race, throughout such a profound work, points to the fact that *race matters* because it is "the most explosive issue in America's life." [13] It "matters so much that it has become almost impossible for one to think outside of 'racial' categories" [14] and work against whiteness as the norm. In short, more than ever before, Americans are compelled to face up to race and racism.

Even though racism is a problem, it is shamelessly argued by many prominent scholars that racism no longer exists in the United States. The denial that racism is alive and well is one way of constituting, what following Judith Butler, I will identify as "the saintly white person" [15] who cannot, by definition, be racist. A big part of the repertoire of commonsense racism is that it is now focused on the individuals and is assembled by such characterizations as uneducated, backwards, and "low-life." [16] Notwithstanding the fact that recently in 2006, a noose was found hanging on the office door of an African American professor Modonna

Constantine of Columbia University, a prestigious institution of higher learning in the supposedly liberal New York City. Hence, when a respected public figure, for example, is accused of racist remarks, there is a great deal of "moral panic,"[17] electrifying public emotions and mesmerizing Americans into opposing camps. What comes to my mind is on April 5, 2007, after a mass criticism of Don Imus for calling members of the women's basket ball team at Rutgers University, "nappy-headed hos," and the aftermath resulted in CBS (rightfully so) firing Imus from his radio program.[18] Imus's assaultive remark about black women was broadcasted for weeks in the media, blogs, and Internet discussion sites and chat rooms, and it created two opposite camps. Many of his defenders anxiously asked us not to think of Imus's remark as racist. Having been so advised, one cannot avoid thinking that his remark is nothing but racist. The fact of the matter is when "we," for a continuous period, read or hear "about some important public figure . . . using racist epithet, that epithet is irrevocably reinscribed in our understanding,"[19] and these comments are easily penetrable.

In the end, one needs to see Imus's racist utterance as embedded in what the sociologist Philip Cohen identifies as "the hidden narratives in theories of racism."[20] In fact, racist practice is always embedded in the theory of racism. While racism, as a prolific form of power that is disseminated across a broad array of institutions, systems, and practice, is not only fashioned and replicated, everyday racist comments are important sites for producing and reproducing of whiteness. Whites, having the right to speak about the constructed social "other" and, conceivably, even so, for all white people, is what Alastair Bonnett defines and describes as "introspection practice."[21] Indeed, "introspection practice" leaves unnoticed something utterly fundamental, that is, the detriments of racist descriptions both for the "self" as well as the "other." While some whites are shocked and disgusted by racist remarks, most blacks and other nonwhites are always ready and waiting for such utterances. Yet the anticipation does not erase the pain and humiliation that nonwhites experience when such continuous occurrences materialize. In fact, a racist remark is performative in the Austin's sense, that is, as a form of utterance, it does what it says—[22] what it sets out to do—which is to debase the nonwhite "other." Most of the time such anguish is experienced in silence because blacks and other people of color are physically and mentally exhausted from perpetual racist assaults and are then less equipped for public retaliation. In this book, I have already identified countless examples of racist assaults on the nonwhite psyche. On the other hand, blacks, other nonwhites, and antiracist whites have been active in resisting and developing proactive positions against racism. However, racism, taking on new forms and continues to overwhelm American society, is daunting.

How can we get beyond race and racism without taking into account America's process of racialization where blacks and other people of color continue to experience discrimination based on race? This question is not new, and Justice Harry Blackmun, in the case of *Regents of the University of California v. Bakke*, shed some light on answering this question when he observed that "in order to get past racism we must first take account of race. There is no other present way. In order to treat people equally, we must treat them differently."[23] I have already drawn on examples where senior citizens in some cases are allowed to ride on the public transit at a reduced price. However, a good illustration is affirmative action programs and the quota system that allow for minority access to job and educational opportunities that are populated by the white majority.

Some outrageous racist comments from whites, telling themselves stories about racial progress and drawing from the presupposition that they themselves are not racists, are made visible by some scholars who have conducted interviews with college students.[24] Yet, we know that these kinds of comments are not limited to public figures and colleges students. They are sometimes more elaborated and show up, for instance, behind the scenes boardrooms, in jokes, opinion pieces, and commentaries, academic and journalistic writings, blogs, and e-mails. The Internet has become perchance the most significant medium made available for racist comments. Bulletin boards on the Internet are posting the most outrageous racist commentaries.[25] Whites acting, writing, and speaking in manners that make the initial design of race and racial thinking in America undyingly accessible to the future populace is a reason for alarm. Racist comments, which have a long history, have extended themselves to include homophobic, anti-Semitic, and sexist statements.

Labels such as *honorary whites* and *model minority* fall prey to the myth that whites who associate and cooperate with individuals from racialized groups "and give them recognition are not racist."[26] In fact, the self-evident truth is that these labels are nothing but racist and, more importantly, are implicated in "the inevitable chatter of benevolence racism."[27] That is, "You are not like the rest of the blacks and Mexicans." "You are an honorary white." "You are the model minority." In creating these labels, there is an additional progression at play, which is the othering of the "other." A somewhat straightforward and accessible example is: You are a CEO, a doctor, a lawyer, or a novelist, with ascribed membership to a racialized ethnic group. Because of your social and economic status, you are made to belief that you are "different" from the other members of that group. Even though, as Stuart Hall would say, it is "the kind of difference that doesn't make a difference of any kind,"[28] you must continuously present yourself like an honorary white or *a* model minority. However, when you are juxtapositioned against whites, you are "different" because of your skin color. "To be different from those that are different," as Homi K. Bhabha puts it, "makes you the same."[29] What this shows is that honorary white and model minority, as emancipator signifiers from the racialized self, cannot be actually accomplished.[30]

The recent development of "whiteness studies," even though it reflects the social settings, debates, legal strategies, and institutional and epistemological provisions that have characterized the creation of whiteness as unraced and unmarked, it is, none the less, charged with assigning race to whites. I have already pointed to dangers of assigning race to whites. By assigning race to whites, racism as an unavoidable and authoritative assignment of race is emaciated into racial identity. Even though, for whiteness studies scholars, a white racial identity, as an unexamined racial formation needs to be examined, normalized whiteness would continue to be treated as cultural expectations. Hence, a change in the meaning of race would depend on stripping whiteness of its authority and power. Is making whiteness visible a way to reducing its power?

"Whiteness studies" and antiracist whiteness signify a profound turn of making whiteness visible to those for whom it is invisible. Given that "whiteness studies" and antiracist whiteness are still positioned within normalized whiteness as such, these practices are not equipped to confront relations of power that remain as institutional norms. What "whiteness studies" and antiracist whiteness do instead, in spite of their intentions, is to rehegemonize whiteness and reproduce white privilege in ways that are ignored. This manifest unawareness has given new urgency for a more in-depth account of the inherent contradictions of "whiteness studies." In chapter 4, I have, in part, highlighted some these contradictions and have concluded that "whiteness studies" seems to have done little to address these challenges. It is only when whites "*get off white*" could they then "get on [*white*] in critical and political transformative ways."[31] Hence, the denormalizing of whiteness is important for whites to "*get off white*" and to reconfigure a post-white identity. However, a post-white identity is not a finished process; it has to constantly work to dehegemonize the *self* by, first and foremost, disengaging with anxious whiteness.

NOTES

1. Butler (1990a), 273.
2. Nonwhites are aware of the genesis of whiteness and the attempts of whiteness to hide its genesis. See W. E. B. Du Bois, *The Soul of Black Folks* (2003); Toni Morrison, *Playing in the Dark: Whiteness and the Literary Imagination* (1997); bell hooks, *Black Looks: Race and Representation* (1992).
3. Beauvoir (1964), 16.
4. See Thomas Jefferson, *Notes on the State of Virginia* (1999).
5. Žižek (2009), 37.
6. Hill (2008), 13.
7. Fuss (1989), 92.
8. Butler (1994), 19.

9. John Hartigan Jr., "Culture Against Race: Reworking the Basis for Racial Analysis," where he demonstrates the historical legacy of race in America; Also, see Thomas Jefferson, *Notes on the State of Virginia*, where he talked about distinct races—First Nations (Indians), blacks, and Chinese. As a matter of fact, it was fixed in Jefferson's mind that blacks and whites could never coexist in the United States of America because the difference between these two races "is fixed in nature . . . And is this difference of no importance," Jefferson reasoned (1999, 6). For a general overview of the emergence of race outside of the United States, see David Theo Goldberg, *The Threat of Race: Reflections of Racial Neoliberalism* (2009, 2–4); and Michel Foucault's 1976 lectures: "Security, Territory Populations Lectures at the Collège de France on race and the formation of the modern state." Lately, several attempts to undo race (move beyond race), as a way of ending racism, have been presented by prominent scholars. See Paul Gilroy, *Against Race: Imagining Political Culture Beyond the Color Line* (2000); Vron Ware and Les Back, *Out of Whiteness: Color, Politics and Culture* (2001).

10. West (2001), 155. Paul Gilroy, on the other hand, argues that we have moved beyond race. See Paul Gilroy, *Against Race: Imagining Political Culture Beyond the Color Line* (2000a) and *Between Camps: Nations, Culture, and the Allure of Race* (2000b).

11. Hanley-López (1994), 5–6.

12. Butler (1990b), 18–20.

13. West (2001), 155–56.

14. Torres et al. (1999), 4.

15. Butler (1995a), 443.

16. Hill (2008), 63.

17. Harris (2008), 43.

18. Before Imus's racist comment, on November 18, 2006, actor Michael Richards, who is famous for portraying the character Kramer on the Television show *Seinfeld*, at the comedy club, The Laugh Factory in Los Angeles, on several occasions, screamed the work nigger at blacks who were present in the audience. The usage of the N-word, in this content, is highly pejorative and should not be defended.

19. Hill (2008), 44.

20. Cohen (1992), 62.

21. Bonnett (2005).

22. See J. L. Austin, *How to Do Things with Words* (1963); and Judith Butler, *Excitable Speech: A Politics of the Performative* (1997b).

23. Kennedy (1986), 1327–28.

24. See Eduardo Bonilla-Silva, "Color-Blind Racism" (2007); Karyn D. McKinney, "I fell 'Whiteness' When I Hear People Blaming Whites: Whiteness as Cultural Victimization" (2003); and Karyn D. McKinney, and Joe R. Feagin, "Diverse Perspectives on Doing Antiracism: The Younger Generation" (2003). For other accounts of racist comments directed at First Nations, see Jane H. Hill, *The Everyday Language of White Racism* (2008), 58–84.

25. Daniels (2009).

26. Hill (2008), 23.

27. Prashad (2001), 4.

28. Hall (2004), 257.

29. Bhabha (1994), 64.

30. Unlike honorary blacks and the white Negro, for example, as self-determining, the agents of existential choice, being ascribed as an honorary white or model minority does the opposite. Each, in its particular orientation, serves to devoid, the individuals so assigned, any form of agency.

31. Fine (1997), 58. Also, see Michele Fine et al., *Off White: Readings on Race, Power, and Society* (1997).

Bibliography

Aanerud, Rebecca. "The Legacy of White Supremacy and the Challenge of White Antiracist Mothering" *Hypatia* 22, no. 2 (2007): 20–38.

———. "Fictions of Whiteness: Speaking the Name of Whiteness in U.S. Literature" in *Displacing Whiteness: Essays in Social and Cultural Criticism*, edited by Ruth Frankenberg. Durham, NC: Duke University Press, 1997.

Abram, Morris B. "Affirmative Action: Eair Shakers and Social Engineers." *Harvard Law Review* 99, no. 6 (April 1986): 1312–26.

Ahmed, Sara. "A Phenomenology of Whiteness." *Feminist Theory* 8, no. 2 (2007): 149–68.

———. "Declaration of Whiteness: The Non-Performativity of Antiracism." *Borderlines* 3, no. 2 (2004). www.borderlandsejournal.adelaide.edu.au/issues/vol3no2.html.

Alcoff, Linda Martín. "What Should White People Do?" *Hypatia* 7, no. 13 (1998): 6–26.

———. "The Problem of Speaking for Others." in *Overcoming Racism and Sexism*, edited by Linda Bell and David Blumefield. Lanham, MD: Rowman and Littlefield, 1995.

Alexander, Bryant Keith. "Black Skin/White Masks: The Performative Sustainability of Whiteness (With Apologies to Frantz Fanon)," *Qualitative Inquiry*, no. 10 (2004): 647

Allen, Theodore W. *The Invention of the White Race: Racial Oppression and Social Control*. New York: Verso Press, 1994.

———. *The Invention of the White Race: Racial Oppression and Social Control*. New York: Verso Press, 1997.

Alpert, Jonathan L. "The Origins of Slavery in the United States—The Maryland Precedent." *American Journal of Legal History* 14, no. 3 (1970): 189–221.

Althusser, Louis. *Lenin and Philosophy and Other Essays*, translated by Ben Brewster. London: New Left Books, 1971.

Analdúa, Gloria E. *Borderlands La Frontera: The New Mestiza*. San Francisco, CA: Aunte Lute Book Co., 1987.

Angelou, Maya. *The Inaugural Poem: On the Pulse of the Morning*. New York: Random House, 1993.

Annals of Congress. *Abridgements of Debates of Congress, 1789–1856* vol. 1. New York: D. Appleton and Co., 1857.

Appiah, Kwame A. "Stereotypes and the Shaping of Identity." Pp 55–71 in *Prejudicial Appearances: The Logic of American Antidiscrimination Law*, edited by Robert C. Post, Judith Butler, Thomas C. Grey, and Reva B. Siegel. Durham, NC: Duke University Press, 2001.

———. "Identity, Authenticity, Survival: Multiculturalism Societies and Social Reproduction." Pp. 149–63 in *Multiculturalism Examining the Politics of Recognition*, edited by Amy Gutmann. Princeton: Princeton University Press, 1994.

———. "But Would that Sill Be Me? Notes on Gender, Race, Ethnicity as a Source of Identity." *Journal of Philosophy* 87, no. 10 (1990): 493–507.

———. "The Uncompleted Argument: Du Bois and the Illusion of Race." In *"Race," Writings, and Difference*, edited by Kwame Anthony Appiah and Henry Louis Gates Jr. Chicago: University of Chicago Press, 1985.

Arnesen, Eric. "A Paler Shade of White." *The New Republic* 226, no. 24 (June 24, 2002): 33–38.

———. "Scholarly Controversy: Whiteness and the Historians' Imagination." *International Labor and Working-Class History*, no. 60 (Fall 2001): 3–32.

Austin, J. L. *How to Do Things with Words.* Oxford, UK: Oxford University Press, 1963.
Babb, Valerie. *Whiteness Visible: The Meaning of Whiteness in American Literature and Culture.* New York: New York University Press, 1998.
Back, Les. "Aryans Reading Adorno: Cyper-Culture and the Twenty-First-Century Racism." *Ethnic and Racial Studies* 25, no. 4 (July 2002): 628–51.
Bailey, Allison and Jacquelyn Zita. "The Reproduction of Whiteness: Race and the Regulation of the Gendered Body." *Hypatia* 22, no. 2 (Spring 2007): 7–15.
Bailey, Thomas. *The American Pageant Revisited: Recollections of a Stanford Historian.* Stanford, CA: Hoover Institute Press.
Baldwin, James. *Collective Essay.* New York: Library of America, 1998.
———. *The Fire Next Text.* New York: Modern Library, 1995.
Balibar, Etienne and Immanuel Wallerstein *Race, Nation, Class: Ambiguous Identities.* London: Verso Press, 1992.
Ballagh, James Curtis. *A History of Slavery in Virginia.* Baltimore, MD: Johns Hopkins University Press, 1902.
Banton, Michael. "The Idiom of Race: A Critique of Presentation," in *Theories of Race and Racism: A Reader,* edited by Les Back and John Solomos. London: Routledge, 2000.
———. "The Race Relations Problematic," *British Journal of Sociology* 42, no. 1 (March 1991): 115–30.
Barkan, Joanne. "Alive and Not Well: Affirmative Action on Campus." *Dissent* (Spring 2008): 49–57.
Bartels, Emily C. "Othello and Africa: Postcolonialism Reconsidered." *William and Mary Quarterly* 54, no. 1 (January 1997): 45–64.
Barthes, Roland. *Writing Degree Zero.* Translated by Annette Lavers and Colin Smith. New York: Hill and Wang, 1977.
Bay, Mia. *The White Image in the Black Mind.* New York: Oxford University Press, 2000.
Beauvior, Simone de. *The Second Sex.* Translated by H.M. Parshley. New York: Alfred Knopf, 1964.
Bell, Daniel. *The Coming of Post-Industrial Society: A Venture in Social Forecasting.* New York: Basic Books, 1973.
Bell, Derrick A. *Race, Racism, and American Law.* Boston: Little Brown, 1980.
Bell, Derrick A., Tracy Higgins, and Sung-Hee Suh. "Racial Reflections: Dialogues in the Direction of Liberation." Pp. 106–11 in *Critical White Studies: Looking Behind the Mirror,* edited by Richard Delgado and Jean Stefanic. Philadelphia: Temple University Press, 1997.
Bellah, Robert N., Richard Madsen, Ann Swidler, and Steven M. Tipton. *Habits of the Heart: Individualism and Commitment in American Life.* New York: Routledge, 1985.
Benedict, Ruth. *Race: Science and Politics.* New York: Modern Age Books, 1940.
Bennett, Lerone. *The Shaping of Black America: The Struggles and Triumphs of African-Americans, 1619–1990s.* Chicago: Johnson, 1975.
Berger, John. *Ways of Seeing.* New York: Penguin Books, 1990.
Bhabha, Homi. *The Location of Culture.* New York: Routledge, 1994.
———. "What Does the Black Man Want?" *New Formations,* no. 1 (1987): 118–24.
Bobo, Lawrence. "Inequalities that Endure? Racial Ideology, American Politics, and the Peculiar Role of the Social Sciences." Pp. 13–42 in *The Changing Terrain of Race and Ethnicity,* edited by Maria Krysan and Amanda E. Lewis. New York: Russell Sage, 2004.
Bonfield, Arthur Earl. "The Origins and Development of American Fair Employment Legislation." *Iowa Law Review* 52 (1967): 1043–92.
Bonilla-Silva, Eduardo. "Color-Blind Racism." Pp. 131–38 in *Race, Class, and Gender in the United States,* edited by Paula S. Rothenberg. New York: Worth Publisher, 2007.
———. *Racism Without Racists: Color-Blind Racism and the Persistence of Racial Inequality in the United States.* Lanham, MD: Rowman and Littlefield, 2006.
———. "Rethinking Racism: Towards a Structural Interpretation." *American Sociological Review* 62, no. 3 (June 1997): 465–80.

Bonnett, Alastair. "From the Crisis of Whiteness to Western Supremacy." *Australia Critical Race and Whiteness Studies Association Journal.* no. 1, (2005): 8–20.

———. "Construction of Whiteness in European and American Anti-Racism." Pp. 200–18 in *Race Identity, and Citizenship A Reader,* edited by Rodolfo D. Torres, Louis F. Miron, and Johnathan Xavier Inda. Malden, MA: Blackwell, 1999.

———. *White Identity and Historical Perspectives.* Hralow, GB: Prentice Hall, 2000.

———. "'White Studies': The Problems and Projects of a New Research Agenda." *Theory, Culture & Society,* 13, no. 2 (1996): 145–55.

Boskin, Joseph. *Into Slavery, Racial Decisions in the Virginia Colony.* Philadelphia: Lippincott, 1976.

Brah, Avtar. *Cartographies of Diaspora: Contesting Identities.* London: Routledge, 1996.

Brah, Avtar and Ann Phoenix. "Ain't I a Woman? Revisiting Intersectionality." *Journal of International Women's Studies* 5, no. 3 (2004): 75–86.

Braitdotti, Rosi. *Metamorphoses: Towards a Materialistic Theory of Becoming.* Cambridge, UK: Polity Press, 2002.

Breen, T. H., ed. *Shaping Southern Society: The Southern Society.* New York: Oxford University Press, 1976.

Brewer, Rose M. "Theorizing Race, Class, and Gender: The New Scholarship of Black Feminist Intellectuals and Black Women's Labor." In *Theorizing Black Feminism: The Visionary Pragmatism of Black Women,* edited by Stanlie M. James and Abena P. A. Busia. New York: Routledge, 1993.

Brodkin, Karen. "Studying Whiteness Shouldn't Be Academic." *Borderlands* 3, no. 2 2004. www.borderlands.net.au/vol3no2_2004/brodkin_studying.htm.

———. *How Jews Became White Folks and What That Says About Race in America.* New Brunswick, NJ: Rutgers University Press, 1998.

Brown, Adam D., Yifat Gutman, Lindsey Freeman, Amy Sodoro, and Alin Coman. "Introduction: Is an Interdisciplinary Field of Memory Studies Possible?" *International Journal of Culture Politics and Society* 22 (2009): 117–24.

Brown, Kathleen M. *Good Wives, Nasty Wenches, and Anxious Patriarchs: Gender, Race, and Power in Colonial Virginia.* Chapel Hill: University of North Carolina Press, 1996.

Brown, Wendy. *State of Injury: Power and Freedom in Late Modernity.* Princeton: Princeton University Press, 1995.

Buchanan, Patrick. *The Death of the West: How Dying Populations and Immigrant Invasions Imperil Our Country and Civilization.* New York: St. Martin's Press, 2002.

Burlingame, Roger. *Machines That Built America.* New York: Signet, 1953.

Burstein, Paul. *Discrimination, Jobs, and Politics: The Struggle for Equal Employment Opportunity Since the New Deal.* Chicago: University of Chicago Press, 1985.

Butler, Judith. "Appearances Aside." Pp. 78–83 in *Prejudicial Appearances The Logic of American Antidiscrimination Law,* edited by Robert C. Post, Judith Butler, Thomas C. Grey, and Reva B. Siegel. Durham, NC: Duke University Press, 2001.

———. "An Affirmative View." Pp. 155–73 in *Race and Representation: Affirmative Action,* edited by Robert Post and Michael Rogin. New York: Zone Books, 1998.

———. *The Psychic Life of Power: Theories in Subjection.* Stanford, CA: Stanford University Press, 1997a.

———. *Excitable Speech: A Politics of the Performative.* New York, Routledge, 1997b.

———. "Collected and Fractured: Responses to Identities." Pp. 439–47 in *Identities,* edited by Kwame Anthony Appiah and Henry Louis Gates, Jr. Chicago: University of Chicago Press, 1995a.

———. "For Careful Reading." Pp. 127–44 in *Feminist Contentions A Philosophical Exchange,* Seyla Benhabib, Judith Butler, Drucilla Cornel, and Nancy Fraser. New York: Routledge, 1995b.

———. "Against Proper Objects: Introduction." *Differences: A Journal of Feminist Cultural Studies* nos. 6.2 and 3 (1994): 1–24.

———. *Bodies That Matters: On the Discursive Limits of "Sex"* London: Routledge, 1993.

————. "Performative Act and Gender Constitution: An Essay of Phenomenology and Feminist Theory." Pp. 270–82 in *Performing Feminisms: Feminists Critical Theory and Theatres*. Baltimore, MD: John Hopkins University Press, 1990a.

————. *Gender Troubles: Feminism and the Subversion of Identity*. New York: Routledge, 1990b.

Cage, Mary Crystal. "Diversity or Quotas? Northeastern U Will Accord Gays and Lesbians Preferential Treatment in Hiring." *Chronicle of Higher Education*, June 8, 1994.

Caldwell, Dan. "The Negroization of the Chinese Stereotype in California." *Southern California Quarterly* 33 (1971): 123–31.

Camus, Albert. *The Plague*. Translated by Stuart Gilbert. New York: Random House, 1948.

Cannon, Katie Geneva. "Slave Ideology and Biblical Interpretation." Pp. 413–20 in *Black Studies Reader*, edited by Jacqueline Bobo, Cynthia Hudley, and Claudine Michel. New York: Routledge, 2004.

Cardyn, Lisa. "Sexualized Racism/Gendered Violence: Outraging the Body Politics in the Reconstruction South." *Michigan Law Review* 100, no. 4 (2002): 675–867.

Carmichael, Stokely and Charles V. Hamilton, *Black Power: The Politics of Liberation in America*. New York: Random House, 1967.

Casey, Marion R. "The Limits of Equality: Racial and Ethnic Tensions in the New Republic, 1989–1986." Pp. 41–62 in *Race and Ethnicity in America: A Concise History*, edited by Ronald H. Bayor. New York: Columbia University Press, 2003.

Catterall, Helen T. *Judicial Cases Concerning American Slavery and the Negro*, vol. 4. New York: Octagon Books.

Chan, Sucheng. *Entry Denied: Exclusion and the Chinese American Community in America, 1882–1943*. Philadelphia: Temple University Press, 1991a.

————. *Asian Americans: An Interpretive History*. New York: Twayne, 1991b.

Chapin, Joyce E. "Natural Philosophy and an Early Racial Idiom in North America: Comparing English and Indian Body." *William and Mary Quarterly* 54, no.1 (January 1997): 229–52.

Charles, Helen. "Whiteness: The Relevance of Politically Coloring the 'Non.'" Pp. 29–35 in *Working Out: New Directions for Women's Studies*, edited by Hillary Hinds, Ann Phoenix and Jackie Stacey. London: Falmer Press, 1992.

Chater, Nancy. "Biting the Hand That Feeds Me: Notes on Privilege from a White Antiracist Feminist." *Canadian Women Studies* 12, vol. 2 (1994): 100–104.

Cohen, Philip. "'It's Racism What Dunnit': Hidden Narratives in Theories of Racism." Pp. 62–103 in *"Race," Culture and Difference*, edited by James Donald and Ali Rattansi. London: Sage, 1992.

Collins, Patricia Hills. *Black Feminist Thought: Knowledge, Consciousness, and the Politics of Empowerment*. London: HarperCollins, 1990.

Correspondences of the *New York Times*. *How Race Is Lived in America: Pulling Together, Pulling Apart*. New York: Times Books, 2002.

Costello, Brannon. "Poor White Trash, Great White Hope: Race, Class and the (De)Construction of Whiteness in Lewis Norton's *Wolfe Whistle*." *Critique: Studies in Contemporary Fiction* 45, no. 2 (2004): 207–23.

Cover, Robert. *Justice Accused, Anti-Slavery and the Judicial Process*. New Haven, CT: Yale University Press, 1975.

Cox, Oliver C. *Caste, Class & Race: A Study in Social Dynamics*. New York: Doubleday, 1948.

Craven, Wesley F. "Twenty Negroes to Jamestown in 1619?" *Virginia Quarterly Review* 47 (1971): 416–20

————. *The Southern Colonies in the Seventeenth Century, 1607–1689*. Baton Rouge: Louisiana State University Press, 1949.

Crenshaw, Kimberlé, "Demarginalizing the Intersection of Race and Sex: A Black Feminist Critique of Antidiscrimination Doctrine, Feminist Theory and Antiracist Politics." *University of Chicago Legal Forum* (1989): 139–67.

Crouch, Stanley. *The All-American Skin Game, or the Décor of Race.* New York: Pantheon, 1996.

Culler, Jonathan. *Barthes: A Very Short Introduction.* New York: Oxford University Press, 2002.

Daniel, G. Reginald. *More Than Black? Multiracial Identity and the New Racial Order.* Philadelphia: Temple University Press, 2002.

Daniels, Jessie. *Cyber Racism: White Supremacy Online and the Attack on Civil Rights.* Lanham, MD: Rowman & Littlefield, 2009.

da Silva, Tony Simoes. "Redeeming Self: The Business of Whiteness in Post-Apartheid South African Writing." Pp. 3–17 in *Transnational Whiteness Matters,* edited by Aileen Moreton-Robinson, Maryrose Casey, and Fiona Nicoll. Lanham, MD: Lexington Books, 2008.

Davis, Adrienne D. "Identity Notes, Part One: Playing in the Light." Pp. 232–37 in *Critical White Studies: Looking Behind the Mirror,* edited by Richard Delgado and Jean Stefanic Philadelphia: Temple University Press, 1997.

Davis, Angela Y. *Women, Race & Class.* New York: Vintage Books, 1983.

———. *With My Mind on Freedom: An Autobiography.* New York: Bantam Books, 1974.

Davis, Natalie Zemon and Randolph Starn. "Special Issue: Memory and Counter Memory." *Representations* 26 (Spring 1989): 1–149.

Davis, T. R. "Negro Servitude in the United States: Servitude Distinguished from Slavery." *Journal of Negro History* 8, no. 3 (1923): 247–83.

Decisions of the General Court. *The Virginia Magazine of History and Biography* 5, no. 3 (January 1898): 233–41.

Degler, Carl N. "Slavery and the Genesis of American Race Prejudice." *Comparative Studies in Society and History* 2, no. 1 (1959): 49–66.

Delany, Martin R. *The Condition, Elevation, Immigration and Destiny of the Colored People of the United States and Official Report of the Niger Valley Exploring Party.* Introduction by Toyin Falola. Amherst, NY: Humanity Books, 2004.

Delgado, Richard and Jean Stefanic. *Critical Race Theory an Introduction.* New York: New York University Press, 2001.

———, eds. *Critical White Studies: Looking Behind the Mirror.* Philadelphia: Temple University Press, 1997.

Dill, Bonnie Thornton, Maxine Baca Zinn, and Sandra Patton "Race, Family Values, and Welfare Reform." Pp. 263–86 in *A New Introduction to Poverty: The Role of Race, Power and Politics,* edited by Louis Kushnick and James Jennings. New York: New York University Press, 1999.

Douglass, Frederick. *Narrative of the Life of Frederick Douglass, an American Slave.* New York: Penguin Classics, 1982.

Drake, W. Avon. "Affirmative Action at the Crossroads: Race and the Future of Black Progress." *Western Journal of Black Studies* 27, no. 1 (2003): 57–64.

D'Souza, Dinesh. *The End of Racism: Principles for a Multicultural Society.* New York: Free Press, 1995.

———. "The Failure of the 'Cruel Compassion.'" *Chronicle of Higher Education,* (September 15, 1995).

———. *Illiberal Education: The Politics of Race and Sex on Campus.* New York: Free Press, 1991.

Du Bois, W. E. B. *The Souls of Black Folk.* Introduction by David Levering Lewis. New York: Modern Library, 2003.

———. *The Philadelphia Negro: A Social Studies.* Introduction by Elijah Anderson. Philadelphia: University of Philadelphia Press, 1996.

———. *Darkwater: Voices from Within the Veil.* New York: Schocken Books, 1969.

———. *Black Reconstruction: An Essay Toward a History of the Part Black Folk Played in the Attempt to Reconstruct Democracy in America, 1860–1880.* New York: Harcourt, Brace and Company, 1935.

Durkheim, Émile. *The Rules of Sociological Methods.* New York: Free Press of Glencoe, 1964.

Duster, Troy. "Individual Fairness, Group Preferences, and the California Strategy." *Representations* 55 (Summer 1996): 41–58.

Dworkin, Ronald. *A Matter of Principle.* Cambridge, MA: Harvard University Press, 1985.

Dyer, Richard. *White.* London: Routledge, 1997.

———. "White," *Screen* 29, no. 4 (1988): 44–64.

Dyson, Eric, Michael. "The Labor of Whiteness, the Whiteness of Labor, and the Perils of Whitewishing." Pp. 219–24 in *Race Identity, and Citizenship A Reader,* edited by Rodolfo D. Torres, Louis F. Miron, and Johnathan Xavier Inda. Malden, MA: Blackwell, 1999.

Early, Gerald, ed. *Lure and Loathing: Essays on Race, Identity, and the Ambivalence of Assimilation.* New York: Penguin Books, 1994.

Elkins, Stanley M. *Slavery: A Problem in American Institutional and Intellectual Life.* Chicago: University of Chicago Press, 1959.

Ellison, Ralph. "Change the Joke and Slip the Joke." *Partisan Review* (Spring, 1958): 212–22.

Equiano, Olaudah. *Interesting Narrative and Other Writings.* New York: Penguin Classics, 1998.

Ezorsky, Gertrude. *Racism and Justice: The Case of Affirmative Action.* Ithaca, NY: Cornell University Press, 1991.

Fanon, Frantz. *Black Skin, White Masks.* Translated by Charles Lam Markmann. New York: Grove Press, 1967.

———. *Towards the African Revolution: Political Essays.* Translated by Constance Farrington. New York: Grove Press, 1964.

———. *The Wretched of the Earth.* Translated by Constance Farrington. New York: Grove Press, 1963.

Farr, Arnold. "Whiteness Visible: Enlightenment Racism and the Structure of Racialized Consciousness." Pp. 143–158 in *What White Looks Like: African-American Philosophers on the Whiteness Question,* edited by George Yancy. New York: Routledge, 2004.

Farrar, Hayward "Woody." "Identity, Patriotism, and Protest on the Wartime Home Front, 1917–1919, 1941–1945." In *A Companion to African American History,* edited by Alton Hornsby, Jr. Malden, MA: Blackwell, 2005.

Feagin, Joe R. *Systemic Racism: A Theory of Oppression.* New York: Routledge, 2006.

———. *Racist America: Roots, Current Realities, and Future Reparations.* New York: Routledge, 2000.

Ferguson, Russell. "Introduction: Invisible Center." Pp. 9–14 in *Out There: Marginalization and Contemporary Cultures,* edited by Russell Ferguson, Martha Gever, Trinh T. Minh-ha, and Cornel West. New York: New Museum of Contemporary Art, 1990.

Fields, Barbara J. "Whiteness, Racism, and Identity," *International Labor and Working-Class History,* no. 60 (Fall 2001): 48–56.

———. "Slavery, Race, and Ideology in the United States of America." *New Left Review,* no. 181 (Summer 1990): 95–118.

Fine, Michele. "Witnessing Whiteness." Pp. 57–65 in *Off White: Readings on Race, Power, and Society,* edited by Michele Fine, Linda Powell, Louis Weis, and L. Mun Wong. New York: Routledge, 1997.

Fine, Michele, Linda Powell, Louis Weis, and L. Mun Wong. *Off White: Readings on Race, Power, and Society.* New York: Routledge, 1997.

Firestone, Shulamith. *The Dialectic of Sex: The Case for Feminist Revolution.* New York, Morrow: 1970.

Fischer, Kirsten. *Suspect Relations: Sex, Race, and Resistance in Colonial North Carolina.* Ithaca, NY: Cornell University Press, 2002.

Fishkin, Shelly F. "Interrogating 'Whiteness,' Complicating 'Blackness': Remapping American Culture." *American Quarterly* 47, no. 3 (1995): 428–66.

Fiss, Owen M. "Group and the Equal Protection Clause." *Philosophy & Public Policy* 5, no. 2 (Winter 1976): 107–77.

Foley, Neil. *The White Scourge: Mexicans, Blacks, and Poor Whites in Texas Cotton Culture.* Berkeley:University of California Press, 1997.

Foner, Eric. *Reconstruction: America's Unfinished Revolution, 1863–1877.* New York: HarperCollins, 1988.

Foster, Sandra. "Difference and Equality: A Critical Assessment of the Concept of Diversity." *Wisconsin Law Review* (January/February 1993): 105–61.

Foucault, Michel. *Security, Territory Populations Lectures at the Collège de France 1977–1978.* Translated by Graham Burchell. New York: Palgrave Macmillan, 2007.

———. *The Ordering of Things: An Archeology of the Human Species.* New York: Vintage, 1994.

———. "A Question of Method." Pp. 73–86 in *The Foucault Effects: Studies in Governmentality with Two Lectures by and an Interview with Michel Foucault,* edited by Graham Burchell, Colin Gordon, Peter Miller. Chicago: University of Chicago, 1991.

———. *Technologies of Self: A Seminar with Michel Foucault,* edited by Luther H. Martin, Huck Gutman, and Patrick H. Hutton. Boston: University of Massachusetts Press, 1988.

———. *Power/Knowledge: Selected Writings and Interviews, 1972–1977.* Translated and edited by Colin Gordon. New York: Pantheon Books, 1980.

———. *The History of Sexuality: An Introduction.* Translated by Robert Hurley. New York: Pantheon Books, 1978.

———. *Disciplining and Punish.* Translated by Alan Sheridan. New York: Vintage Books, 1977.

Frankenberg, Ruth. "Mirage of an Unmarked Whiteness." Pp. 72–96 in *The Making and Unmaking of Whiteness,* edited by Birgit Brander Rasmussen, Erik Klineberg, Irene Nexica, and Matt Wray. Durham, NC: Duke University Press, 2001.

———. "Introduction: Local Whiteness, Localizing Whiteness." Pp. 1–33 in *Displacing Whiteness: Essays in Social and Cultural Criticism,* edited by Ruth Frankenberg. Durham, NC: Duke University Press, 1997.

———. "'When We Are Capable of Stopping, We Begin to See': Being White, Seeing Whiteness." Pp. 3–18 in *Names We Call Home: Autobiography on Racial Identity,* edited by Becky Thompson and Sangeeta Tyagi. New York: Routledge, 1996.

———. "Whiteness and Americanness: Examining Constructions of Race, Culture, and Nation in White Women's Life Narratives." Pp. 62–67 in *Race, Culture, and Nation In White Women's Life Narratives,* edited by Steven Gregory and Roger Sanjek. New Brunswick, NJ: Rutgers University Press, 1994.

———. *White Women, Race Matters: The Social Construction of Whiteness.* Minneapolis: University of Minnesota Press, 1993.

Franklin, Benjamin. "Observations Concerning the Increase of Mankind and Peopling of Countries." In *The Papers of Benjamin Franklin,* vol. 4, edited by Leonard W. Labaree. New Haven, CT: Yale University Press, 1961.

Fredrickson, George M. *Racism a Short History.* Princeton: Princeton University Press, 2002.

———. "Towards a Social Interpretation in the Development of American Racism." Pp. 240–54 in *Key Issues in the Afro-American Experience,* vol. 1, edited by Nathan I. Huggins, Martin Kilson, and Daniel M. Fox. New York: Harcourt Brace Jovanovich, 1971.

Freire, Paulo. *Pedagogy of the Oppressed.* Translated by Myra Bergman Ramos. New York: Continuum, 2000.

———. *Teachers as Cultural Worker.* Boulder, CO: Westview Press, 1998.

Fuss, Diana. "Interior Colonies: Frantz Fanon and the Politics of Identification." *Diacritics* 21, nos. 2–3 (1994): 19–43.

———. *Essentially Speaking: Feminism, Nature, and Difference.* New York: Routledge, 1989.

Gallagher, Charles. "White Reconstruction in the University." Pp. 299–318 in *Privilege: A Reader,* edited by Michael Kimmel and Abby Ferber. Boulder, CO: Westview Press, 2003.

————. "White Like Me? Methods, Meaning, and Manipulation in the Field of White Studies." Pp. 678–92 in *Racing Research, Researching Race: Methodological Dilemmas in Critical Race Studies*, edited by France Winndance Twine and Jonathan W. Warren. New York: New York University Press, 2000.

————. "White Racial Formation: Into the Twenty-First Century." Pp. 6–11 in *Critical White Studies: Looking Behind the Mirror*, edited by Richard Delgado and Jean Stefancic. Philadelphia: Temple University Press, 1997.

Gans, Herbert. "Deconstructing the Underclass." Pp. 102–8 in *Race, Class, and Gender in the United States*, edited by Paula S. Rothenberg. New York: Worth Publisher, 2007.

Garner, Steve. *Whiteness: An Introduction*. London: Routledge, 2007.

Gates, Henry Louis and Anthony Appiah, eds. *The White Issue: A Special Issue of Transition*. Durham, NC: Duke University Press, 1998.

————. *Loose Cannons: Notes on the Culture War*. New York: Oxford University Press, 1992.

Gilroy, Paul. *After Empire: Melancholia or Convivial Culture*. London: Routledge, 2004.

————. *Against Race: Imagining Political Culture Beyond the Color Line*. Cambridge, MA: Belknap Press of Harvard University Press, 2000a.

————. *Between Camps: Nations, Culture, and the Allure of Race*. London: Allen Lane, 2000b.

Giroux, Henri. "Rewriting the Discourse of Racial Identity: Toward a Pedagogy and Politics of Whiteness." *Harvard Educational Review* 67, no. 2 (Summer 1997): 285–320.

Glazer, Nathan. *We Are All Multiculturalists Now*. Cambridge, MA: Harvard University Press, 1997.

————. *Affirmative Discrimination: Ethnic Inequality and Public Policy*. Cambridge, MA: Harvard University Press, 1987.

Goldberg, David Theo. *The Threat of Race: Reflections of Racial Neoliberalism*. Malden, MA: Blackwell, 2009.

————. "Introduction: Multicultural Conditions." In *Multiculturalism: A Critical Reader*, Oxford: Blackwell, 1994.

Goldstein, Eric L. *The Price of Whiteness: Jews, Race, and American Identity*. Princeton: Princeton University Press, 2006.

Goodell, William. *Slavery and Anti-Slavery: A History of the Great Struggles in Both Hemispheres, with a View of the Slavery Question in America*. New York: Negro Universities Press, 1962.

Gordon, Lewis R. "A Questioning Body of Laughter and Tears: Reading Black Skin, White Masks Through the Cat and Mouse of Reason and a Misguided Theodicy." *Parallax* 8, no. 2 (2002): 10–29.

Gossett, Thomas F. *Race: The History of an Idea in America*. Dallas, TX: Southern Methodist University Press, 1963.

Gross, Ariela J. "Like Master, Like Man: Constructing Whiteness in the Commercial Law of Slavery, 1800–1861." *Cardozo Law* Review no. 18 (1996): 263–99.

Gutman, Yifat, Adam D. Brown, and Amy Sodoro, eds. *Memory and the Future: Transnational Politics, Ethics and Society*. New York: Palgrave Macmillan, 2010.

Gyory, Andrew. *Closing the Gate: Race, Politics, and the Chinese Exclusion Act*. Chapel Hill, NC: University of North Carolina Press, 1998.

Hacker, Andrew. *Two Nations: Black and White, Separate, Hostile, Unequal*. New York: Scribner, 2003.

Hage, Ghassan. "White Self-Racialization as Identity Fetishism: Capitalism and the Experience of Colonial Whiteness." Pp. 185–206 in *Racialization: Studies in Theory and Practice*, edited by Karim Murji and John Solomos. New York: Oxford University Press, 2005.

Hall, Stuart. "What Is This 'Black' in Black Popular Culture?" Pp. 255–64 in *Black Studies Reader*, edited by Jacqueline Bobo, Cynthia Hudley, and Claudine Michel. New York: Routledge, 2004.

————. "Culture, Community, Nation." *Cultural Studies* 7, no. 3 (1993): 349–63.

Hancock, Ange-Marie. "When Multiplication Doesn't Equal Quick Addition: Examining Intersectionality as a Research Paradigm." *Perspectives on Politics*, no. 5, (2007): 63–79.

Handlin, Oscar and Mary Handlin. "Origins of the Southern Labor System." *William and Mary Quarterly* 7, no. 2 (1950): 199–222.

Haney López, Ian F. *White by Law: The Legal Construction of Race*. New York: New York University Press, 1996.

Harlan, John M. *Plessy v. Ferguson: A Brief History with Documents*, edited by Brook Thomas. Boston: Bedford/St. Martin's, 1997.

Harris, Cheryl I. "Finding Sojourner's Truth: Race, Gender, and the Institution of Slavery." *Cardozo Law Review* 18, no. 309 (November 1996): 1–89.

———. "Whiteness as Property." *Harvard Law Review* 106, no. 8 (June 1993): 1707–91.

Harris, Geraldine. *Staging Femininities: Performance and Performativity*. Manchester, UK: Manchester University Press, 1999.

Harris, Laura A. "Notes from a Welfare Queen in the Ivory Tower." Pp. 372–80 in *This Bridge We Call Home*, edited by Gloria E. Anzaldúa and AnaLouise Keating. New York: Routledge 2002.

Hartigan, John, Jr. "Culture Against Race: Reworking the Basis for Racial Analysis." *South Atlantic Quarterly* 104, no. 3 (2005): 543–60.

———. "Establishing the Fact of Whiteness." Pp. 183–99 in *Race, Identity, and Citizenship: A Reader*, edited by Rodolfo D. Torres, Louis F. Mirón, and Jonathan Xavier Inda. Malden, MA: Wiley-Blackwell, 1999a.

———. *Racial Situations: Class Predicaments of Whiteness in Detroit*. Princeton, NJ: Princeton University Press, 1999b.

Hawthorne, Nathaniel. *The House of the Seven Gables*. New York: Oxford University Press, 1991.

Hegel, Georg Wilhelm Friedrick. *Lectures on the Philosophy of World History*. Translated by Hugh Barr Nisbet with introduction by Duncan Forbes. Cambridge, MA: Cambridge University Press, 1975.

Hernandez, Roger. "Racism with Good Intensions a Misguided Policy." *Victoria Advocate*, October 10, 1997.

Herrnstein, Richard J. and Charles Murray. *The Bell Curve: Intelligence and Class Structure in American Life*. New York: Free Press, 1994.

Higginbotham, A. Leon Jr. *In the Matter of Color Race and the American Legal Process: The Colonial Period*. New York: Oxford University Press, 1978.

Higginbotham, Evelyn Brooks. "African-American Women's History and the Metalanguage of Race." Pp. 183–208 in *Feminism and History*, edited by Joan Wallach Scott. New York: Oxford University Press, 1996.

Higham, John. *Strangers in the Land: Patterns of American Nativism, 1860–1925*. New Brunswick, NJ: Rutgers University Press, 1994.

Hill, Herbert. "Race, Ethnicity and Organized Labor: The Opposition to Affirmative Action." *New Politics* 1, no. 2 (Winter 1987): 31–82.

Hill, Jane H. *The Everyday Language of White Racism*. Malden, MA: Wiley-Blackwell, 2008.

Hill, Mike. *After Whiteness: Unmaking an American Majority*. New York: New York University Press, 2004.

———, ed. *Whiteness A Critical Reader*. New York: New York University Press, 1997.

Hing, Bill Ong. "Beyond the Rhetoric of Assimilation and Cultural Pluralism: Addressing the Tension of Separatism and Conflict in an Immigration-Driven Multiracial Society." *California Law Review* 81, no. 4 (1993): 863–925.

Hispanic Coalition on Higher Education. "An Open Letter to the Regents of the University of California." *New York Times* (July 20, 1995): A11.

Hochschild, Jennifer. *Facing up to the American Dream: Race, Class, and the Soul of the Nation*. Princeton: Princeton University Press, 1995.

Hoffman, Frederick L. *Race Traits and Tendency of the American Negro*. New York: AMS Press, 1973.

hooks, bell. *Black Looks: Race and Representation.* Boston: South End Press, 1992.
———. *Ain't I a Woman: Black Woman and Feminism.* Boston: South End Press, 1981.
Huck Eugene R. and Edward H. Moseley, eds. *Militarists, Merchants, and Missionaries.* Tuscaloosa: University of Alabama Press, 1970.
Huntington, Samuel P. *Who Are We? The Challenges to America's National Identity.* New York: Simon and Schuster, 2004.
Ignatiev, Noel. *How the Irish Became White.* New York: Routledge, 1995.
Ignatiev, Noel and John Garvey. *Race Traitor.* New York: Routledge, 1996.
Ingram, Penelope. "Racializing Babylon: Settler Whiteness and the 'New Racism.'" *New Literary History* 32 (2001): 157–76.
Jacobson, Matthew F. *Whiteness of a Different Color: European Immigrants and the Alchemy of Race.* Cambridge, MA: Harvard University Press, 1998.
Jefferson, Thomas. "Notes on the State of Virginia." In *Documents of American Prejudice: An Anthology of Writings from Thomas Jefferson to David Duke,* edited by S. T. Joshi. New York: Basic Books, 1999.
Johnson, Lyndon Baines. "To Fulfill These Rights: Commencement Address at Howard University." Pp. 635–40 in *Public Papers of the Presidents of the United States.* Washington, DC: U.S. Government Printing Office, 1966.
Johnson, Whittington B. "The Origins and Nature of African Slavery in Seventeenth Century Maryland." *Maryland Historical Magazine* 73, no. 3 (September 1978): 236–45.
Jones, Marvin D. "Darkness Made Visible: Law, Metaphor, and the Racial Self." Pp. 78–82 in *Critical White Studies: Looking Behind the Mirror,* edited by Richard Delgado and Jean Stefanic. Philadelphia: Temple University Press, 1997.
Jordan, Winthrop D. "Unthinking Decision: Enslavement of Negroes in America to 1700." Pp. 100–15 in *Shaping Southern Society: The Colonial Experience,* edited by T. H. Breen. New York: Oxford University Press, 1976.
———. *White Over Black: American Attitudes Toward the Negro, 1550–1812.* Chapel Hill: University of North Carolina Press, 1968.
———. "Modern Tensions and the Origins of American Slavery." *Journal of Southern History* 28 (February 1962): 18–32.
Joshi, S. T., ed. *Documents of American Prejudice: An Anthology of Writings on Race from Thomas Jefferson to David Duke.* New York: Basic Books, 1999.
Kallen, Horace M. *Cultural Pluralism and the American Idea: An Essay in Social Philosophy.* Philadelphia: University of Pennsylvania Press, 1956.
Katz, Judy. *White Awareness: Handbook for Anti-racism Training.* Norman: University of Oklahoma Press, 2003.
Katz, William L. *The Invisible Empire: The Ku Klux Klan's Impact on History.* Washington, DC: Open Hand Publications, 1986.
Katznelson, Ira. *When Affirmative Action Was White: An Untold History of Racial Inequality in Twentieth Century America.* New York: W.W. Norton, 2005.
Keating, AnaLouise. "Interrogating 'Whiteness,' (De)constructing 'Race.'" *College English* 57, no. 8 (1995): 901–18.
Kennedy, Randall. "Persuasion and Distrust: A Comment of the Affirmative Action Debate." *Harvard Law Review* 99, no. 6 (April 1986): 1327–46.
Kennedy, Stetson. *Jim Crow Guide to the U.S.A.: The Laws, Customs, and Etiquette Governing the Conduct of Nonwhites and Other Minorities as Second-Class Citizens.* Westport, CT: Greenwood Press, 1959.
Kimmel, Michael and Abby Ferber, eds. *Privilege: A Reader.* Boulder, CO: Westview Press, 2003.
King, Martin Luther, Jr. *Why We Can't Wait.* New York: New American Library, 1964.
Kivel, Paul. *Uprooting Racism: How White People Can Work for Racial Justice.* Philadelphia: New Society Publishers, 1995.
Kupperman, Karen Ordahl. "Presentment of Civility: English Reading of American Self-Preservation in the Early Years of Colonization." *William and Mary Quarterly* 54, no. 1 (January 1997): 193–228.

Kymlicka, Will. *Multicultural Odysseys: Navigating the New International Politics of Diversity*. New York: Oxford University Press, 2007.

Lau, Don. "S.F. School Board Reduces Lowell Admission Score for Chi-Ams: Change Affects Only Those Coming from Public School." *Asianweek* (March 3, 1993).

Lauretis, Teresa, de. "Difference Embodied: Reflections on Black Skin, White Masks." *Parallax* 8 (2002): 54–68.

Lawlor, Steph. "Getting Out and Getting Away: Women's Narrative of Class Mobility." *Feminist Review* 63, no. 5 (1999): 3–24.

Lazarre, Jane. *Beyond the Whiteness of Whiteness: Memoir of a White Mother of Black Sons*. Durham, NC: Duke University Press, 1996.

Lee, Harper. *To Kill a Mockingbird*. New York: Grand Central Publishing, 1960.

Litwack, Leon F. "The Jim Crow Blues." *OAH Magazine of History* (January 2004): 7–58.

———. *Trouble in the Mind: Black Southerners in the Age of Jim Crow*. New York: Knopf, 1998.

———. *North of Slavery: The Negro in the Free States, 1790–1860*. Chicago: University of Chicago Press, 1965.

Lipsitz, George. *The Possessive Investment in Whiteness: How White People Profit From Identity Politics*. Philadelphia: Temple University Press, 1998.

———. "The Possessive Investment in Whiteness: Racialized Social Democracy and the 'White' Problem in American Studies." *American Quarterly* 47, no. 3 (1995): 369–87.

Lorde, Audre. *Sister Outsider: Essays and Speeches*. Trumansburg, NY: Crossing Press, 1984.

Luxton, Meg. *More than a Labor of Love: Three Generation of Women's Work in the Home*. Toronto, ON: Women's Press, 1980.

MacMillan, Liz. "Lifting the Veil of Whiteness: Growing Body of Scholarship Challenges Racial Norm." *Chronicle of Higher Education* (September, 1995).

Mailer, Norman. "The White Negro: Superficial Reflections on the Hipster." *Dissent* 4, no. 3 (1957): 276–93.

Malcomson, Scott L. *One Drop of Blood: The American Misadventure of Race*. New York: Farrar, Straus Giroux, 2000.

Mann, Arthur. "From Immigration to Acculturation." In *Making America: The Society & Culture of the United States*, edited by Luther S. Luedtke. Chapel Hill: University of North Carolina Press, 1992.

Marable, Manning. "Racism and Sexism." Pp. 160–65 in *Race, Class, and Gender in the United States: An Integrated Study*, edited Paula S. Rothenberg. New York: Worth Publishers, 2004.

———. *Problems in Race, Political Economy, and Society: How Capitalism Underdeveloped Black America*. Cambridge, MA: South End Press, 2000.

Marable, Manning and Leith Mullings, eds. *Let Nobody Turn Us Around*. Lanham, MD: Rowman & Littlefield, 2009.

Marx, Gary T. "The White Negro and the Negro White." *Phylon* 28, no. 2 (1967): 168–77.

Marx, Karl and Friedrich Engels. *The Communist Manifesto*. Translated by Samuel Moore with introduction by David Harvey. London: Pluto Press, 2008.

McGary, Howard. *Race and Social Justice*. Malden, MA: Blackwell, 1999.

McIntosh, Peggy. "White Privilege: Unpacking the Invisible Knapsack." Pp. 177–82 in *Race, Class, and Gender in the United States: An Integrated Study*, edited by Paula S. Rothenberg. New York: Worth Publishers, 2007.

McIntyre, Alice. *Making Meaning of Whiteness: Exploring Racial Identity with White Teachers*. Albany: State University of New York Press, 1997.

McKinney, Karyn D. "I Feel 'Whiteness' When I Hear People Blaming Whites: Whiteness as Cultural Victimization." *Race and Society*, no. 6 (2003): 39–55.

McKinney, Karyn D. and Joe R. Feagin, "Diverse Perspectives on Doing Antiracism: The Younger Generation." In *White Out: The Continuing Significance of Racism*, edited by Ashley "Woody" Doane and Eduardo Bonilla-Silva. New York: Routledge, 2003.

McLaren, Peter. "Wayward Multiculturalists: A Reply to Gregor McLennan." *Ethnicities* 1, no. 3 (2001): 408–18.

———. "Unthinking Whiteness, Rethinking Democracy: Critical Citizenship in Gringolandia." Pp. 10–55 in *Becoming and Unbecoming White: Owning and Disowning a Racial Identity*, edited by Christine Clark and James O'Donnell. Westport, CT: Bergin and Garvey, 1999.

McMillen, Neil R. *Dark Journey: Black Mississippians in the Age of Jim Crow*. Urbana: University of Illinois Press, 1990.

Mercer, Kobena. "Skin Head Sex Thing: Racial Difference and the Homoerotic Imaginary." Pp. 188–200 in *The Masculinity Studies Reader* edited by Rachel Adams and David Savran. Malden, MA: Wiley Blackwell, 2002.

———. *Welcome to the Jungle: New Positions in Black Cultural Studies*. New York: Routledge, 1994.

———. "'1968': Periodizing Postmodern Politics and Identity." Pp. 424–49 in *Cultural Studies*, edited by Lawrence Grossberg, Cary Nelson, and Paula Treichler. New York: Routledge, 1991.

Michaels, Walter Benn. "Autobiography of an Ex-White Man." *Transition* 73, no. 1 (1998): 122–43.

———. "Posthistoricism: The End of History." *Transition* 70, no. 2 (1996): 4–19.

———. "Race into Culture: A Critical Genealogy of Cultural Identity." *Critical Inquiry* 18, no. 4 (1992): 655–85.

Miles, Robert. *Racism*. London: Routledge, 1989.

Miles, Robert and Rodolfo D. Torres. "Does 'Race' Matter? Transatlantic Perspectives on Racism After 'Race Relations.'" Pp. 19–38 in *Race, Identity, and Citizenship: A Reader*, edited by Rodolfo D. Torres, Louis F Mirón, and Jonathan Xavier Inda. Malden, MA: Blackwell, 1999.

Millet, Kate. *Sexual Politics*. Garden City, NY: Doubleday, 1970.

Mills, Charles W. "Racial Exploitation and the Wages of Whiteness." In *What White Looks Like: African American on the Whiteness Question*, edited by George Yancy. New York: Routledge, 2004.

———. "White Supremacy as Sociopolitical System." Pp. 35–48 in *White Out: The Continuing Significance of Racism*, edited by Ashley "Woody" Doane and Eduardo Bonilla-Silva. New York: Routledge, 2003.

———. *Blackness Visible: Essays on Philosophy and Race*. Ithaca, NY: Cornell University Press, 1998.

———. *The Racial Contract*. Ithaca, NY: Cornell University Press, 1997.

Min-ha, Trinh T. "Outside In Inside Out." Pp. 133–45 in *Questions of Third Cinema*, edited by Jim Pines and Paul Willemen. London, UK: British Film Institute Publishing, 1990.

Mirón, Louis F. "Postmodernism and the Politics of Racialized Identities." Pp. 79–99 in *Race, Identity, and Citizenship: A Reader*, edited by Rodolfo D. Torres, Louis F. Mirón, and Jonathan Xavier Inda. Malden, MA: Wiley-Blackwell, 1999.

Mirsky, Jeannette and Allan Nevins. *The World of Eli Whitney*. New York: Macmillan, 1952.

Mohanty, Chandra, Talpade. *Feminism Without Borders*. Durham, NC: Duke University Press, 2004.

Montagu, Ashley. *Man's Most Dangerous Myth: The Fallacy of Race*. Lanham, MD: AltaMira Press, 1997.

Moon, J. Donald. "The Moral Basis of the Democratic Welfare State." In *Democracy and the Welfare State*, edited by Amy Gutmann. Princeton: Princeton University Press, 1988.

Moore, Wilbert E. and Robin M. Williams. "Stratification in the Ante-Bellum South." *American Sociological Review* 7, no. 3 (1942): 343–51.

Moreton-Robinson, Aileen. "Writing off Treaties: White Possession in the United States Critical Whiteness Studies Literature." In *Transnational Whiteness Matters*, edited by Aileen Moreton-Robinson, Maryrose Casey, and Fiona Nicoll. Lanham, MD: Lexington Books, 2008.

Moreton-Robinson, Aileen, Maryrose Casey, and Fiona Nicoll, eds. *Transnational Whiteness Matters*. Lanham, MD: Lexington Books, 2008.

Morgan Edmund S. *American Slavery, American Freedom: The Ordeal of Colonial Virginia*. New York: Norton, 1975.

Morgan, Jennifer. "'Some Could Suckle Over Their Shoulders': Male Travelers, Female Body and the Gendering of Racial Ideology, 1500–1770." *William and Mary Quarterly* 54, no. 1 (January 1997): 167–92.

Morrison, Toni. "Black Matters." Pp. 265–282 in *Race Critical Theories: Text and Context*, edited by Philomina Essed and David Theo Goldberg. Malden, MA: Blackwell, 2002.

———. *Playing in the Dark: Whiteness and the Literary Imagination*. Cambridge, MA: Harvard University Press, 1993.

———. "Unspeakable Things Unspoken: The Afro-American Presence in Literature." Presented at the Tanner Lecturers on Human Value, Michigan: University of Michigan, October 1988.

Mouffe, Chantal. *The Return of the Political*. New York: Verso Press, 2005.

Murray, Charles. "Affirmative Racism." *New Republic* 191, no. 26 (December 31, 1984): 18–23.

Myrdal, Gunnar. *Challenge to Affluence*. New York: Pantheon Books, 1963.

———. *An American Dilemma: The Negro Problem and Modern Democracy*. New York: Harper & Row, 1962.

Nafficy, Hamid. *The Making of Exile Cultures: Iranian Television in Los Angeles*. Minneapolis: University of Minnesota Press, 1993.

Nash, Gary B. "The Image of the Indian in the Southern Colonial Mind." Pp. 75–99 in *Shaping Southern Society: The Colonial Society*, edited by T.H. Breen. New York: Oxford University Press, 1976.

Najmi, Samina and Rajini Srikanth. *White Women in Racialized Spaces: Imaginative Transformation and Ethical Action in Literature*. Albany: State University of New York Press, 2002.

Nelson, Dana. *The World in Black and White: Reading "Race" in American Literature 1630–1802*, New York. Oxford University Press, 1994.

New York Times. "Police Officer Starts to Defend White Men" (November 19, 1995).

Newitz, Annalee and Matt Wray. "Introduction." Pp. 1–12 in *White Trash: Race and Class in America*, edited by Annalee Newitz and Matt Wray. New York: Routledge.

Noel, Donald L., ed. *The Origins of American Slavery and Racism*. Columbus, OH: Merrill, 1972.

Nora, Pierre.*Realms of Memory: The Construction of the French Past*. New York: Columbia University Press, 1996.

———. "Between Memory and History: *Les Lieux de Mémoire*." *Representations*, 26, no. 26 (1989): 7–24.

Offe, Claus. *Contradictions of the Welfare State*. London, UK: Hutchinson, 1984.

Omi, Michael. "Racialization in the Post–Civil Rights Era." Pp. 178–86 in *Mapping Multiculturalism*, edited by Christopher Newfield and Avery F. Gordon. Minneapolis: University of Minnesota Press, 1996.

Omi, Michael and Howard Winant. *Racial Formation in the United States from the 1960s to the 1990s*. New York: Routledge, 1994.

Outlaw, Lucius T., Jr. "Rehabilitate Racial Whiteness?" Pp. 159–72 in *What White Looks Like: African-American Philosophers on the Whiteness Question*, edited by George Yancy. New York: Routledge, 2004.

Owen, David S. "Whiteness in Du Bois's 'The Souls of Black Folk.'" *Philosophia Africana* 10, no. 2 (August 2007): 107–26.

Parekh, Bhikhu. "Multiculturalism." Pp. 45–56 in *What More Philosophers Think*, edited by Julian Baggini and Jeremy Strangroom. London: Continuum.

Pateman, Carol. *The Sexual Contract*. Stanford, CA: Stanford University Press, 1988.

Patterson, Orlando. "Affirmative Action, on the Merit System." *New York Times* (August 7, 1995).

———. *Slavery and Social Death: A Comparative Study*. Cambridge, MA: Harvard University Press, 1982.

Perry, Pamela. *Shades of White: White Kids and Racial Identities in High School*. Durham, NC: Duke University Press, 2002.

Phillips, Kendall R. "The Failure of Memory: Reflections on Rhetoric and Public Remembrance." *Western Journal of Communication* 74, no. 2 (March–April 2010): 208–23.

———. "Introduction." Pp. 1–14 in *Framing Public Memory*, edited by Kendall R. Phillips. Tuscaloosa: University of Alabama Press, 2004.

———, ed. *Framing Public Memory*, Tuscaloosa: University of Alabama Press, 2004.

Phillips, Ulrich B. *American Negro Slavery: A Survey of the Supply, Employment and Control of the Negro Labor as Determined by the Plantation Regime*. New York: D. Appleton, 1918.

Pinder, Sherrow O. *The Politics of Race and Ethnicity in the United States: Americanization, De-Americanization and Racialized Ethnic Groups*. New York: Palgrave Macmillan, 2010.

———. "Notes on Hurricane Katrina: Rethinking Race, Class, and Power in the United States," *21st Century Society Journal of the Academy of Social Science* 3, no. 4 (2009): 241–56.

———. "Anti-Lynching Movement." *Encyclopedia of Activism and Social Justice*, edited by Gary L. Anderson. Thousand Oaks, CA: Sage Publications, 2007a.

———. *From Welfare to Workfare: How Capitalist States Create a Pool of Unskilled Cheap Labor (A Marxist-Feminist Social Analysis)*. Lewiston, NY: Edwin Mellen Press, 2007.

Piper, Adrian. "Passing for Black, Passing for Whites." *Transition* 58 (Summer 1992): 4–32.

Post, Robert C. "Prejudicial Appearances: The Logic of American Antidiscrimination Law." Pp. 1–53 in *Prejudicial Appearances: The Logic of American Antidiscrimination Law*, edited Robert C. Post, Judith Butler, Thomas C. Grey, and Reva B. Siegel. Durham, NC: Duke University Press, 2001.

Prashad, Vijay. *The Karma of Brown Folks*. Minneapolis: University of Minnesota Press, 2001.

President's Advisory Board on Race, "Executive Order 13050." *The Multiracial Activist* (June 13, 1997). http://www.multiracial.com/government/whitehouse-eo13050.html.

Quadagno, Jill. *The Color of Welfare: How Racism Undermined the War on Poverty*. New York: Oxford University Press, 1994.

Radstone, Susannah. "Memory Studies: For and Against." *Memory Studies* 1 (2008): 31–39.

Rai, Amit S. "'Thus Spake the Subaltern': Postcolonial Criticism and the Scene of Desire." Pp. 91–119 in *The Psychoanalysis of Race*, edited by Christopher Lane. New York: Columbia University Press, 1998.

Rasmussen, Birgit Brander, Irene J. Nexica, Eric Klinenberg, and Matt Wray, eds. *The Making and Unmaking of Whiteness*. Durham, NC: Duke University Press, 2001.

Rawls, John. *A Theory of Justice*. Cambridge, MA: Belknap Press of Harvard University Press, 1971.

Reed, Adolph Jr. "The Underclass as Myth and Symbol: The Poverty of Discourse about Poverty." *Radical America* 24, no. 1 (January 1992): 21–40.

Regents of the University of California, SP-1: *Adoption of Resolution Policy Ensuring Equal Treatment–Admissions* Section 9 (July 20, 1995).

Revel, Judith. "Identity, Nature, Life: Three Biopolitical Deconstructions." *Theory, Culture & Society* 26, no. 6 (2009): 45–54.

Ricoeur, Paul. *Memory, History, Forgetting*. Translated by Kathleen Blamey and David Pellauer. Chicago: University of Chicago Press, 2004.

Riggs, Damien. "We Don't Talk About Race Anymore: Power, Privilege and Critical Whiteness Studies." *Borderlands* 3, no. 2 (2004). www.borderlands.net.au/vol3no2_2004/riggs_intro.htm.

Roediger, David R. "Whiteness and Its Complications." *Chronicle of Higher Education* (July 14, 2006): 6–8.

———. *Working Towards Whiteness: How America's Immigrants Became White, The Strange Journey from Ellis Island to the Suburbs.* New York: Basic Books, 2005.

———. *Colored White: Transcending the Racial Past.* Berkeley, CA: Berkeley University Press, 2002.

———. *Black on White: Black Writers and What It Means to Be White.* New York: Schocken Books, 1998.

———. *Towards the Abolition of Whiteness: Essays on Race, Politics, and Working Class History.* New York: Verso Press, 1994.

———. "Race and the Working-Class Past in the United States: Multiple Identities and the Future of Labor History." *International Review of Social History,* no. 38 (1993): 127–43.

———. *The Wages of Whiteness: Race and the Making of the American Working Class.* New York: Verso Press, 1991.

Russell, John H. *The Free Negro in Virginia, 1619–1895.* New York: Negro University Press, 1913.

Said, Edward W. *The Politics of Dispossession: The Struggle for Palestinian Self Determination, 1969–1994.* New York: Vintage Books, 1994.

———. *Culture and Imperialism.* New York: Knopf, 1993.

———. *Orientalism.* New York: Pantheon Books, 1978.

Sander, Ronald. *Lost Tribes and Promised Lands: The Origins of American Racism.* New York: HarperCollins, 1992.

Sartwell, Crispin. *Act Like You Know: African American Autobiography and White Identity.* Chicago: University of Chicago Press, 1998.

Schlesinger, Arthur M. *The Disuniting of America: Reflections on a Multicultural Society.* New York: W.W. Norton, 1998.

Schuman, Howard, Charlotte Steeh, and Lawrence Bobo. *Racial Attitudes in America: Trends and Interpretation.* Cambridge, MA: Harvard University Press, 1985.

Schwartz, Barry and Horst-Alfred Heinrich. "Shadings of Regret: America and Germany." Pp. 115–44 in *Framing Public Memory,* edited by Kendall R. Phillips. Tuscaloosa: University of Alabama Press, 2004.

Schwartz, Bernard. *Behind Bakke. Affirmative Action and the Supreme Court.* New York. New York University Press, 1988.

Sears, David O. "Symbolic Racism." Pp. 53–84 in *Eliminating Racism: Profiles in Controversy,* edited by Phyllis A. Katz and Dalmas A. Taylor. New York: Plenum, 1988.

Seligman, Katherine. "Ethnic Concerns Cloud Lowell." *San Francisco Examiner* (April 3, 1993).

Seshadri-Crooks, Kalpana. "The Comedy of Domination: Psychoanalysis and the Conceit of Whiteness." Pp. 353–79 in *The Psychoanalysis of Race,* edited by Christopher Lane. New York: Columbia University Press, 1998.

Siegel, Reva B. (2001). "Discrimination in the Eyes of the Law: How 'Color Blindness' Discourse Disrupts and Rationalizes Social Stratification." Pp. 99–153 in *Prejudicial Appearances The Logic of American Antidiscrimination Law,* edited by Robert C. Post, Judith Butler, Thomas C. Grey, and Reva B. Siegel. Durham, NC: Duke University Press, 2001.

Simien, Evelyn M. "Doing Intersectionality Research: From Conceptual Issues to Practical Examples." *Politics and Gender* 3, no. 2, (2007): 264–71.

Sio, Arnold A. "Interpretations of Slavery: The Slave Status in the America." *Comparative Studies in Society and History* 7, no. 3 (1965): 289–308.

Smith, J. Owen. "The United States Supreme Court's Human Rights Violation in the University of Michigan Case." Pp. 120–35 in *Contemporary Patterns of Politics, Praxis, and Culture,* edited by Georgia A. Persons. New Brunswick, NJ: Transaction Publishers, 2005.

Smith, Rogers M. "Towards a More Perfect Union: Beyond Old Liberalism and New Liberalism." Pp. 327–52 in *The new Liberalism and our Retreat from Racial Equality Without for All*, edited by Adolph Reed Jr. Boulder, CO: Westview Press, 1999.

———. "Beyond Tocqueville, Myrdal, and Hartz: The Multiple Traditions." American Political Science Review 87, no. 3 (1993): 549–66.

Snead, James. "European Pedigrees/African Contagions: Nationality, Narrative, and Communality in Tutuola, Achebe, and Reed." Pp. 231–49 in *Nation and Narration*, edited by Homi Bhabha. New York: Routledge, 1990.

Snowden, Frank M. Jr. *Before Color Prejudice: The Ancient View of Blacks*. Cambridge, MA: Harvard University Press, 1983.

Solow, Barbara Lewis and Stanley L. Engerman, eds. *British Capitalism and Caribbean Slavery: The Legacy of Eric Williams*. New York: Cambridge University Press, 1987.

Spelman, Elizabeth. *Inessential Women Problems of Exclusion in Feminist Thought*. Boston: Beacon Press, 1988.

Spencer, Martin E. "Multiculturalism, 'Political Correctness,' and the Politics of Identity." *Sociological Forum* 9, no. 4 (1994): 547–67.

Spencer, Stephen. "The Discourse of Whiteness: Chinese-American History, Pearl S. Buck, and *The Good Earth*." *Americana: The Journal of American Popular Culture, 1900 to Present* 1, no. 1. www.americanpopularculture.com/journal/index.htm.

Spivak, Gayatri C. "Race Before Racism: The Disappearance of the American." *Boundary 2* 13 no. 2 (Summer 1998): 35–53.

———. "Diasporas Old and New: Woman in Transnational World." *Textual Practice* 10, no. 2 (1996): 245–69.

———. *The Spivak Reader: Selected Works of Gayatri Chakravorty*, edited by Donna Landry and Gerald Maclean. New York: Routledge, 1995.

———. "Theory in the Margin: Coetzee's Foe Reading Defoe's Crusoe/Roxana" Pp. 154–80 in *Consequence of Theory: Selected Papers from the English Institute, 1987–1988*, edited by Jonathan Arac and Barbara Johnson. Baltimore, MD: Johns Hopkins University Press, 1991.

———. *The Post-Colonial Critic: Interview, Strategies, Dialogues*, edited by Sarah Harasym. New York: Routledge, 1990.

———. "Can the Subaltern Speak?" Pp. 271–313 in *Marxism and the Interpretation of Culture*, edited by Cary Nelson and Lawrence Grossberg. Urbana: University of Illinois Press, 1988.

Sowell, Thomas. *Civil Rights, Rhetoric or Reality?* New York: Morrow, 1984.

Stampp, Kenneth M. *Peculiar Institution: Slavery in the Ante-Bellum South*. New York: Knopf, 1956.

Steele, Shelby. *Content of our Character: A New Vision of Race in America*. New York: St. Martin's Press, 1991.

Stomajor, Sonia. "A Latina Judge's Voice." *Berkeley La Raza Law Journal* 13, no. 1 (2002): 87–93.

Takaki, Ronald T. *A Different Mirror: A History of Multicultural America*. Boston: Little, Brown, 1993.

———. *Iron Cages: Race and Culture in 19th-Century America*. New York: Alfred A. Knopf, 1979.

Talbot, Margaret. "Getting Credit for Being White" *New York Times* (November 30, 1997): 116–18.

Tardon, Raphael. "Richard Wright Tells Us the White Problem in the United States." *Action* 24 (October 1946).

Taylor, Paul C. "Silence and Sympathy: Dewey's Whiteness." Pp. 227–41 in *What White Looks Like: African-American Philosophers on the Whiteness Question*, edited by George Yancy. New York: Routledge, 2004.

Tehranian, John. *Whitewashed: America's Invisible Middle Eastern Minority*. New York: New York University Press, 2008.

Terdiman, Richard. "The Mnemonics of Musset's Confession." *Representations*, no. 26 (Spring 1989): 26–48.

Thernstrom, Stephen and Abigail Thernstrom. *America in Black and White: One Nation Indivisible.* New York: Simon and Schuster, 1997.

Thomas, Clarence. "An Afro American Perspective: Towards a Plain Reading of the Constitution—The Declaration of Independence in Constitutional Interpretation." *Howard Law Journal* (1987): 691–703.

Tingfang, Wu. *America Through the Spectacles of an Oriental Diplomat.* New York: Frederick A. Stokes Co, 1914.

Tocqueville, Alexis de. "Democracy in America." Pp. 12–16 in *Documents of American Prejudice: An Anthology of Writings on Race from Thomas Jefferson to David Duke,* edited by S. T. Joshi. New York: Basic Books, 1999.

———. *Democracy in America* vol. 2. New York: Knopf, 1945.

Torres, Rodolfo D., Louis F. Mirón and Jonathan Xavier Inda, edited by *Race, Identity, and Citizenship: A Reader.* Malden, MA: Wiley-Blackwell, 1999.

Towers, Frank. "Projecting Whiteness: Race, and the State of Labor History." *Journal of American Culture* 21, no. 2 (1998): 47–57.

Traub, James. "The Way We Live Now." *New York Times Magazine* (February 16, 2003).

Twine, France Winddance and Charles Gallagher. "Introduction The Future of Whiteness: A Map of Third Wave." *Ethnic and Racial Studies* 31, no. 1 (January 2008): 4–24.

van de Berghe, Pierre. *Race and Racism: A Comparative Perspective.* New York: John Wiley and Sons, 1967.

Van Evrie, John H. *Negroes and Negro "Slavery": The First on Inferior Race: The Latter Is the Normal Condition.* New York: Van Evrie, Horton & Co., 1863.

Vaughan, Alden T. "The Origins Debate: Slavery and Racism in Seventeenth Century Virginia." *Virginia Magazine of History and Biography,* 97 no. 3 (1989): 311–54.

———. "Blacks in Virginia: A Note on the First Decade." *William and Mary Quarterly* 3, series 29 (1972): 469–78.

Verba, Sidney and Gary R. Orren. *Equality in America: The View from the Top* (Cambridge, MA: Harvard University Press, 1985.

Wacquant, Loïc. "From Slavery to Mass Incarceration: Rethinking the 'Race Question' in the US." *New Left Review,* no. 13 (2002): 41–60.

Waldinger, Roger. "Rethinking 'Race.'" *Ethnicities* 1, no. 19 (2001): 19–21.

Ware, Vron and Les Back, *Out of Whiteness: Color, Politics and Culture.* Chicago, University of Chicago Press, 2002.

Wells-Barnett, Ida B. *Southern Horrors Lynch Laws in All Its Phases.* New York: New York Age Print, 1992.

———. *The Red Record.* Cirencester, UK: Echo Library, 2005.

West, Cornel. *Race Matters.* New York, Vintage Books, 2001.

———. *Keeping Faith: Philosophy and Race in America.* New York: Routledge, 1993.

———. "Learning to Talk of Race." *New York Times Magazine* (August 2, 1992).

White, Hayden. "The Practical Past." *Historien* 10 (2010): 10–19.

Wiegman, Robyn. "Witnessing Whiteness: Articulating Race and the 'Politics of Style,'" *Borderlines* 3, no. 2 (2004). www.borderlands.net.au/vol3no2_2004/westcott_witnessing.htm.

———. "Whiteness Studies and the Paradox of Particularity." *Boundary* 26, no. 2 (1999): 115–50.

Wilkins, Roger. 2000. "Racism Has Its Privileges." Pp. 335–45 in *The Best of the Nations,* edited by Victor Navasky and Katrina V. Heuvel. New York: Thunder's Month Press, 2000.

Williams, Eric. *Capitalism and Slavery.* Chapel Hill: University of North Carolina Press, 1994.

Williams, Patricia. "Alchemical Notes: Reconstructing Ideals form Deconstructed Rights." *Harvard Civil Rights and Civil Liberties Review* 22, no. 1 (1987): 401–33.

Wilson, Pete. "Why Racial Preferences Must End." *San Francisco Chronicle* (January 18, 1996).

Wilson, William Julius. *The Declining Significance of Race.* Chicago: University of Chicago Press, 1980.

———. "What Shall We do with the White People?" Pp. 58–66 in *Black on White: Black Writers on What It Means to Be White*, edited by David R. Roediger. New York: Schocken Press, 1999.

Wimsatt, William Upski. *Bomb the Suburbs*. New York: Soft Skull Press, 2008.

Winant, Howard. *The New Politics of Race: Globalism, Difference, Justice*. Minneapolis: University of Minnesota Press, 2004.

———. "Behind Blue Eyes: Whiteness and Contemporary U.S. Racial Politics." Pp. 40–53 in *Off White: Readings on Race, Power, and Society*, edited by Michele Fine, Linda Powell, Louis Weis, and L. Mun Wong. New York: Routledge, 1997.

Wittig, Monique. *The Straight Mind and Other Essays*. Boston, MA: Beacon Press, 1992.

Wood, Ellen Meiksins. *Empire of Capital*. New York: Verso Press, 2003.

Woodward, C. Vann. *The Strange Career of Jim Crow*. New York: Oxford University Press, 1955.

———. *Origins of the New South, 1877–1913*. Baton Rouge: Louisiana State University Press, 1951.

Woolley, John T. and Gerhard Peters. *The American Presidency Project*. www.presidency.ucsb.edu/ws/?pid=58863.

Wray, Matt. *Not Quite White: White Trash and the Boundaries of Whiteness*. Durham, NC: Duke University Press, 2006.

Wright, James M. *The Free Negroes in Maryland, 1634–1860*. New York: Columbia University Press, 1921.

Wright, Richard. *Black Boy*. New York: Harper and Row, 1937.

Wu, Frank H. *Yellow: Race in America Beyond Black and White*. New York: Basic Books, 2002.

Yancy, George. "Whiteness and the Return of the Black Body." *Journal of Speculative Philosophy* 19, no. 4 (2005): 215–41.

———. "Introduction: Fragments of a Social Ontology of Whiteness." In *What White Looks Like: African-American Philosophers on the Whiteness Questions*, edited by George Yancy. New York: Routledge, 2004a.

———, ed. *What White Looks Like: African-American Philosophers on the Whiteness Questions*. New York: Routledge, 2004b.

Young, Marion, Iris. "Polity and Group Difference: A Critique of the ideals of Universal Citizenship." *Ethics* 99, no. 2 (January 1989): 250–74.

Žižek, Slavoj. *First as Tragedy, Then as Farce*. London: Verso Press, 2009.

———. "Multiculturalism, Or, the Cultural Logics Multinational Capitalism." *New Left Review* 1, no. 225 (September–October, 1997): 28–51.

Index